THE EDUCATION OF RONALD REAGAN

COLUMBIA STUDIES IN CONTEMPORARY AMERICAN HISTORY

FIGURE 1 The September 1958 cover of GE's monthly magazine, *The Monogram*. The company used "Better Business Climate" to describe civic programs for greater voter involvement, but to some top corporate political strategists such as Ralph Cordiner and Lemuel Boulware, it was code for a comprehensive campaign to move employees, and cities where Ronald Reagan toured as "GE's Goodwill Ambassador," to the right.
Source: Schenectady Museum.

THE EDUCATION OF
RONALD REAGAN

THE GENERAL ELECTRIC YEARS
and the Untold Story of His Conversion to Conservatism

Thomas W. Evans

COLUMBIA UNIVERSITY PRESS   NEW YORK

COLUMBIA UNIVERSITY PRESS

Publishers Since 1893

NEW YORK   CHICHESTER, WEST SUSSEX

Copyright © 2006 The Mentor Center, L.C.

Library of Congress Cataloging-in-Publication Data

Evans, Thomas W., 1930–

The education of Ronald Reagan : the General Electric years and the untold story

of his conversion to conservatism / Thomas W. Evans.

p. cm.—(Columbia Studies in contemporary American history)

Includes bibliographical references and index.

ISBN 0–231–13860–1 (cloth : alk. paper)—ISBN 0–231–51107–8 (e-book)

1. Reagan, Ronald.   2. Reagan, Ronald—Political and social views.

3. Conservatism—United States—History—20th century.   4. General Electric

Company—Biography.   5. General Electric Company—History—20th century.

6. Presidents—United States—Biography.   7. United States—Politics and

government—1953–1961.   8. United States—Politics and government—1961–1963.

I. Title.   II. Series.

E877.2.E93 2006

973.927092—dc22   2006017594

[B]

∞

Columbia University Press books are printed on permanent and durable acid-free paper.

Printed in the United States of America

c 10 9 8 7 6 5 4 3 2 1

To Lois

CONTENTS

PART I
Background

PART II
A Postgraduate Course in Political Science

PART III
An Apprenticeship for Public Life

PART IV
Encouraging an Increasing Majority of Citizens

APPENDIX
Speeches of Reuther, Boulware, and Reagan

If you believe, as Ronnie does, that everything happens for a purpose, then certainly there was a hidden purpose in Ronnie's job for General Electric.
—Nancy Reagan, *My Turn*, 1989

━━━━

For eight years [1954–1962], I hopskotched around the country by train and automobile for GE and visited every one of its 139 plants, some of them several times. Along the way, I met more than 250,000 employees of GE. . . . Looking back now I realize that it wasn't a bad apprenticeship for someone who'd someday enter public life. . . . Those GE tours became almost a postgraduate course in political science for me. . . . by 1960 I had completed the process of self-conversion.
—Ronald Reagan, *An American Life*, 1990

━━━━

It's the job of every businessman—every citizen—to go back to school on economics individually, in small groups, in big groups. . . . to learn from simple text books, from organized courses, from individual discussions with business associates, in neighborhood groups, at the club or bar, on train or bus. . . . that we are each going to study until we understand this wonderful system of ours. . . . that we are going to preserve and improve it rather than let it be damaged or even perish along with our free market and our free persons. . . . that we are publicly going to encourage an increasing majority of citizens. . . . toward the greatest and surest further attainment of our material and spiritual needs and desires.
—Lemuel Boulware, GE vice president, 1944–1960,
"Salvation Is Not Free" address, Harvard Business School, 1949

THE EDUCATION OF RONALD REAGAN

PART I

BACKGROUND

ONE

A NEW DEALER TO THE CORE

On October 27, 1964, Ronald Reagan delivered his famous, nationally televised speech in support of conservative Republican presidential candidate Barry Goldwater. David Broder, the dean of the Washington press corps, and his coauthor Stephen Hess, senior fellow at the Brookings Institution, later wrote that it was "the most successful political debut since William Jennings Bryan's Cross of Gold speech in 1896."[1]

Biographers and historians are unanimous in the finding that "The Speech," as it became known to both admirers and critics, was developed while Reagan toured the country for General Electric during the eight years that he was employed by the company (1954–1962). He served as host of GE's Sunday-night television show and spent a quarter of his time as traveling ambassador, visiting GE's 250,000 workers in 139 plants and speaking from civic platforms to the employees and their neighbors in the forty states covered by GE's far-flung industrial empire.

But during his years with General Electric, Reagan developed more than a set of prepared remarks. He eventually became an integral part of the company's elaborate political initiative, probably the most comprehensive in corporate America. The program extended from the executive suites to GE's employees on the plant floor to the voters in the towns and cities where the plants were located. Reagan later described his experience as "an apprenticeship for public life."

Toward the end of his years with GE, when transcripts of still-evolving versions of "The Speech" were made available to the public for the first time, Reagan felt he had experienced a conversion. He wrote in *An American Life*, "I wasn't just making speeches—I was preaching a sermon."[2]

Reagan was a self-confessed Democrat and New Dealer when he arrived at GE. After his eight-year "postgraduate course in political science," conducted largely under the aegis of GE's vice president and labor strategist, Lemuel Boulware, Ronald Reagan came to expound on the need to reduce taxes and limit government. He described international communism, as Boulware and GE president Ralph Cordiner did, as "evil." He observed Boulware, who was regarded by many in corporate America as the most successful labor negotiator of all time, and Reagan himself became a knowledgeable negotiator during this period, equally at ease with corporate executives and blue-collar workers. His education stretched well beyond the bargaining table. He became familiar with such diverse thinkers as von Mises, Lenin, Hayek, and the Chinese military strategist Sun Tzu. He read and reread the practical economics of Henry Hazlitt. He quoted Jefferson, Madison, and Hamilton.

Lemuel Boulware believed that it was not enough to win over company employees on narrow labor issues. They must not only accept the offer but pass on GE's essentially conservative message to others, helping the company to win voters at the grass roots who would elect officials and pass legislation establishing a better business climate. In short, they would become "communicators" and "mass communicators," (Boulware's words)[3] as they went through the company's extensive education program. In time, the program would also help to produce a "great communicator."

And yet, for all the recent interest in the Reagan presidency, little has been written about how his change from liberal to conservative, from actor to politician, came about. A veil of secrecy has been drawn over this crucial period of Ronald Reagan's education. Part of the reason for this was Cordiner and Boulware's concern that GE's political efforts might come under attack as violating federal and state statutes that made partisan corporate political activity a crime. They also felt that GE's unions might find Boulware's aggressive negotiating posture—dubbed *Boul-*

warism and still referred to as such in labor-law texts—the basis for an unfair-labor-practice charge.

During this same period, GE's pricing system, especially for the heavy equipment it sold to cities and utilities, was under attack from a Senate investigating committee and federal grand juries sitting in Philadelphia. The investigators and prosecutors maintained that GE used illegal price-fixing and that certain high-ranking executives should go to jail. Civil suits following the federal criminal actions could lead to hundreds of millions of dollars in damages. While Ronald Reagan had no involve-ment in this situation, some of the litigation extended beyond Reagan's years with the company, as he entered the political arena in California. Neither he nor his mentors saw any advantage in publicizing his connec-tion to General Electric or to the political apparatus they had created while there.

Fortunately, several recent events bring new light to this study of Ronald Reagan's "education": the discovery of a collection of hitherto unpublished papers and a repository of GE corporate documents last published during the 1950s and 1960s; interviews with GE personnel who had been silent until now; and a reexamination of other publications and oral histories that now have a more meaningful context.

Many observers consider the changes in Ronald Reagan during his GE years to be profound. Others see them as superficial and opportunistic. To truly understand Ronald Reagan during and after the GE years, it is important to know what he was like when he came to the company. It is also important to know what the company was like—as later chapters will make clear—at the time when Reagan was an employee. An appro-priate point of departure for both inquiries would be 1945, when the country emerged from war and a generation of Americans returned to resume lives that had been interrupted in a way that everyone hoped would never occur again.

When Captain Ronald Reagan, recently honorably discharged from the U.S. Army Air Corps, returned to civilian life on July 11, 1945, he didn't have far to go. His extreme near-sightedness had kept him from combat duty. While his career had been disrupted, his military service had been in Hollywood, making training and motivational films. Industry insiders referred to the duty station as "Fort Roach" after producer Hal Roach, who had turned his studio over to the government.[4] Reagan was thirty-four years old when he left the service.

"When the war was over," television journalist Tom Brokaw wrote, "the men and women who had been involved, in uniform and in civilian capacities, joined in joyous and short-lived celebrations, then immediately began the task of rebuilding their lives and the world they wanted." He was emphatic in his appraisal of them: "This is the greatest generation any society has produced."[5]

Not content simply to take life as it came, Ronald Reagan, like many returning veterans, became active in civic affairs. As he returned to his job at Warner Brothers, he joined the left-leaning American Veterans Committee and was on the board of the Hollywood Independent Citizens Committee of Arts, Sciences, and Professions. He was concerned about the threat posed by the atom bomb that had been dropped on Hiroshima and Nagasaki. He believed HICCASP had been formed as "a support group for President Franklin D. Roosevelt."[6]

In 1947, Reagan was elected president of the Screen Actors Guild, the actors' union. He joined other leaders of AFL-CIO unions in opposing Republican-sponsored "Right-to-Work" legislation. At the same time, he "took the initiative in organizing for the state of California the Labor Committee for Truman."[7] His prominence in the Screen Actors Guild continued, and he was elected to four more successive one-year terms as president of the union in the years before he came to work for General Electric.[8]

Reagan campaigned for Democrats. In addition to President Harry Truman in 1948, he vigorously supported civil rights advocate Hubert Humphrey, and in 1950 he backed Helen Gahagan Douglas in her quest for a U.S. Senate seat from California (against Richard Nixon). Although he supported war hero Dwight Eisenhower, the Republican candidate for president in 1952, it was as a "Democrat for Eisenhower." He called himself a "liberal Democrat" and a "New Dealer to the core."[9]

What was it in his background that led to these political leanings and, for that matter, his ability to go out on the hustings and campaign for candidates who felt as he did? Reagan's first recorded public speech might be an appropriate starting point for understanding his political inclinations and his natural gifts. Former president Gerald Ford once observed that Ronald Reagan "was one of the few political leaders I have met whose public speeches revealed more than his private conversations."[10]

FIGURE 2 At the Truman White House on April 1, 1949, waiting to see the president are Holly-wood labor leaders and Truman supporters (*left to right*) Roy Brewer of the International Alliance of Stage Employees; Kenneth Thompson, the first executive secretary of the Screen Actors Guild; Ronald Reagan, president of the guild; and Dick Walsh, international president of IATSE. Walsh introduced the motion at the AFL-CIO convention the prior spring to endorse Truman for reelection. Reagan campaigned as part of Labor for Truman.
Source: Screen Actors Guild Archives, Los Angeles, California.

There is some irony in this subject matter because as a gubernatorial candidate in 1966, and later as California's governor, Reagan gained popular support from his criticism of Governor Pat Brown's handling of the student protests at Berkeley. Reagan's first public address occurred in the course of another protest on another campus at another time, almost four decades earlier, when he himself was a student.

"Dutch" Reagan (as he was then known) entered Eureka College in 1928. The college had been founded in 1855 and was the major institution in the town that bore its name. Like many farm belt communities, Eureka, Illinois, was already suffering the economic downturn that would soon engulf the entire country in the Great Depression.[11]

Reagan "fell head over heels in love with Eureka," as he later wrote, and regarded it as "another home."[12] He soon learned that many of his fellow students did not share his enthusiasm. In an economy move, college president Bert Wilson announced that he planned to drop several courses, making it difficult for some of the undergraduates to amass enough credits to graduate. Wilson met the ensuing controversy head-on by offering to resign. The board of trustees rejected his tender, giving him, in effect, a vote of confidence.

The students disagreed. Thanksgiving vacation was beginning, and instead of traveling home for the holiday, they held a mass meeting in the largest hall available, the college chapel.[13] The student leaders chose freshman Dutch Reagan, who had only been on campus for two months, to speak for them. It was almost midnight when young Reagan rose. He had been briefed by students far more familiar with the issues than he was, but Reagan's persuasive speaking style was all his own. At the end of his remarks, the audience "came to their feet in a roar," endorsing a motion which would have been extreme even in the 1960s: "We, the students of Eureka College, on the 28th of November, 1928, declare an immediate strike pending the acceptance of President Wilson's resignation by the board of trustees."[14]

The vote was recorded as "unanimous." Many of the students saw it as a protest against Wilson's "domineering personality and his outmoded rules governing student behavior." In any event, they felt strongly enough about it to lay their academic careers on the line. When the students returned from the delayed Thanksgiving break, all but six (two of whom were Wilson's daughters) refused to attend class. The strike attracted national attention. A press headquarters was set up for the reporters who arrived from all over the country.

On Thursday, December 6, the United Press reported a rumor "that the school would be moved to Springfield," causing consternation among the local merchants. The Alumni Committee pleaded "for a quick end to the turmoil." The students refused to budge, and the next day President Wilson resigned. An acting president was named. Wilson's changes were abandoned, and the college adopted a more liberal code of student behavior—permitting college dances, among other things. By Monday, the "campus had returned to its usual routines."

There were no more protest rallies at Eureka where Reagan could hone his speaking skills, but he became one of the stars of the Dramatic Club, continuing a path he had embarked on at North Dixon High. As one biographer notes, "No microphones were used in those days and Dutch could always be heard. His college reviews repeat the word 'presence.' He had a way 'of sauntering across the stage' that drew all eyes to him even when he was not speaking."

His "ear for words" and his "startling memory" enabled him to slide by with passing grades and very little effort at Eureka. His major was economics, which he described as an "instinctive science for him." His real interests were extracurricular. In addition to drama, they included debating, football, swimming, and student government.

Although his family was poor—his father was often out of work—both Dutch and his older brother Neil (often called "Moon") went to Eureka. Their mother, Nelle, was determined to give her boys a better life. She insisted that they continue their education after high school, even though only about 8 percent of their classmates did. Moon got a football scholarship, and Dutch arranged for financial aid and a deferment of tuition. Both boys had part-time jobs.

Biographers credit Nelle Reagan with Ronald's early development of significant skills, as well as his moral beliefs and his character.[15] She read *The Three Musketeers* and other adventure stories to her boys when they were very young, and Reagan became a reader well before he started school.[16] (One wonders whether his youthful enthusiasm for the works of Edgar Rice Burroughs—which included the series about Carson of Venus and earthling John Carter who fought the Martian warlords—may have stimulated his interest in a defense shield in space.)[17] He maintained his enthusiasm for reading throughout his life.[18]

Nancy Reagan confirms that her husband was a constant reader. In her autobiography, she recalls the "small library" that she and her husband carried in their suitcases when Reagan began his short-lived career as a nightclub entertainer. The owner of the Last Frontier hotel was astonished; he'd never seen an entertainer bring books to Las Vegas before.[19] Reagan's coworkers noticed his reading, too. A consultant in Reagan's first gubernatorial campaign was impressed that his client's personal library "was stacked with books on political philosophy."[20] Moreover, Reagan retained what he read. White House staff member David Gergen described the fortieth president's "steel-trap mind" for what he read.[21] Gergen also noted Reagan's slow reading rate, which he attributed to Reagan's tendency, possibly derived from his years as an actor, to memorize what he read.

Reagan was an equally enthusiastic writer. As early as 1947, a movie magazine observed, "In private life, Reagan is most interested in writing."[22]

A recent collection of his speeches contains a chapter giving examples of his writings from 1925 to 1994, although the primary example of Reagan's facility for writing is the collection itself. It contains 670 radio speeches he wrote "in his own hand" in the years between his governorship and the presidency.[23]

Anne Edwards, in *Early Reagan*, traces to his mother another major component of Reagan's ability to communicate. "Perhaps the one physical attribute Dutch inherited from Nelle was his voice. . . . a distinctive, mellow voice, tinged with a hopeful cadence—a voice that had a timbre to it that impressed people with the honesty of the words he spoke. Because he believed in himself and his voice so conveyed his confidence, others picked up on it."[24]

Edwards also credits Nelle with teaching her son how to use his voice. "When trying to be persuasive, he would lower the volume," she writes, "speaking 'barely above a whisper' to win a confidential intimacy, and he instinctively knew just the right moments to raise that volume and lower the pitch for intensity. . . . Dutch's voice had the humility and passion of a true believer, a manly, ingratiating voice made for promises."

Dutch had another, far more famous, model for his manner of speaking. The Reagans were Democrats. Dutch's father worked hard as a volunteer to defeat Herbert Hoover in 1932, and the family often huddled around the radio to listen to *their* candidate, Franklin Delano Roosevelt. They were thrilled by Roosevelt's "fireside chats." In a mellow voice and friendly manner, FDR tried to raise the spirits of the nation from the Great Depression into which it had fallen. Throughout his life, Ronald Reagan continued to revere Roosevelt as a communicator and a leader, even after he came to disagree with almost every economic component of the New Deal.

Like FDR, Reagan polished his speaking style on radio. After college, he became a sportscaster on Des Moines radio station WHO. He broadcast Chicago Cubs games. In those days, broadcasters sat in the studio, fashioning detailed narratives of what transpired on the field from a barren line on the Western Union tape. "Single to center," for example, might become two minutes of exciting description.[25] The verbal agility necessary to do the job would serve Reagan well on the stump and at the podium in the future.

While no one ever doubted Reagan's ability to communicate, his political opponents and critics later in his career were quick to question his ability to think. The insights of those who had an opportunity to observe him in office are necessary in order to weigh his performance at that time. One or two are set out here, however, to demonstrate the native skills that he brought to learn and use the information dispensed by Lemuel Boulware and others at General Electric during this crucial period in his education.

David Gergen, who served under a few presidents, tried to categorize Reagan's mental capacity when he worked for him. He began with the premise that exceptional verbal skills indicate a certain kind of intelligence. Gergen examined the concept of "multiple intelligences" promulgated by Harvard psychologist Howard Gardner. He believed that Reagan ranked high in "inter-personal intelligence," as contrasted with the "logical-mathematical intelligence," at which lawyers and professors often excel. He quotes from Gardner's book, *Leading Minds: An Anatomy of Leadership*: "effective leaders of institutions and nations lead directly, through the stories and acts they address to an audience." Gergen concludes that "emotional intelligence"—a term used by Daniel Goleman— is a clear fit for Reagan. He cites Goleman's study of 188 companies in the *Harvard Business Review*, which concludes "that the higher up one climbs in the corporate world, the more important emotional intelligence is to effective leadership."[26]

In Ronald Reagan's conversion from actor to politician, from liberal to conservative, Lemuel Boulware played the role of a teacher. But he was more than that. "Mentor" might be an accurate description, with its four classic aspects of tutor, sponsor, motivator, and role model.[27] Sometimes it is hard to calibrate the extent of a mentor's influence in the development of a protégé. It is especially important to understand this process in the case of Boulware and Reagan, for the men worked in close proximity for seven years.[28] How did they affect each other? How important was Boulware to Reagan's "postgraduate" education?

Did Ronald Reagan have a role model? There was no film-industry figure or military superior officer that he looked up to in this way, and his father was certainly not one to emulate. An alcoholic and a binge drinker who was often fired as he disappeared from his job for a prolonged period, Jack Reagan's public drunkenness had embarrassed and saddened his younger son on more than one occasion. If there was a void here, it may well have been filled by Lemuel Boulware, who was sixteen years older than his protégé.

As Reagan traveled the country, the affection and admiration he had formed for Boulware was undoubtedly enhanced as he met with Boulware's employee relations managers. These executives, some three thousand whose jobs had been created by Boulware, reported directly to him; their loyalty and enthusiasm for their leader knew no bounds. Reagan also witnessed Boulware's unbroken series of successes as he went over the heads of the union leaders directly to the workers.

At the beginning of this chapter, you read of the reasons why Boulware, Reagan, and others at GE did not comment publicly on their joint experience with the company. Ronald Reagan did not mention Lemuel Boulware's contribution to his political ascendancy until after he had reached the presidency. Then he was generous and emphatic, but primarily in highly personal communications with his mentor.

After the Reagan presidency, historians and political commentators discovered that even their close personal observations of the president were often distorted by a personal trait that few of them had witnessed before, particularly in a public man. Reagan had a sign on his desk that read, "There's no limit to what a man can do or where he can go if he doesn't care who gets the credit." Reagan truly believed this, and he had sufficient self-confidence not to rush to assert that a particular plan or program attributed to an assistant or colleague was really his.

Such conduct is rare, especially at a time when we witness presidents acting to expand their "legacies," even after they have left office. Consider two quick examples for now. "Mr. Gorbachev, tear down this wall!" was one of the most famous statements of the fortieth president. The speechwriter who conceived it has written a book about it and his years in the Reagan White House. He came up with the line on his own well before Reagan's visit to Berlin and is justly proud.[29] Reagan never told him or the media that he had spoken a similar line in a debate with Robert Kennedy two decades before.[30]

Another Reagan concept, the Strategic Defense Initiative—invariably attributed to scientist Edward Teller or a general under Reagan's command—was discovered by Reagan in a GE publication in 1962, and he discussed it with his close friend and foreign policy adviser before the 1980 election. Reagan never went public with his early personal discovery of SDI. You will read more about it later.

For all of their brilliant offerings at podiums all over the country, Reagan and Boulware were very private men. Each had many friends and a handful of influential mentors. Few people really knew them well. It went against their respective natures to broadcast their personal relationships. Ironically, we discover their cherished beliefs not in private conversations, but in the words they uttered, again and again, in public. In Boulware's case, we have his writings and thousands of GE documents to flesh out his beliefs and plans.

But what of Reagan? In recent years, two volumes have been published presenting, respectively, radio talks and letters that Reagan had "written in his own hand." The editors of these books have commented, however, that "nothing has thus far been found in [Reagan's] own hand of the speeches he gave to [GE] employees. . . . It is quite possible that they were his own creations, but we cannot be sure."[31]

In his first autobiography, Ronald Reagan acknowledges that he was part of General Electric's extensive "Employee and Community Relations Program."[32] This was the intracompany title given to Boulware's program, the vehicle for Reagan's self-styled "apprenticeship for public life" and his "postgraduate education in political science."[33]

A few sharp-eyed observers of the company have speculated about Reagan's exact role at GE. Journalist Rick Perlstein notes that "Reagan was an integral component of the Boulwarite system,"[34] but he does not expand the point much further. Labor-law professor David Jacobs observes that "Ronald Reagan had played a role in Boulware's strategy. . . . addressing employee groups as well as consumers,"[35] but Jacobs focuses on his own particular legal field. Jacobs *does* go on to describe Reagan's "basic GE speech as a compact and persuasive appeal to conservative policies."

Ronald Reagan's education at GE will be set out in detail in the chapters that follow. But can a mature adult *really* develop a set of beliefs and skills after his years of formal education have long passed? More to the point: Was Reagan's education for world leadership unique—and therefore unlikely or even a charade?

There are a number of examples that buttress the plausibility of Reagan's education, but only two will be referred to here, and those only briefly: Dwight Eisenhower and Winston Churchill. Toward the end of his presidency, Eisenhower was asked to name the ablest man he had ever known. It was a good question for Ike, who had worked with some of the most prominent figures of the twentieth century—Roosevelt, Churchill, Truman, and de Gaulle among them. Eisenhower answered: "Fox Conner."[36]

As an army major, Eisenhower went to Panama to serve under General Fox Conner in the 1920s. Ike already had a solid service record. He had not obtained the combat command he had sought in the First World War, however, and he felt that a successful military career might be beyond him. While his ability as a drafter of battle plans had already been observed, his academic attainments at West Point were middling.

On his arrival in Panama, the major was impressed with the huge library in the general's home. Conner fostered the younger officer's latent reading habit by starting his protégé with three historical novels, including *The Adventures of the Brigadier Gerard*, the classic fictional treatment of Napoleon's battles.[37] Map studies and other readings followed. Ike again went through von Clausewitz's *On War*, the full impact of which had escaped him when he first encountered the book at the Point. He read the memoirs of the great soldiers, including Grant (whose single literary work would become a model for Eisenhower's own memoirs after World War II). Philosophic writers, such as Plato and Cicero, were also part of his fare.[38]

After the major had read a volume from the general's well-stocked library, the older man would quiz the younger about what he had read, and he and Ike would engage in spirited discussions about military strategy. Conner held firm views about how the next war would be fought—he believed that the Treaty of Versailles virtually insured that Germany would commence a war, that America would be drawn into it, and that the war would be won by a coalition of allies operating under a unified command—and these views became Eisenhower's. By the time Eisenhower had completed his three-year tour in Panama, he had gained a commanding knowledge of strategy, tactics, and military history.[39]

If there was any doubt about the effect of Conner's tutelage, it was resolved by Ike's performance at the highly competitive Command and General Staff School in Fort Leavenworth, Kansas, after his return from Panama to duty in the states. The designation "Hon. Grad." in the *Army Register*, which applied to the first 10 percent of the class, was a distinction that counted heavily in an officer's future assignments and promotion. For this reason, competition to simply get into the school was intense. Eisenhower finished first among the 244 students in the class.[40]

Fox Conner was more than Eisenhower's teacher. He was a role model as well. A highly respected officer—he was chief of staff to General "Black

Jack" Pershing in France in World War I—he was everything a career soldier should be.

Winston Churchill had selected *his* role model early in life—his father, Lord Randolph Churchill, who might have become prime minister had disease not destroyed his brain and his career. Winston had little doubt as to his inevitable career in politics. But he realized that he knew almost nothing about the operations of the British government. His education at Harrow and Sandhurst (Britain's West Point) had provided meager fare in this regard. Accordingly, when he was stationed in India in the course of his military service, he had his mother send him records of parliamentary proceedings. He spent years studying these transcripts in the off hours when his cohorts were playing polo or cards.

A random background check would have given Lemuel Boulware some understanding of Reagan's natural skills in the course of Boulware's review of the various candidates for the job that Reagan eventually filled. In addition, Boulware might have read speeches that Reagan had given in the years before he came to General Electric, including his endorsements and campaign rhetoric on the hustings for Democratic candidates. There were also the speeches from platforms provided by the liberal veterans' groups to which he belonged in the late 1940s, SAG membership meetings and industry functions, and local civic groups concerned about communist attempts to take over the film industry.[41]

Immediately after his presidency, Ronald Reagan published a collection of his speeches. Other than the speech he gave for Goldwater in 1964, Reagan included only one public address from his prepresidential (in fact, pre-electoral) career. Entitled "Remarks at the Kiwanis International Convention," delivered in St. Louis, Missouri, on June 21, 1951, Reagan described the offering as his "basic Hollywood speech."[42] He explained that: "If you didn't sing or dance in the Hollywood of my day, you wound up as an after-dinner speaker."

His editorial comment notes that the object of his basic speech was "to correct some of the misimpressions about the gaudy, bawdy Hollywood lifestyles created by gossip columnists and fan magazines." In his speech, he points out that the divorce rate in Hollywood is less than the national average; that there are roughly three times as many high school graduates in the industry as in other American businesses; and that over 60 percent of his fellow workers are regular members and attendees of the churches in their communities.

In the course of his remarks, he observes that the Kremlin had focused on American films as "the worst enemy" of communism. He proudly states that "we now have [the Communists] licked" in their attempt to invade the motion picture industry. He sees Hollywood as a bastion of free enterprise, where the heights one can climb are "unlimited," and success based only on "your ability and your talent." This, he proclaims, is "the American way."

While Reagan was unstinting in his efforts to find public platforms to defend his industry, the pre-GE public speech most cited by historians was his commencement address at William Woods College (now William Woods University) in Fulton, Missouri, in 1952. This speech made no attempt to refute the gossip columnists and the fan magazines. Rather, it "revealed his view of America and his philosophy as an American."[43]

Reagan received the invitation to speak at William Woods through Dr. Raymond McCallister, a Protestant minister from St. Louis.[44] McCallister, a fellow Eureka alumnus, had been in the dramatic society and on the debating team with young Reagan, and he now sat on the William Woods board.[45] Reagan was introduced by Dr. T. T. Swearingen, president of the all-female college.[46] Of course, Reagan really needed no introduction. His face and his name were known to most Americans, certainly to every one of the thousand people who sat before him.

In front, dressed in black caps and gowns, were the 109 young women of the class of 1952 who were graduating that day. Behind them sat their families. It was a clear day, filled with sunshine. The speaker, wearing an academic gown over a white shirt that displayed his California tan to advantage, was forty-one years old. He was still playing romantic leads in the movies, and the smile with which he began his remarks caused a ripple in the audience.

Ronald Reagan began with a reference to the hymn that was sung at the start of the commencement ceremonies. As a result, the remarks have become known as the "America the Beautiful speech."[47] Right from the outset, Ronald Reagan made it clear that this was not going to be conventional commencement fare: "I feel duty bound to inform you that I am going to try to give you some remarks from my mind and heart; but they certainly will not be an address."[48]

Perhaps Dr. Swearingen had warned Reagan to be cautious. Ronald and Nancy Reagan had arrived in Fulton the night before. Nancy was pregnant with their first child, Patricia Ann. The guests of honor stayed with the college president, and, after a reception, the Swearingens and the Reagans relaxed in informal talk. In an interview years later, Dr. Swearingen admitted that he "got a lot of flack for inviting [Reagan] to give the commencement address because they had never had an actor before. They thought we were going out of the realm of where you go to get speakers."[49]

In fact, faculty opposition may have been spurred by two other campus appearances by Reagan within the past year. These were on celluloid. In *Bedtime for Bonzo*, he appeared with Diana Lynn and a precocious chimpanzee; Reagan was cast as a college professor. In *She's Working Her Way Through College*, he costarred with Virginia Mayo. The blonde, leggy Ms. Mayo played a burlesque queen who sought an education. Reagan was cast as a sympathetic pedagogue.[50]

If some of the faculty felt it was inappropriate to have a movie actor at commencement, the students certainly did not agree. Nancy Statton Korcheck, a member of the class of '52, has kept until this day a handwritten letter from Ronald Reagan dated April 28, 1952, in response to her invitation to join the local chapter of Phi Beta Kappa. In his letter, Reagan confirms that he will be coming for commencement, although he is "somewhat frightened at the idea that any words of mine can be interesting to you and your classmates." He gratefully declines her invitation.[51]

At the beginning of his remarks, Reagan made it clear that he was proud of America and that "if [he] had a text for anything [he] was going to say, you have heard it in the opening hymn." He recalled the signing of the Declaration of Independence and the crucial role played by a stranger, who addressed the group but then disappeared from the scene. He observed to the graduates that "you young ladies are getting ready to set foot in [a] man's world." He referred to the term "momism," which had been used to deplore the influence of women on the men in this man's world, particularly on those young men who had been "unable or unwilling to face the test of war in behalf of their country."

The speaker took issue with this view. He said that if "women are going to be blamed under the term of 'momism' for this group of men who could not meet the test, then certainly credit must be due [and] momism must be responsible for the sixteen million young men who did meet those tests." He then gave a stirring example—the pilot of a B-17 bomber that had been disabled by anti-aircraft fire, who chose to go down with the plane rather than abandon the wounded and trapped ball turret gunner. The pilot, Reagan noted, was posthumously awarded the Congressional Medal of Honor.

While he had focused on the fight against Hitlerism, the speaker observed that it was only a part of the "same old battle" America had been waging back through the ages. He mentioned the "ideological struggle that we find ourselves engaged in today" and said that he "thought of America as a place in the divine scheme of things that was set aside as a promised land."

The fight was not over. At the end of his impassioned speech, Reagan told the graduates: "We need you, we need your youthful honesty, we need your courage, we need your sweetness, and with your help I am sure we can come much closer to realizing that this land of ours is the last best hope of man on earth. God bless you!" The audience rose in a standing ovation. Then many of them rushed forward with their yearbooks, hoping to get his signature.

Some of the elements of "The Speech" with which Reagan made his national political debut in 1964 were already apparent: unmitigated patriotism, steadfast anticommunism, effective use of anecdotes and examples, the ability to inspire an audience, and a low-key style. The phrase "the last best hope of man on earth" actually appears at the end of both the 1952 commencement speech and the 1964 national telecast.[52]

The description of the commencement remarks in the *Fulton Daily Sun Gazette* could well have been a report on "The Speech": "Reagan spoke in a forceful but unassuming way, and throughout his talk, he told both humorous and serious stories. His friendly manner reflected his screen personality which is known to all who have attended his screen performances."[53]

Reagan's "America the Beautiful" speech was not an untrammeled success. Had the actor not embarked on a political career, the alleged imperfections would undoubtedly have gone unnoticed. But as Reagan entered public life, critics questioned the authenticity of the examples he had cited. In *Sleepwalking Through History*, for example, journalist-author Haynes Johnson quotes Reagan's version of the events in Independence Hall and then observes: "Such an incident [the intervention of the stranger], of course, never happened. . . . Ronald Reagan seems to have made it up out of whole cloth." He goes on to say about the B-17 account that no Congressional Medal of Honor was awarded for "anything resembling this story. . . . The story was either the product of Reagan's imagination or a scene he remembered from a World War II Hollywood movie."[54] Whether myth or reality, the story was a favorite of Reagan's, and he repeated it in a letter to a constituent during his governorship, which was later published in a collection of his correspondence in 1976.[55]

Certain aspects of the "America the Beautiful" speech would have appealed to Lemuel Boulware, although there is no clear evidence that he had read it or read about it. The patriotic theme and the press reports of the effectiveness of the speaker's style would have been attractive to Boulware, even though he probably had no intention, as he planned Reagan's early tours of the plants, of providing a public platform to GE's "traveling ambassador." The anecdotal inaccuracy could have been dealt with by proper instruction and vetting. Boulware was extremely careful about the items issued by his office. They were thoroughly checked and rechecked by his extensive staff. The use of persuasive, commonsense examples would have struck a responsive chord. They were a major part of Boulware's technique.

The legendary "Reagan Luck" was at work with Fulton, the locale of this oft-cited public speech. The actor had a personal connection with the city on which events were to confer a place in history. Fulton was the background for the novel *King's Row*. (The book's author, Henry Bellaman, was a resident of Fulton.) Reagan considered his role in the movie based on the book to be among the finest work he had ever done in films.[56] A line from the movie—"Where's the rest of me?"—became the title of Reagan's first autobiography.

The city's fame came from more than the renowned novel or Reagan's movie, however. Fulton was also the site, at Westminster College in 1946, of one of the most famous speeches of the twentieth century. It was there that former British Prime Minister Winston Churchill, with his host President Harry S. Truman by his side, proclaimed that the Soviet Union had drawn an "Iron Curtain" over the nations of Eastern Europe.

On November 9, 1990, Reagan returned to Fulton for the dedication of a "magnificent sculpture" called *Breakthrough*, by Churchill's granddaughter Edwina Sandys, commemorating the fall of the Berlin Wall. (The sculpture actually included a part of the wall.) It had been three years since Reagan's famous call in Berlin: "Mr. Gorbachev, tear down this wall." In his 1990 remarks, the former president stressed the importance

FIGURE 3 Ronald Reagan is shown after his 1952 commencement address at William Woods College (now William Woods University) in Fulton, Missouri. Entitled "America the Beautiful," after the hymn sung by the students as he went to the podium, this is the speech most often cited from Reagan's pre-GE days. He felt that it "revealed his view of America" at that time.
Source: William Woods University.

of Churchill's classic speech. "The road to a free Europe that began here in Fulton led to the Truman Doctrine and the Marshall Plan, to N.A.T.O. and the Berlin Airlift, through nine American presidencies and more than four decades of military preparedness."[57]

Events came full circle on May 6, 1992, when Mikhail Gorbachev came to Fulton to receive an honorary degree. In his speech, Gorbachev did not mention Reagan by name, but he did describe the longstanding Soviet-U.S. conflict as one "presented as the inevitable opposition between good and evil—all the evil, of course, being attributed to the opponent." This was, inescapably, a reference to Reagan's famous characterization of the USSR as the "evil empire." Yet Reagan believed that Gorbachev, in the words of British prime minister Margaret Thatcher, was a "man with whom I could do business."[58] And the Soviet premier and the American president "did business" together so effectively that the "Iron Curtain," came down.

Reagan's first encounter with communists came soon after his return to civilian life. Not long after he joined the board of the Hollywood Independent Citizens Committee of Arts, Sciences, and Professions, he learned that the organization had become a communist front. He and eleven other prominent board members tried to wrest control and, failing that, resigned. It soon became clear to Reagan that HICCASP and other front organizations were attempting to "take over Hollywood."[59]

At about the same time, SAG asked Reagan to mediate a dispute between two rival unions. The leader of one of them, the Conference of Studio Unions, was Herb Sorrell, who many people thought was a communist. The CSU went out on strike and brought violence to the studio gates. Reagan witnessed it firsthand—buses overturned, windows smashed, blood in the streets. When Reagan crossed the picket lines, Sorrell called for a boycott of his movies.[60]

The FBI soon came to see Reagan. One of their informants had reported that one member at a Communist Party meeting had asked, "What the hell are we going to do about that son-of-a-bitching bastard Reagan?" The actor received an anonymous phone call, threatening, "Your face will never be in pictures again." He understood that they planned to throw acid in his face. The Burbank police put a twenty-four-hour guard on his house and insisted that he carry a gun in a shoulder holster.[61]

Reagan later wrote that "I knew from the experience of hand-to-hand combat that America faced no more insidious or evil threat than that of Communism."[62] Like Reagan, Boulware also fought communists within the labor movement, as will be developed in greater detail later. Boulware's position at the bargaining table and elsewhere was simple. He described the blandishments being offered by the communists as "evil."[63]

Reagan and Boulware's opposition to communism was deeply ingrained. Reagan believed, however, that "some members of the House Un-American Activities Committee came to Hollywood searching more for personal publicity than they were for Communists. Many fine people were accused wrongly of being Communists simply because they were liberals."[64] And Boulware distributed to GE employees a book entitled *The Road Ahead*, in which author John T. Flynn contended that American Communist Party members were not the real problem. "I insist that if every Communist in America were rounded up and liquidated," he wrote, "the great menace to our form of social organization would be still among us."[65] Both the actor and the executive had had direct, personal experiences with communists in this country; each was deeply concerned about communism as an *international* threat and as a corrosive influence on American economic policy.

Their mutual opposition to communism was not the only potential bond between the two men. Reagan's interest in labor matters ensured that he would watch closely the steps that Boulware would take in labor negotiations. His fascination with labor issues, of course, went back years before his association with GE. One of the reasons Jane Wyman gave for the rift that had grown between her husband and herself as their divorce litigation unfolded was his preoccupation with SAG matters and related political issues. When they married, they had a common focus on their screen careers; Reagan soon seemed more concerned with union issues. She found his constant conversation about the subject a point of increasing irritation.[66] Richard Nixon once reminded Reagan that they had discussed "labor relations in the motion picture industry" when they first met in 1947.[67] This was more than a casual interest.

There is an intriguing possibility of a third reason—in addition to their opposition to communism and their deep interest in labor matters—as to why Lem Boulware was interested in Ronald Reagan. In the spring of 1950, two years before she married Reagan, Nancy Davis met Boulware. According to a letter in Boulware's collected papers, the meeting took place at the Arizona Biltmore, and Nancy was with her parents.[68] Her stepfather, Dr. Loyal Davis, was a devoted conservative. The Davises had a home in Phoenix, where Reagan first met Barry Goldwater.[69] Nancy adored her stepfather, and her husband came to respect Dr. Davis and his conservative views, as well. One wonders if Loyal Davis might have played a part in Boulware's hiring of the man who, by 1954, had become his son-in-law.

In time, the strong mutual interests of Boulware and Reagan would have a bearing on their relationship. But they may not have been a factor when Reagan was hired, in light of the limited fare the actor was expected to dispense on the GE plant tour. The general likeability he projected on the screen undoubtedly weighed positively in GE's decision to hire him. But the principal factor in his hiring might well have been his willingness to undertake the demanding tour and, frankly, his availability.

There is a dispute as to whether others were considered for the GE job before Reagan. Frances Fitzgerald states flatly that other actors had rejected GE's offer. Anne Edwards writes that others were "considered." Reagan himself maintains that the "package" was created with him in mind.[70]

Reagan's career had not been going particularly well. In the past two years, he had made three movies: *Law and Order*, *Prisoner of War*, and *Cattle Queen of Montana*.[71] The first two had only limited success at the box office; in the third, he did not even get top billing. In the RKO film scheduled for release the following year, he was to receive third billing. He had turned down the few recent parts his agent had sent to him because they were so bad.[72]

His last job, before the GE offer, was as an emcee in Las Vegas. Although he was to recall in his first autobiography that the act was "a sellout every night" and that the income was welcome during a period when the revenue stream had gone dry, neither he nor Nancy, who accompanied him on the two-week stint, enjoyed the experience.[73] Soon thereafter, he felt that he had "hit rock bottom" and told his agent, "Never again will I sell myself short."[74]

Ronald Reagan's frustration at this point had little to do with any political aspirations. He *did* believe that his civic activities revealed a gravitas that was being ignored by producers, who should be giving him more substantive parts. As a biographer noted, "He could not have helped but feel that his potential had never been realized, that the power and charisma he exuded in his [Screen Actors Guild] dealings and in his [speeches] should have been transferred to his image on film."[75]

It would be years before Reagan's true potential would be recognized, and then in a job that had little to do with the movies. He would, in time, be cast as a soldier in a kind of warfare he had never encountered on the screen. Lemuel Boulware was a leader of that ideological combat.

There were many possible reasons why Boulware saw to it that right from the start Ronald Reagan was put on *his* payroll.[76] He may have been concerned that the company spokesman would espouse his liberal beliefs in the message that he brought to the plants. The actor would bear watching. Or, alternatively, as he considered the talents of GE's new employee, Boulware may have foreseen the role Ronald Reagan could play in GE's political campaign.

But why was politics the business of business in the first place?

TWO

POLITICS:WAR BY DIFFERENT MEANS

Context is key in the process of education. In Ronald Reagan's case, the context was politics, with emphases on economics and frequent forays into foreign policy. The size of government, the extent of taxation, and the competition of foreign ideologies were all major themes in his political education. Much of this came from the policies of the company he worked for and the role that company chose to play in the politics of the nation. A lot of it came from the times in which he lived and the epochal events that formed them.

As Tom Brokaw points out, this generation was different. Tempered by the Great Depression, they had gone on to defeat a powerful fascist military coalition. They sought now to create a society that would preserve the values for which they had fought. The logic of Carl von Clausewitz's famous statement—"War is not an independent phenomenon, but a continuation of politics by different means"[1]—remained true. But with the coming of peace, the process would be reversed, and the arena now would be politics.

During the war, management and labor fought side by side to defeat a common fascist foe. Their goals seemed compatible, almost identical.

Now, with the cessation of their joint efforts against the Axis powers, significant differences began to emerge. Labor leader Walter Reuther's goal of "equal and equitable distribution of wealth"[2] and corporate executive Lemuel Boulware's quest to maintain "our free markets and our free persons"[3] became points of embarkation for another contest, this one to take place at the bargaining table, on the campaign trail, and in the voting booth.

Although the post–World War II confrontation began with a crippling national strike, both sides soon declared that their own war—the one between labor and management—to be truly effective, must go beyond the bargaining table to the country's grass roots. In 1947, Reuther announced that "unions can no longer operate as narrow pressure groups, concerned only with their own selfish interests. The test of democratic trade unionism in a democratic society is its willingness to lead the fight for the welfare of the whole community."[4]

Lemuel Boulware's answer came two years later when he said that "a majority of us, *as citizens at the grass roots* [italics his] . . . [must] get our representatives in government, unions and elsewhere to act with economic and political horse sense."[5]

Ronald Reagan's education would proceed in the midst of this epochal national contest.

———

There were millions of people, at every level of the workforce, who, at the end of World War II, left disappearing defense industries and now-superfluous government agencies to find new jobs or rejoin the companies that had employed them before hostilities began. Remarkably, three of the highest-ranking officials from one of the most powerful wartime regulatory arms—the War Production Board—went to the same company: General Electric.[6]

The executive vice chair of the WPB, Charles E. Wilson (known as "Electric Charlie" to distinguish him from General Motors CEO Charles E. Wilson, who was dubbed "Engine Charlie") resumed his duties as GE president, bringing with him WPB vice chairs Ralph Cordiner (who was his heir apparent and had been with the company before) and Lemuel Boulware (who had managed other corporations prior to his government service). Wilson gave his younger charges—both of whom became GE vice presidents—directions to establish long-range plans for

FIGURE 4 Charles E. ("Electric Charlie") Wilson, executive vice chairman of the War Production Board, with the four high-ranking military officers who constituted the WPB's executive committee. Board vice chairmen Ralph Cordiner and Lemuel Boulware later replaced two of the officers. All three of the civilians went to GE as the war ended. In war and peace, Wilson was deeply committed to long-range planning.
Source: Franklin D. Roosevelt Library.

corporate management and employee relations, respectively. Cordiner and Boulware were the men who would shape GE's policies regarding politics and the economy.

Some of the emerging leaders of management and labor could be seen in the last years of the war. Each of the government agencies regulating the wartime economy had its own adherents and critics. The WPB, the recent domain of Wilson, Cordiner, and Boulware, was described as favoring "those social forces that stood in historic opposition to the industrial union movement," while the National War Labor Board was regarded by most businessmen as "a bastion of New Deal liberalism."[7]

Before World War II, organized labor had grown under the Wagner Act and other favorable New Deal policies. Part of the reason was the emergence of industrial unionism, under the banner of the CIO (Congress of Industrial Organizations), as distinguished from the craft-oriented

AFL (American Federation of Labor). Labor's power increased with stepped-up production during wartime, but the unions' wartime "no strike" pledge reduced the public awareness of the extent to which labor's new strength could be used against management.

Some of labor's increased muscle was apparent during the war. As historian Nelson Lichtenstein notes in *Labor's War at Home: The CIO in World War II*, "the up-and-coming Walter Reuther of the UAW [United Auto Workers, a CIO union] captured headlines with a program to convert Detroit auto factories into 'one great production unit' to fulfill Roosevelt's ambition to manufacture 50,000 aircraft a year."[8] Although the plan was never put into effect as such—in part because it was opposed by the conservatively oriented WPB[9]—it drew considerable national attention and support from Harry Hopkins and other New Deal liberals.

Reuther's bold plan for greater wartime production, as well as a forceful civil rights initiative adopted by the UAW, were created in the cauldron of international conflict. This did not diminish their domestic political significance, however. Automotive executive and future Michigan governor George Romney described Reuther as "the most dangerous man in Detroit because no one is more skillful in bringing about the revolution without seeming to disturb the existing forms of society."[10]

Reuther's beliefs and practices have a special importance in any understanding of the education of Ronald Reagan because so many of the policies—within GE and nationally—of Reagan's mentor, Lemuel Boulware, were honed in response to the leadership that Reuther gave the other side of the contest. Reuther's background and education were rooted in socialism. His deep faith in unionism was a family birthright.

Walter Philip Reuther was born in Wheeling, West Virginia, in 1907. Both of his parents had emigrated from Germany. His mother, Anna, was a devout Lutheran. His father, Valentine, has been described as "a fervent unionist and Socialist: an active member of the Brewery Workers Union, one of the few industrial unions in the AFL, and an ardent supporter of Eugene Debs' Socialist Party of America."[11] He believed that American society was divided into warring classes of capitalists and workers. He followed Debs's conviction that workers had to use their political power to create a "cooperative commonwealth," which would replace capitalism.

The Reuther home was an active learning center. Walter, his three brothers, and his sister had access to their father's well-stocked library of socialist tracts. Family debates on social issues were the order of the day. Their mother's "religious commitments" and their father's convictions became the foundation of the children's beliefs.

At his father's urging, Walter dropped out of high school at sixteen to work as a tool-and-die apprentice in a Wheeling machine shop. Valentine Reuther thought this demanding specialty would bring his son to a higher level of skill and authority than most mass-production workers. After completing his apprenticeship, Walter moved to Detroit, the vibrant center of the auto industry, in 1927. He finished high school at night, but his plans to go right on to college collapsed with the U.S. economy at the onset of the Great Depression in 1929.

The automobile manufacturers were "staunchly anti-union." (Their leaders would later become regular participants in Boulware's monthly meetings of executives to coordinate activities and exchange ideas to defeat "union officials.") Their plants were marked by open shops and networks of informants. Violence was frequent. Walter and his younger brother Victor, who had just completed a year at West Virginia University, allied themselves with socialist organizations such as the League for Industrial Democracy and the students at City College of Detroit, who were active in the local Socialist Party. In 1932, the Reuthers campaigned for the Socialist Party candidate for president, Norman Thomas. Valentine was extremely pleased with his sons' activities. He wrote them that "socialism is the star of hope that lights the way."[12]

Walter's active socialist political activity was not without cost. In 1932, he was fired by the Ford Motor Company. He and Victor decided to use their savings to pay for a two-and-a-half-year world tour, which included working for fifteen months in the Soviet Union's Gorki auto plant. While they were impressed by the Russian effort to create a Soviet workers' state, they did not become communists. When they got home, they attended the socialist-oriented Brookwood Labor College, which, as it turned out, was very much a family affair. Brother Roy Reuther was an instructor to the 1935–36 class, and Roy and Victor's future wives were students.

After Brookwood, brothers Roy, Victor, and Walter joined the UAW. Walter soon demonstrated skill as an organizer and "bureaucratic infighter." He was able to move ahead simultaneously on both his political agenda and his union career. His youthful debates at home paid dividends as he developed a reputation as a stump speaker. Not everyone was pleased with his quick ascension within organized labor, however. CIO founder and president John L. Lewis—himself a renowned orator—described Reuther as "an earnest Marxist chronically inebriated by the exuberance of his own verbosity."[13]

Still, Reuther moved rapidly into positions of leadership. In 1936, he was elected to the UAW's International Executive Board and was also named president of the union's newly created West Side Local 174. At the time, the local had hardly any members, but within a year it expanded dramatically. The UAW became "one of the largest and most influential unions in the United States."[14]

Walter Reuther used his growing power to turn the UAW in two new directions. First, he and others moved to expunge the communists from positions of leadership. In the late 1930s, he condemned their subservience to Soviet Russia and at the union's national convention in 1940, he sponsored a resolution barring from union office any "member of an organization whose loyalty [is] to a foreign government." During this same period, he resigned from the Socialist Party, which had, over his objection, refused to support Frank Murphy, Michigan's Democratic governor, for reelection in 1938. In 1940, he enthusiastically backed FDR for president. His fame grew during the war, and at about the same time that Japan's defeat led to the end of the world conflict, Reuther became president of the UAW.

Attacks based on his background and past actions continued even after Reuther changed his party affiliation. But his response suggested a broader, more inclusive posture. When a General Motors executive accused him of trying to create "a socialistic nation," Reuther answered: "If fighting for equal and equitable distribution of wealth in this country is socialistic, I stand guilty of being a socialist."[15]

James B. Carey was another prominent labor leader who would make frequent appearances in the careers of both Boulware and Reuther. In 1933, Carey was twenty-one years old and had worked as a tester-inspector in Philco's radio laboratory for only a short time. He helped to form a local union and was elected its first president. Carey was fiercely proud of the part he had played in the growth of the labor movement. Years later, in the course of a meeting with other union officials, he remarked that "industrial unionism started here at the Fort Pitt Hotel where we had a meeting in 1933."[16]

That same year, Carey's local and others in the radio industry formed the Radio and Allied Trades National Labor Council, which then affiliated with the AFL. Carey was elected president.[17] His efforts to have his council recognized as a national union were rebuffed by the AFL, however. Several craft unions objected to the new organization. In 1936, the AFL went further, suspending all CIO unions. The council, now renamed the United Electrical and Radio Workers, was chartered as a union by the CIO. Carey was elected its first president, and Julius Emspak, a leader of the GE local at Schenectady, became its first secretary-treasurer.[18]

Carey was clearly an electable young man. He has been described as "a good speaker . . . quite capable of moving crowds and at debate."[19] His highly emotional character and the attendant outspokenness made him a poor administrator and an ineffective bargainer, however, and in the words of Walter Galenson, a historian of the labor movement, he "gradually relinquished the running of the union's daily affairs, including negotiations with employers, to his willing associates."[20] In 1938, Carey was elected secretary-treasurer of the CIO, where he would often serve as an ally of Walter Reuther.

Although he was moving away from United Electrical activities, Carey could not resist occasionally reinserting himself in the negotiating process. As *Business Week* magazine later observed, "the personal instability of James Carey . . . made him maneuverable by GE strategists."[21] His flamboyance and comments, many of them highly personal and profane, would, over time, prove grist for Boulware's mill.

As Carey's national prominence grew, UE leadership fell to Julius Emspak and his close associate James Matles of the International Association of Machinists. The addition of the machinists to the membership (and the title) of the UE provided a further wedge into the auto industry. It also brought Communist Party members to the union's leadership.

Emspak and Matles were identified as Communists on numerous occasions, most notably in testimony by Louis Budenz, onetime editor of the party's newspaper, the *Daily Worker*.[22] The UE drew great public attention at the outset of World War II because at that point in history, the American Communist Party slavishly followed the line dictated in Moscow. When Soviet dictator Joseph Stalin entered a nonaggression pact with Adolf Hitler, the UE opposed the U.S. defense effort.[23] After Hitler invaded Russia, however, the UE joined the war effort with unbridled enthusiasm. And its Communist Party–trained leaders proved to be extremely effective organizers. From its modest representation of 10,000 workers in 1936, the UE grew to represent 600,000 employees in

1,375 plants over the next ten years. Eighty-six of these plants and 110,000 employees were part of GE. The UE had become the company's largest union and the third largest in the CIO.

Walter Reuther's fame from his wartime proposal to produce "50,000 planes a year" may have gone to his head. He badly overplayed his hand during the national strike of 1946. He seized headlines when he brought out GM's 320,000 hourly workers. The UAW's demands far exceeded other unions. They included a call for a 30 percent increase in hourly wages, which was described at the time as "extraordinary."[24] Although Reuther's move put the UAW on the front pages, it also created a major opportunity for his archenemies within the CIO, the communist leaders of the UE.

Early in 1946, while the UAW was still on strike, the UE and the United Steelworkers accepted an 18.5–cents-per-hour wage increase from their employers. Although this was viewed by members of both unions and by their employers as a "significant union victory,"[25] it fell far short of Reuther's demand. (The UE settlement was apparently reached without Reuther's knowledge.)[26] The UAW leader kept his members out for 113 days, eventually settling for the same figure as the electrical workers and the steelworkers. A labor historian called it "one of the most dramatic defeats" in Reuther's career.[27]

Reuther's defeat at the bargaining table did not deter him from pursuing one of his most cherished objectives. The war had opened the eyes of Reuther and some other leaders of organized labor to new openings for minorities in the work force. During the Great Depression, it had been difficult to "effect change in the Negro's employment" due to the scarcity of jobs. "It was not until the demands of war created a national labor shortage," Reuther later wrote, "that Negro workers really won new opportunities for employment and upgrading."[28]

When Reuther was elected to the union presidency at the UAW convention eleven days *after* the GM strike ended, the issue of communist control and *not* his tactical error during the strike dominated the election. Reuther won by the razor-thin margin of 114 votes out of 8,761 cast. He staked his career on defeating the "left-wing caucus" within the union, with its significant component of communist leadership.[29] Ironically, many of the African American members of the GM locals felt that Reuther's victory depended on the allegiance of "white southern transplants" who constituted a "prejudiced element" within the UAW.[30] The changes made at the union's 1946 constitutional convention would do much, eventually, to allay these concerns.

The tenth UAW constitutional convention, in 1946, was the occasion for passage—this time unanimously—of Article 25 of the union's constitution. This established a Fair Practices Committee in every local and confirmed that "equal opportunity" and "anti-discrimination" were major initiatives of the union. Funding was provided by automatic monthly contributions from dues-paying members.[31] Reuther's wartime condemnation of discrimination against Negroes and Mexicans by certain locals—even to the extent of expelling recalcitrant locals—now became part of the union's constitution. Reuther himself assumed directorship of the UAW's Fair Practices and Anti-Discrimination Department.

Walter Reuther's victories in 1946 did *not* give him control of the union. The left-wing caucus retained both vice presidencies, the secretary-treasurer's office, and ten of the eighteen regional directorships. After all, they had played a major role in the success of the national strike. Reuther's campaign to gain ascendancy at the union's 1947 convention drew strength from the decline of Soviet-American relations and the beginning of the Cold War.

"The American Communist party is not a political party in the legitimate sense," Reuther wrote. "Communist party members in America and in our union are governed by the foreign policy needs of the Soviet Union, and not by the needs of our union, our membership, or our country."[32] Reuther took great care in selecting his candidates for regional directorships, choosing men with strong local support, and winning fourteen of the eighteen contests. His faction also captured the vice presidencies, and the two-fisted, militant Emil Mazey, who would remain his ally for years to come, was elected secretary-treasurer. Reuther's margin in his reelection to the presidency climbed to two-thirds of the vote.

Buoyed by the change of leadership at the UAW and President Truman's surprising election victory in 1948, Reuther, CIO leader Philip Murray, and like-minded union officials began a two-year purge of the organizations that followed the left-wing caucus. Eleven unions, with a total membership of 900,000 were expelled from the CIO during this period. Former "stalwarts," such as the International Longshoreman's Union and the United Electrical Workers, were among those forced out.[33]

It was during this period that Walter Reuther and Lemuel Boulware found themselves on the same side. The CIO's purge of communists had been aided in part by weaponry provided in the Taft-Hartley Act passed by the Republican-dominated eightieth Congress. The UE's expulsion from the CIO had a profound effect on its bargaining status at GE.

In 1949, the CIO chartered a new union, the International Union of Electrical, Radio, and Machine Workers. The UE was swept entirely out of the General Motors electrical division and out of most Westinghouse and General Electric plants. There were no communists in the leadership of the new union, the IUE. In fact, Jim Carey was back, first as temporary head and then as IUE president, a position he continued to hold during the years of Boulware's tenure at GE. While the UE was still a factor at GE, remaining as bargaining agent at the company's largest plant (Schenectady), the IUE became GE's major employee union.[34]

Boulware believed that the communists were motivated by hatred of the free-enterprise system, as much as they were in trying to get a better deal for their members. He insisted that "there is an inescapable *moral* requirement for our continued freedom and the enjoyment of the rest of the material and non-material well-being open to us."[35] This requirement, in his view, was not met in communist doctrine.

While union power burgeoned during the final years of the war, the War Production Board's hesitation to expedite reconversion to peacetime industry "guaranteed that the wartime growth of the [corporate] industrial giants would not be endangered by new competition in the postwar period."[36] While the country's largest companies appeared satisfied by this policy and even looked forward to harmonious industrial relations during the postwar period, a group of middle-sized manufacturing firms, located largely in the South and Midwest, were uneasy with the wartime surge of union power. They did their best to defeat it, even when they were condemned by the National War Labor Board.

Leaders of this effort to thwart the organizing efforts of the CIO were Sewell Avery, chairman of Montgomery-Ward, and Fred Crawford, of Cleveland's Thompson Products. Crawford was elected president of the National Association of Manufacturers in 1943. Other companies in the conservative vanguard were Hughes Tool, Kohler Industries, and Humble Oil.[37]

Early in 1946, the Truman administration "scuttled" wartime price controls,[38] creating a target of higher profits that labor sought to share. The "no strike pledge," which had masked union power during the war, no longer existed. Corporate leaders who had expected a calm transition to peacetime production were rudely awakened. Unions now shut down entire industries. Similar actions had followed the First World War, leading one labor historian to conclude that "1946 was the greatest year of strike activity since 1919."[39] The crippling national strike taught corporate managers throughout the country an important lesson: organized labor had emerged from the war with new power and resolve.[40]

This was certainly true at the General Electric Company. Herbert Northrup, a former GE employee-relations consultant and later a university professor wrote: "1946 [was] the year of the greatest strike wave in our history. . . . [It] demonstrated to the company that its then method of bargaining was no match for . . . the union's."[41]

PART II

A POSTGRADUATE COURSE
IN POLITICAL SCIENCE

THREE

===

BOULWARISM

In 1946, the leadership team within General Electric learned the lesson that every management in corporate America learned that year—that they did not possess the political and negotiating skills of the union leaders. At GE, however, they learned a second lesson as well. Even as the strike led to acceptance of union demands in GE plants, one part of the company—which involved thousands of workers and millions of dollars of annual revenues—suffered no direct losses from the strike. In fact, it did not go out on strike at all. Its manager was Lemuel Boulware.

Boulware was just a year shy of his fiftieth birthday when he came to General Electric in 1944. Charles Wilson had given him two separate jobs. He was a "marketing consultant" to the company president. He was also responsible for GE's seven wholly owned subsidiary manufacturing companies, which sold their products under other names. These "Affiliated Manufacturing Companies" (which included Hotpoint and Carboloy) had 16,000 employees and did $150 million in business annually.[1] A company organization directory of July 1945 reveals that Boulware served on GE's select Advisory and Operations Committees, along with the other two former WPB officials. Cordiner had a second title, "assistant to the president," which presaged his later succession to the GE presidency.[2]

When none of the workers at the subsidiaries under Boulware's supervision joined the employees of the parent company in the seven-week strike, Charles Wilson and the GE board did what bold corporate leaders might be expected to do: Boulware was made "vice president, employee relations" of the General Electric Company, and he soon added "community relations" and "public relations" to his portfolio as well.[3] Wilson then directed Boulware to expand his successful policies into a long-range plan for the company.

Boulware once told a colleague that Boulwarism "was a terrible word for a good idea."[4] The word was coined by a writer for *Fortune* in an article describing policies of major companies in their continuing battle with organized labor.[5] "Crawfordism" was used to describe the policies of Frederick C. Crawford, chief executive of TRW (formerly Thompson Products), and "Fairlessness" was named after U.S. Steel's head Ben Fairless. Only "Boulwarism" survives as part of the language, and largely in labor-law cases and texts.

Boulwarism was *not* a narrow agenda for bargaining with labor. Boulware's program went over the heads of union officials directly to the blue-collar workers, their families, and their neighbors. It had two main components: an ideology that set out in some detail what America should be and a methodology that prescribed how these goals could be achieved. These twin threads became what Ronald Reagan later called his "postgraduate education in political science" and his "apprenticeship for public life."

―――――

Lemuel Boulware was described in many ways in the course of his career. He was certainly a manager extraordinaire. He was a renowned negotiator. A journalist writing about Harvard Business School's legendary class of 1949 described Boulware, their commencement speaker, as "one of the era's most influential executives."[6] The IUE's Jim Carey, who was a prominent adversary for over a decade, called him a propagandist (on a par with "Hitler, Mussolini, and Khrushchev") and accused him of "brainwashing."[7] But Boulware saw himself as a teacher.

After receiving his B.A. (with a major in political economy) from the University of Wisconsin in 1916, Boulware stayed on as a teaching assistant at the university's business school. With the advent of World War I, he gave up that post and entered the army. Still, after a transfer to the New York region, he managed to find time to teach in Brooklyn's Plymouth Institute at night while performing his duties as a captain in the infantry during the day. He loved the give and take of the education process. (Almost fifty years later, in a very active retirement, he lectured at Florida Atlantic University).[8]

When World War I ended and Lemuel Boulware returned to civilian life, he decided to enter the world of business. He had more to learn. He worked in a variety of capacities—accountant, purchasing agent, comptroller, and factory and marketing manager—as he moved up the corporate ladder. In 1935, he became vice president and general manager of Carrier Corporation and in 1940, vice president and general manager of Celotex Corporation. From there, he went on to his World War II service as vice chairman of the War Production Board.

When he joined General Electric, teaching was at the core of his work. In order to make the changes he desired in the company, the country, and the national economy, he felt that a process of education must first be initiated and continued, even as the contest proceeded into its most intense stages. He had to teach economic precepts and political fundamentals to his workers, his fellow executives within the company and in other companies, and the public at large. In the course of this work, he would be aided by thousands of employees, recruits from the media, and a variety of leaders within the community. He would create one of the most powerful and sophisticated news-management operations in the country. He would teach, and an expanding universe of students from all walks of life would learn.

In devising his program, Boulware had visited all of his companies' plants. He spoke not only with local management but also *with the workers*. His inquiries went beyond the usual industrial-warfare shibboleths to probe the economic and social interests and concerns of the employees. The materials and speeches he developed hit home. His expertise in marketing was an important part of his work. He was among the first to employ sophisticated surveys of market (and employee) reactions. He constantly sought feedback and revised the *form* of his message when he found it was missing its mark. He was always the first to know how changing conditions affected the attitudes of GE workers.

FIGURE 5 In 1946, General Electric suffered the consequences of a crippling nationwide strike. But none of the 16,000 workers under vice president Lemuel Boulware went out on strike. Consequently, Boulware (pictured here at about this time) was put in charge of all of GE's labor, public, and community relations and was directed by Charles Wilson to create a comprehensive plan to deal with these matters.
Source: Lemuel Boulware Papers, Rare Book and Manuscript Library, University of Pennsylvania.

On June 11, 1949, Lem Boulware addressed a group of graduating students and alumni at the Harvard Business School. It was five years before Ronald Reagan would come to work for GE and fifteen years before his nationally televised political debut. As you will see—because in this book speeches, especially those written by the speakers themselves, are given careful scrutiny—Boulware's remarks that day were very similar to "The Speech" that Reagan delivered in 1964. In fact, Boulware's words came much closer to "The Speech" than Reagan's own "America the Beautiful," presented in the first chapter.

At the time of his speech in Cambridge, Boulware was a hero of American business. He was reputed to understand blue-collar workers better than anyone in the country. His speech at Harvard was a clear statement of his (and GE's) basic position and, in part, how he planned to achieve his objectives. Boulware also had a reputation as a compelling speaker. (One executive from another company was so impressed that he made it a point to learn Boulware's schedule and to travel around the country to hear him.)[9] It became apparent as Boulware spoke that he welcomed the opportunity to make his message known. His enthusiasm was a big part of his effectiveness.

The occasion for his speech in Cambridge was the Alumni Day Program of the Harvard Business School. The subject for the day-long session captured the students' attention: "Developing Executives for Business Leadership." And since the speakers were described as "the all-time, all-star team"[10] of management, and the students would get to mingle with them at a reception and dinner at the Harvard Club of Boston, the soon-to-be graduates turned out in high numbers. Boulware spoke to a packed hall. In addition to the forty-niners, the reunion classes were present as well.

After a fulsome introduction, Boulware rose from his place and moved to the lectern at the center of the stage. Although he wore horn-rimmed glasses and his brown hair was thinning, he exuded power. His face had a ruddy glow from weekends spent on the golf course in Westchester. He was tall, three inches over six feet, and his muscular build recalled his years, now three decades behind him, as a stellar athlete at Wisconsin. His voice was deep, still holding a touch of his Kentucky home. He wore his customary uniform of the day for such events, an elegantly tailored navy blue, pinstriped, three-piece suit and a maroon Countess Mara tie.[11]

As Boulware faced his audience in Cambridge, he was already contemplating a mission that went beyond the boundaries of his own company. He knew that to be truly effective he had to enlist executives from other corporations in his program of worker education. At this high point of union-management warfare in America, state legislatures were passing laws that, in Boulware's view, aided organized labor. He needed help to fight such laws. But first, he had to influence his fellow executives to reverse the public's picture of the American businessman as greedy, un-caring, and untrustworthy.

"Here we are," Boulware told his audience, "with incredible achieve-ments to show for our management of the business side of our wonderful system of freedoms, incentives, and competition. . . . We are phenome-nal manufacturers. We have been fabulous financiers. We are superb at individual selling and mass marketing." His listeners positively glowed. Then he turned to his real message for the day:

> But taken as a whole man of business, each of us is too likely to be condemned by a majority of the public as anti-social. We always seem to be coldly against everything. . . . As a result, too many of our employees and too many of their friends and representatives—in unions, in government, among educators and clergy, in the whole public . . . not only do not respect us but also do not like us. They do not understand or appreciate what we are trying to do. And let's be frank about it—there are times when it looks like *we* don't, either.[12]

Boulware lamented the failure of American businessmen to understand the workings of the economy that produced their success. "The penalty of such economic ignorance," he said, "can be—is already—very great in both the economic and political fields. Our free markets and our free persons are at stake." He then embarked on his core message, which he and his minions were to repeat again and again. "We don't like the proposals for further greatly enlarged government expenditures now being urged on the public by a combination of government and union officials. . . . The size of taxes—now and proposed—is bad enough." Noteworthy in Boulware's rhetoric was his method of addressing his audience as "we." *Together* they would share defeat if they could not rouse themselves for victory.

In describing his program to his listeners, Boulware presented a brief outline of exactly what he planned: "It's the job of every businessman—every citizen—to go back to school on economics individually, in small groups, in big groups . . . to learn from simple text books, from organized courses, from individual discussions with business associates, in neigh-borhood groups, at the club or bar, on the train or bus." This was a sum-mary of the process that became the education of Ronald Reagan, and, as Reagan became increasingly a participant, the beginning of his role in the conservative revolution in America. Boulware made it clear: the campaign could not be the work of only one company or one community; it must be a national effort.

Boulware wanted businessmen to do more than clean up their images. He wanted them to make an effort to learn how their system worked and to become engaged in the process of conveying this message to others. He was talking not only about influencing their employees but about gaining support from "citizens at the grass roots." He wanted them to get involved, to be politically active. Now he was recruiting them. In just a few years, he would marshal them for action in the field. He chided them: "We businessmen are bold and imaginative before commercial competition. We are cowardly and silent in public when confronted with union and other economic and political doctrines contrary to our beliefs."[13]

It would be impossible to measure the effect of Boulware's words on his audience. This was a special time in the history of American education. Many of the students were World War II veterans whose college expenses were paid in whole or in part by the GI Bill—which Tom Brokaw described as "the greatest investment in higher education that any society ever made."[14] They tended to be more mature, more dedicated than their predecessors. Interviewed fifty years after the event, one class member commented that Boulware was "much discussed." Another did not recall the speech but remembered "Boulwarism" from the school's course in labor relations. A third recalled that Boulware's tone was "tough" and that the room was "very crowded."[15]

Fortune Magazine described the class of forty-nine, at its twenty-fifth reunion in 1974, as "Harvard Business School's most successful class."[16] (That reputation has stood the test of time. A book published in 2002 proclaims that the class has "transformed American business.")[17] The forty-niners have been called "The Class the Dollars Fell On"[18]—after "The Class the Stars Fell On," Dwight Eisenhower's class at West Point, which had more than its share of generals.

Career accomplishments are easily exaggerated at reunion time, but here the evidence is compelling. Class members headed Xerox, Johnson & Johnson, Bloomingdale's, and many other major U.S. corporations. About half the class were either the CEOs or COOs of the companies that employed them. The annual revenues of these companies exceeded $50 billion. The class's collective net worth was about $2 billion. One of their number was the largest shareholder in General Dynamics, and others were presidents of colleges and senior partners of investment banking firms. The reunion chairman, John Shad, an investment banker who was then near the top at E. F. Hutton, was later appointed chairman of the SEC by President Reagan.[19]

One member of the class recalls that at commencement he joked with his roommates, both of whom had also been Harvard undergraduates with him, about Boulware's conservatism. They viewed themselves as "liberals."[20] It was a time, after all, when most Americans described themselves as liberals or moderates. This included a majority of Republican officeholders.

By 1974, of course, much of this had changed. By then, a growing number of Americans thought of themselves as conservatives. A conservative had captured the Republican presidential nomination a decade before. The south, a traditional Democrat stronghold, was becoming conservative and Republican. The change had resulted in part from the campaign of American businessmen, discussed at greater length in later chapters, to counter the efforts of union leaders at the grass roots. Boulware and Cordiner had been leaders in this movement. Gerald Ford, a moderate Republican president, would soon face a fight from conservative Ronald Reagan for the party nomination.

The prevailing attitude on campus can be seen in the *New York Times* account of the undergraduate experience of Supreme Court Chief Justice John G. Roberts Jr., who arrived at Cambridge in the fall of 1973. The Harvard Young Republicans found a 25 percent increase in interest among incoming freshman of over the previous year. Founders of the conservative Federalist Society arrived on campus during Roberts's time at Harvard. Two of the professors at the law school later gained a measure of fame as conservatives: Charles Fried, who became President Reagan's solicitor general, and Douglas Ginsberg, whom Reagan nominated for the Supreme Court in 1987 and who withdrew when it was revealed that he had once smoked marijuana. Young John Roberts's senior paper on Daniel Webster was entitled "The Utopian Conservative."[21]

Boulware had spent years developing his 1949 mission statement. He "went public" in the "Salvation Is Not Free" speech that he gave on Alumni Day. Soon after the commencement, he gave the same speech at the Chicago and Detroit Economic Clubs and at seventeen other distinguished forums. These organizations and others distributed thousands of copies of Boulware's remarks. GE itself sent "many thousands" to employees and their neighbors.[22] The average citizen, he wrote, "*cannot afford to leave politics to the politicians.*"[23]

Boulware saw the need to educate the citizenry in three areas: "economic *understanding, moral fortitude and political sophistication*" (emphasis in original).[24] By 1949, he was well on his way to implementing the long-range plan that "Electric Charlie" Wilson had directed him to establish. A review of its evolution from collective bargaining to "political bargaining" (his term) to the broader arena of politics is crucial to understanding its effectiveness as a mature doctrine. Even today, some fifty years later, it is hard to find a company that has come even close to what Boulware created.

IUE president Jim Carey and other union officials employed the term "Boulwarism," in a derogatory manner, to describe General Electric's negotiating posture, which they maintained was intransigent. They said that Boulware laid the company's offer on the table and told them to "take it or leave it." Boulware liked to point out that with the exception of the company's 1948 offer (which the union accepted without change), "all subsequent ones were revised in major or minor ways" during his "fourteen years on the job."[25] The validity of the union's charge that Boulwarism was an unfair labor practice was in litigation for over a decade. Boulware, in retirement, wrote a comprehensive defense in his first book, *The Truth About Boulwarism.*[26]

It is important to understand that GE *did* intend to place a "truthful" first offer on the bargaining table early in negotiations. Boulware did not believe in starting with an offer presented as "final," which would then be raised (as the company had intended all along) after threat of a strike by the union. Boulware called these "trick offers." His surveys found that the process led employees to distrust management and to give full credit to their own leaders for results achieved.[27]

Instead, GE began negotiations with an extended study of working conditions and corporate profits. "Then," Boulware said, "when it finally seemed evident that all items of current interest, together with all the available related information of real significance, had been fully considered and discussed to the point of exhausting all possibilities, we made a comprehensive and complete offer."[28] GE would then go directly to the workers in a program of "education" that Boulware called "Job Marketing," described more fully below. Ronald Reagan became an integral part of this effort. Changes in GE's first offer could and did occur, but only if new facts ("information of real significance") were later presented.[29]

While the preparation of the company's offer was conducted at GE's own pace and within the boundaries of its offices, the process was made known in some detail to its employees. Immediately after placing one such offer on the table, for example, Boulware sent out to all plant newspapers an article headlined "Proposal Result of Much Research, Fact-Gathering."[30] The full-page text detailed the research that went into the proposal, identifying many of the individuals involved in the process, with accompanying photos and credentials.

Chief Judge Irving Kaufman , who would later write the Second Circuit decision on Boulwarism (which he insisted on spelling as "Boulwareism") described the program in the following way: The "early publicity phase . . . employing virtually all media, from television and radio, to newspaper, plant publications and personal contact" came first. Later, he wrote, "the Boulware approach swung into high gear."[31] When collective bargaining negotiations approached the final months of the contract period, "a typical employee received over 100 written Company communications." On many days, this employee might get "two, and sometimes three or four GE messages, not including oral discussions and meetings with Company supervisors."

One text on labor negotiations provides the following definition: "Boulwarism is an attempt to win and hold the loyalty of the workers so as to counter-balance the power of the union."[32] Boulware would probably agree, although he was always careful to point out that he was not "antiunion." He once told a group of executives at a National Association of Manufacturers conference, "We believe in the union idea. We think unions are here to stay. We think some among even the best of employers might occasionally fall into short-sighted or careless employee practices if it were not for the presence or distant threat of unions."[33]

Boulwarism was a persistent, continuous process. As *Business Week* noted, "GE's policy of year-round communication with its employees (another component of Boulwarism) gives it more influence with its work force than most companies have."[34] Of course, this policy put pressure on the company's "traveling ambassador from Hollywood," who had to be able to answer questions about these messages as he visited the plants throughout the country. The elements of "Job Marketing"[35] were so simple and straightforward that it is difficult to believe, today, that the concept was revolutionary when promulgated. Boulware cited as the inspiration for GE's novel approach to employee relations a remark of a professor from his undergraduate days who had suggested that "the principles and practices in marketing should be examined for possible use in employee and community relations."[36] He had a "sudden recollection" of the professor's advice as he considered an ongoing study of the Marketing Executives Society (in which he had been active for many years). The study, which was finally published in 1962, did not deal directly with labor matters. It traced the revolution that had occurred in marketing *products*. Boulware's contribution was to apply the lessons thus learned to employee relations.

The Marketing Executives Society's history described the old way of selling as designing a product, manufacturing it, and then turning it over to the salesmen. This was a "hit-or-miss" procedure that began to change in 1926, when Henry Ford had trouble selling cars the way *he* wanted to build them, without considering the preferences of his customers. As the society's report pointed out, "For the most observant, there had occurred back there in 1926 the final confirmation of the revolution from the old 'me' kind of *selling* to the new 'you' kind of *marketing* with emphasis especially on pre-sales preparation extending to the product as well as to the other elements in sales planning."[37] Armed with a customer survey, Henry Ford grudgingly abandoned his Model T and produced the Model A, a car made the way the customers wanted it.

Over the ensuing decades, industry developed the science of "market research," utilizing customer surveys, focus groups, and similar techniques in product planning. The latest in-depth methods were being used on campuses in New York City at the time of GE's contest with the IUE, and Boulware had had the opportunity to see their initial development in Washington during his years with the War Production Board

The "Likert Format" came out of World War II testing in German and Italian communities. The measurement was of quantum of commitment and used a five-point scale. This was a qualitative survey, vastly different from the old-fashioned, head-to-head survey model the IUE often employed. The war also gave birth to focus groups, which Paul Lazarfeld used to test radio propaganda scripts. After the war, Lazarfeld came to Columbia University, and Robert Merton and others colleagues memorialized his seminal work in *The Focused Interview*. At this time, the techniques were used at the Bureau of Applied Research at Teachers College at Columbia.[38]

Research into individual preferences—what Boulware referred to as "man-to-man information transfers"—had been used by General Electric for twenty years when Boulware arrived at the company. Now he asked whether GE "could pass on to our employees—our 'job customers'—the benefits of what we had learned in many years of pleasing product customers through . . . market research" and other elements of product planning, training, and sales.[39] Occasionally, historians perceived the importance of this new approach. Kim McQuaid in *Uneasy Partners*, after singling out Boulware, goes so far as to say that the application of "industrial psychology's techniques and tools" to the labor-management contest "helped spark a revolution."[40]

When Boulware first came to General Electric, he initiated his own version of focus groups (among them, book clubs that involved spouses as well as the workers themselves, and that are discussed more fully below). The process took years. Boulware began by redefining the American worker. As most companies approached the end of their labor agreements, they viewed their employees as one-dimensional. The focus was almost entirely on compensation. Boulware's starting point was, "Our employee did not live by bread alone. He did not work for bread alone. He would not or could not do his work well if he thought his return for what it was to be in bread alone."[41]

Boulware saw the employee as broader than previously defined. Each was a "contributor claimant," who might fill a number of different roles under that broader classification. As he explained, "The people who did things for each other in private [i.e., nongovernmental] business, then [1947] as now, did so in five contributor-claimant roles: investor, customer, employee, supplier, and neighboring or more distant citizen." Boulware maintained that each of these contributor-claimants was demanding something of business. He analyzed these demands in three categories:

1. The basic material satisfactions
2. The extra human satisfactions
3. The assurance that the balanced best-interests were being served

A durable piece of Boulware literature is the checklist he prepared to guide his management colleagues in their understanding of the expectations of GE workers. At this point, it should probably be browsed. It will be revisited from time to time throughout the book.

THE NINE-POINT JOB—OLD AND NEW
OCTOBER 15, 1947

1. COMPENSATION, which includes:
   a. Pay that is right—all things considered—for the skill, care, and full day's effort as measured by reasonable modern standards, and
   b. Extra financial benefits such as pensions, awards for ideas, free life insurance, scholarships, and paid vacations.
2. WORKING CONDITIONS that are as good as they can be made at the moment, that are regularly improved, that are being constantly studied for further improvement, and about which all suggestions as to additional improvements are always welcome.
3. SUPERVISION, which is:
   a. Competent technically to aid the employee to get the most out of the machine or other facilities with reasonable physical effort, and
   b. Competent as a leader to make the employee understand promptly, clearly, and easily the reasons behind the direction or advice given so he can do his job intelligently and voluntarily, and
   c. Competent as a counselor or as a guide to good counsel where the employee seeks aid in personal matters.
4. JOB SECURITY to the greatest degree possible through the teamwork of employees, management, stockholders, and loyal customers.
5. RESPECT for basic human dignity, which is protected along with the rest of the employee's stake as a free, upstanding, good American citizen.
6. PROMOTION as fast as opportunities arise or can be created and on a strictly fair basis in view of the skill, care, and effort of the individual employee, with the employee's own ability and ambition being aided to every extent possible by training on the job.
7. INFORMATION on management's objectives, plans, problems, successes, and failures, and current expectations for the section, the department, and the company as a whole.
8. BELIEF in the individual job's importance, significance, and

challenge, and in the employee's contributions to the great good accomplished by the final GE product.

9. SATISFACTION that comes from going home to the family after a day's work with the feeling that something has been accomplished, that the accomplishment has gained the attention and earned the respect and gratitude of one's fellow employees at all levels, and that the job is a good one to return to the next and following days.

Boulware probably took some good-natured ribbing about the 1947 date that appeared on the handout, even as it was used in the 1950s and 1960s. He did not hesitate, however, to continue a policy for years, so long as it still worked. (Similarly, he had no reluctance in giving the same speech, such as "Salvation Is Not Free" at many locations over many years.) This commitment to the long-term was, he believed, a lesson in itself. Certainly it was one which was eventually practiced by his most famous protégé.

As vice president of public and community relations, Boulware developed a managed-news program that was the envy of corporate America and undoubtedly an inspiration for the Reagan White House. Newspapers in towns and cities where GE plants were located—the *Berkshire Eagle*, for example, which covered the Lynn, Massachusetts, plant—often, published articles favorable to the company, which was among their largest advertisers and often the city's largest employer. It was not surprising, then, when an editorial in the *Eagle* proclaimed that other employers were reluctant to move into Pittsfield because GE's salary and other working conditions at its Lynn plant were hard to compete with. "TRYING TO LURE NEW BUSINESS HERE WON'T BE EASY," an *Eagle* headline said.[42] In later years, when Reagan, as GE's traveling ambassador, became a more significant part of the program, the papers routinely featured articles on his local appearances and, often, on the conservative message that he preached.

The most impressive publications, however, were the newspapers and magazines put out by the company itself. There were four, not counting the countless bulletins issued from Boulware's headquarters directly to the workers in the course of bargaining: *Works News*, *Employee Relations News Letter*, *Monogram*, and *The General Electric Forum*. *Works News* was distributed every Friday. Workers could take it home over the weekend to share with their families. It was included in the respective plant newspapers—the *GE Schenectady News*, for example—so that Boulware's messages on government or the economy or pending labor legislation could be interspersed among the results of the company's bowling league or the pending contest for the community's representative in the Miss General Electric competition. As bargaining entered its final days, this local news was supplemented by teletypes posted on the plant bulletin board, presenting GE's version of what had transpired that day in contract negotiations.

Mats were sent out to the local *Works News* each week. Boulware left little to chance. Test pages were often distributed in advance, and "formal surveys" were used to ensure employee understanding and interest. This turned out to be an effective and cost-efficient way to literally bring the company's message home.[43] For example, when Boulware learned from random reports that employees thought that the owners of the company made an annual profit of fifteen to twenty cents per dollar of sales, he conducted surveys that confirmed the reports. He then distributed material which pointed out that the owners received only four cents per dollar. Handbills sent directly to workers and articles in company publications underlined the point. (Great care was used in the manner in which this point was made because Boulware's research revealed that a majority of GE's workers, in their "contributor-claimant" roles, were also investors in the company.)[44]

The substantive content of Boulwarism will be reviewed throughout this book. But a sampling of the mats would include such topics as "How General Electric Keeps Trying to Make Jobs Better"; "How Big Are General Electric Profits—Are They Too Big?"; and "Should Pay Be Equal Everywhere?" Some of the articles involved national and international social and political concerns, for example: "What Is Communism? What Is Capitalism? What Is the Difference to You?" and "Let's Learn from Britain."[45]

Mailings to the employee relations managers reflected the subjects set out in *Works News* mats but were updated and tended to focus more on narrow union-management issues, for example: "Why employee 'expectations' should be realistically modest in 1960"; "Building Employee Understanding"; "The Why and How of Curbing Inflationary Settlements"; and "The Fallacy of Using 'Ability to Pay' as a Guide to Wage and Benefit Levels"; "Show how employees not represented by unions get their wage and benefit improvements without the possible delay of waiting for union acceptance"; "Why employees can expect their union officials to 'demand' a strike from them"; and "Why the company has no choice but to 'take' a strike rather than be forced beyond what is right."

The *Employee Relations News Letter* was another important weapon. The publication began with a circulation of 15,000, essentially GE's 12,000 supervisors and 3,000 ERMs. Its four pages were written late every Friday, then printed and shipped by midnight so they were in the hands of supervisors on Monday morning. It was the glue that held the program together and kept the troops motivated. Eventually, the *News Letter* became part of the Cordiner-Boulware political outreach program and added "thought leaders" throughout the country to the distribution list. These included clergymen and officials in GE towns but also media personalities, academics, and others who could carry GE's message to a wider public. His respect for Ronald Reagan's profession is apparent in Boulware's writings. In the category of those who should be the "sources of corrective guidance," he lists teachers, editors, and clergymen, as might be expected, but also includes "broadcasters" and "entertainers."[46] Circulation of the *News Letter* increased to "several times the original 15,000."[47]

The articles in GE publications were often addressed to major issues of governmental policy. The narrow "labor" issue was buried within the broader context of the policy discussion. Each publication, Boulware wrote, would include "controversial issues of acute current interest and impact on employee cooperation."[48] In late 1957, for example, an issue of the *Employee Relations News Letter* was devoted to the question of how the federal government could allocate its spending between defense and "better living."[49] The GE employee must come to the discussion in his capacity as a taxpayer (i.e., an aspect of his contributor-claimant role) trying to understand the considerations affecting these items of the federal budget.

Of course, GE was in the defense business, and the article urged the "weapons-system" approach that favored the element of private risk capital. The government was seen as a customer and not a manager. In the midst of the analysis, the article focused on "the part union officials and union members play."[50] Managers and supervisors were put on the alert that "in 1958 the debate on worker interests will be on a new note" as a result of the Soviet launching of *Sputnik* into space. A large wage increase would fall on employees as consumers. Workers must understand that their "balanced best interests" (a benchmark in Boulware's three-part analysis of contributor-claimant interests) must include a calculation of real wages, with their key component of increased productivity.

In addition to the *News Letter*, all managers and other concerned "thought leaders" were encouraged to read the *Wall Street Journal* editorial page each day and Hazlitt's and Fertig's weekly columns. *National Review* and *Freeman Magazine* were also on the list, as were columns by William Buckley and David Lawrence.

Monogram was GE's monthly publication. A slick, small magazine, it was highly readable and covered a panoply of subjects of interest to the company's employees and their neighbors. Coverage of television's *General Electric Theater* was a staple, along with articles about the program's star, Ronald Reagan.[51]

Finally, there was *The General Electric Forum*, a "Defense Quarterly," subtitled *"For National Security and Free World Progress."* It carried articles by leading scientists, government officials, and experts in the field. At least one article by a GE executive or scientist would appear every quarter alongside the other prestigious contributors. Each issue had a theme, such as "Frontiers of Human Progress" and "Education and Leadership for World Progress."[52] (GE's corporate motto at the time was "Progress Is Our Most Important Product.") Just before Ronald Reagan left GE, the publication contained an article on the nuclear-defense shield, anticipating the Strategic Defense Initiative by some twenty years.[53] When president, Reagan made one of the article's coauthors a U.S. ambassador.

General Electric also maintained book clubs for its employees and their spouses, which met every week over a sixteen-week period.[54] The books were often texts on economics, and usually conservative. The featured authors included Lewis Haney (*How You Really Earn Your Living*) and *Wall Street Journal* columnist Henry Hazlitt (*Economics in One Lesson*). Hazlitt was a close friend of Lemuel Boulware.[55] Some of the other books on Boulware's list were Hazlitt's *What You Should Know About Inflation* and *Failure of the New Economics*; *Understanding Profits* by Claude Robinson; *The New Argument on Economics* by Schoeck and Wiggins; *Economics of the Free Society* by William Roepke; *Prosperity Through Freedom* by Lawrence Fertig; and *The Fateful Turn* by Clarence E. Carson.[56]

Occasionally, Boulware would send his managers a book not on the list. *The Road Ahead*, by John T. Flynn, "was distributed to all managers as an unpleasant and unpalatable beginning lesson" in how far thought leaders could stray from their professed aims.[57] Flynn begins his book by saying that his "purpose in writing this book is to attempt to describe the road along which this country is traveling to its destruction." He uses Great Britain (in 1950, when the book was published) as a warning of America's impending doom. In words that Boulware might have written, Flynn states that the downward path in this country "is being carried out with startling fidelity and promptness with the aid of the ignorance of the American businessman and politician."[58]

The book clubs did two important things for GE. First, they carried Boulware's basic message not only to GE's workers but to their spouses. The company found that spouses often influenced the employees to accept GE's positions. The clubs also presented GE with a unique tool for understanding its workers. They were de facto focus groups.[59] Boulware was way ahead of most of his colleagues in understanding the real reasons a worker held his or her beliefs. As noted earlier, he was a pioneer in the use of sophisticated marketing techniques and a very active member of the Marketing Executives Society.[60] His ability to understand the attitudes of IUE members better than their leaders led to some of his greatest victories over the union. Pure and simple, he knew more about the strength of members' resolve to strike than their leaders did.

A 120-page manual entitled *Supervisor's Guide to General Electric Job Information* was sent to the company's 12,000 supervisors and 3,000 employee relations managers. The ERMs were particularly loyal to Boulware and enthusiastic about his teachings. While still with GE's independent companies, as he fashioned his approach to blue-collar workers, he created the post of vice president of employee and community relations," or as they were more familiarly known, ERMs.

The position, he observed, was

a very significant departure from prior practice in and out of General Electric. It had naturally been quite a mental and emotional wrench for many of the managers, professional specialists and others—who had been going conscientiously about their work as they saw it— suddenly to have to face the now obvious fact that the employee and community relations function not only had been too long neglected at all levels but also had become, if it had not always been, equal in importance to engineering, manufacturing, marketing, and finance.[61]

The ERMs and supervisors were often Boulware's eyes and ears in the field.

Boulware's specially selected troops were trained in his tactics as well as his philosophy. The tactics, too, differed from methods used by most other companies. Boulware's point of departure is spelled out in his second book, *What You Can Do About . . . Inflation, Unemployment, Productivity, Profit, and Collective Bargaining*, published in 1972. There he uses the following diagram:

$$B\text{———}M\text{——————————————}G$$
$$B_1 \quad G_1$$

Boulware explained that the politician running for election can campaign between B_1 and G_1, where B represents the bad—the spurious and damaging something-for-nothing position—and G represents the good—the honest and rewarding something-for-something course. The politician will not risk losing, so he stays very close to the voting majority (M), between the far more limited positions of B_1 and G_1.[62]

Within the context of collective bargaining, if the company wants to get support for G—its offer—it has to move M between contract-bargaining sessions. It must go over the heads of the union's representatives, directly to the workers. It must try to attract independent locals and to encourage their establishment. It must involve spouses and workers who are not members of the union. It must explain its position to neighbors and to thought leaders in the community in which the plant is located. It must maintain a constant campaign, going on each day for years, and not limited to the few months before the contract expires.[63]

Applying this approach in the broader context of government, a governor or president must appeal *directly to the voters* and not focus exclusively on legislative representatives and party leaders. The most effective work must be accomplished *between elections*. How Ronald Reagan, as governor and then as president, applied this lesson will be reviewed later.

Boulware's job-marketing program and his publications supplied information that became part of "The Speech" and, later, a staple of Reagan-administration policy. Boulwarism had been in place for seven years when Ronald Reagan joined the General Electric Company. GE employees had received thousands of pages of information on economic and political issues and were getting more every day. As he toured the country, Reagan met people in his audiences who would "cite examples of government interference and snafus."[64] In time, Reagan became a leader in the company's ideological contest. At the beginning, however, he played a different role.

FOUR

THE PLANT TOUR

When he first came to work for GE in 1954, Ronald Reagan's principal role was to host the *General Electric Theater* on television. But he was also committed to spend a quarter of his time touring all of the plants in GE's far-flung, decentralized corporate empire. The premise for the tour was simple enough: the appearance of Reagan—GE's new employee and soon to be its most familiar face—at each of the company's locations would give the workers a sense of unity under the GE banner. As will be seen in later chapters, there *was* a significant political element in the plant tour, but it was not apparent at the outset to Reagan or to those handling the day-to-day scheduling, accommodations, and travel arrangements.

The *GE Theater* soon became the country's top-rated Sunday evening prime-time program. One of the reasons for the show's popularity was the stars it was able to attract, in large part because of Reagan's popularity among his fellow actors. Friends who shared his background in radio—like Bob Hope and Jack Benny—were happy to accept his invitation to appear. His SAG leadership had also endeared him to a wide spectrum of professionals of all ages, everyone from James Dean to Ethel Barrymore. Reagan could go on for hours on the tour with anecdotes about the program's stars. When he took on the presidency of the Motion Picture Industry Council, which was formed to combat "unflattering stories about Hollywood," he added industry accounts of good works. GE dubbed him "the Ambassador from the Film World."[1]

The actor was proud of the accomplishments of the show. It was "the first to emanate from both New York and Hollywood on a regular basis and the first to alternate between live and filmed shows."[2] Fifty Academy Award winners appeared on the show, many for the first or only time on television. Reagan had a significant part in script selection, and in later years scripts reflected the philosophy for which he became famous. The company occasionally rejected a program idea if product promotion might be compromised. For example, management vetoed a script in which a plane's instruments—one of GE's businesses—were not working satisfactorily in a storm.[3]

Reagan's tour of GE plants presented many challenges. The announced premise of the tour was simple, but the execution was not. As the "goodwill ambassador" himself observed, "No large corporation [had] ever attempted decentralization on the scale attempted by GE."[4] Reagan recalled that he had personally met all of the employees in locations in "some forty states."[5] He estimates that of the two years that were spent traveling during his eight years with the company, he was "on [his] feet in front of a 'mike' for about 250,000 minutes."[6]

The tour began almost immediately after he was hired, even before the fall premiere of the *General Electric Theater*. The format of Reagan's appearances at the plants did not include any ideological content at the outset; in fact, the only "speeches" included were informal chats with workers along the assembly lines. The staple was Hollywood patter and enthusiasm for company products. The company sent an aide to travel with its corporate spokesman. He would see that appointments were kept and that the tight schedule was met. The first such aide was Earl Dunckel, who served during the first year of the tour.

They started in August. The big turbine plant in Schenectady was the first stop. Reagan was impressed by the size of the operation, with some thirty-eight acres of factory under one roof.[7] The decibel level was as intimidating as the sheer size. The smoke and fumes were so great that Reagan's eyes were irritated and he had to take out his contact lenses. When he started to walk around the factory floor, a group of workers recognized him, and the word spread. Suddenly all of the machines ground to a halt. The tour of the huge facility took four hours.[8]

Another stop on that first swing was Erie, Pennsylvania. The actor stopped at each machine and talked with just about everyone. He signed a lot of autographs and seemed to be really enjoying himself. "The people were most amusing," Dunckel reported. "The women would come running up—mash notes, autographs and all that kind of thing. The men would all stand . . . looking at him, obviously saying something very derogatory—'I bet he's a fag,' or something like that. He would carry on a conversation with the girls just so long . . . then he would leave them and walk over to these fellows and start talking to them. When he left them ten minutes later, they were all slapping him on the back saying, 'That's the way, Ron.'"[9]

The routine on the plant tour could be physically and mentally taxing. As occasional traveling aide Ed Langley reported, however, "There is [a] way that Ron stays fresh on these trips. He makes them an adventure. There has to be a set pattern to the talks, but he always seems to find a way to vary the routine. Consider what happened today."[10] At a reception for middle-management employees, one of the wives asked Reagan what she could do about her young son. The boy was depressed. He thought he might want to be an actor, but that was about the only bright spot on an otherwise bleak horizon. Nothing she tried seemed to lift the boy out of the dumps. The company spokesman thought about it for a moment and then said he would call on Saturday morning but that the boy should not be told.

Saturday was supposed to be Reagan's day off. He had finished a full schedule on Friday, with another reception that night. He had every right just to stay in bed, but he kept his promise to the boy's mother. He wanted the meeting to seem spontaneous, so aides George Dalen (who had replaced Earl Dunckel) and Langley were enlisted in a scheme to poll every other house on the boy's street. Reagan would ring a doorbell and say, "I'm Ronald Reagan and I'm conducting a survey on the *General Electric Theater*."

The report continued: "At the target house, we bounded into a cramped living room and confronted an incredulous mother and her sullen, furtive, indeed loutish son. Reagan's performance was astounding. Laughing, rumpling the brat's hair, spieling his cleaned-up dirty jokes, Reagan said he'd show the two of them how movie fights were staged.

George Dalen and I had been through this routine lots of times before audiences of GE workers. Coats off, George and I attacked Ronnie with fake punches, but the White Knight, supposedly wiping blood from his lips, laid into us, and George and I took our falls over the furniture and skidded across the rugless floor."

"The boy was so captivated," Langley continued, "he wanted to try a pulled punch on Reagan, and did. Reagan went back on his heels, disbelief on his face, staggered and fell on the sofa. Bouncing up immediately, he hugged the boy and told him he'd make a great film actor. Then he sat down, and became a father and a father confessor. He had the kid and his mother crying and begging him not to go, to stay for supper, to keep in touch. There's no doubt in my mind that he will."

Reagan welcomed opportunities to vary the routine, and some of these forays went further afield than he or his traveling aide had anticipated. After one scheduled appearance in Rhode Island, for example, he decided he wanted to visit the nearby state house. There, he ran into a group of about thirty grade-school children, escorted by their teacher. The students recognized the television star and gathered around.

As Langley wrote years later, "He gave the damnedest impromptu talk I've ever heard. It was part Jack Kennedy, part William Jennings Bryan." He then quoted Reagan: "'If we believe nothing is worth dying for, when did this [gesturing around the local symbol of democracy, the state house] begin? Should Moses have told the children of Israel to live in slavery rather than dare the wilderness? Should Christ have refused the cross? You and I, my young friends, have a rendezvous with destiny. If we flop, at least our kids can say of us that we justified our brief moment here. We did all that could be done.'"

The report concluded that GE had picked up thirty grade-school supporters and their teacher that day. Langley did not comment that the "rendezvous with destiny" phrase had been made famous by Franklin Roosevelt two decades earlier or that the phrase was one of Reagan's favorites. One wonders, when Langley watched "The Speech" on national television in 1964 if he recalled that he had first heard Reagan use its phrases—the "rendezvous with destiny" and the invocation of Moses and Christ—years before to a group of children in a state capitol.

We cannot be sure exactly what Ronald Reagan said to GE's employees and their neighbors on the plant tour. No texts, handwritten or otherwise, survive. But the reports of traveling aides, local publications, and

The General Electric News

Outdoor Lighting Department

| VOL. II | HENDERSONVILLE, N. C., MARCH 8, 1957 |

Reagan Here March 19

RONALD REAGAN, who is scheduled to visit Outdoor Lighting Department on March 19, has covered over 50 cities, where he speaks before employees and local civic groups (shown addressing a group of General Electrical employees on one of his many tours).

All members of the Outdoor Lighting Department are looking forward with eagerness to the coming visit of Ronald Reagan, motion picture star and host on TV's General Electric Theatre. It will be one of the highlights of the year, both for the plant and the community.

Ever since the popular actor and good-will ambassador from Hollywood will make several appearances at functions in Hendersonville as well as spend considerable time in the Department.

Plans for the day's program on Tuesday, March 19, have been completed. From 9:00 to 10:30 a.m. our distinguished visitor will breakfast with the local press and radio officials at the Skyland Hotel, after which he will leave for the plant. From 10:45 to 11:15, he will meet with General Manager J. T. Bailey and the Section Managers. He will talk to hourly employees in the cafeteria from

Salaried employees will have an opportunity to hear Mr. Reagan in the cafeteria from 12:00 to 12:15. At one o'clock he will have lunch and address members of Rotary, Lions, and Kiwanis at the hotel, after which he will return to the plant.

From 2:30 to 3:30 employees will have another opportunity to see and chat with the actor as he tours the plant. Second and third shift employees will hear him in the cafeteria from 3:30 to 3:45

In order to give the families of employees a chance to see and hear Mr. Reagan a program at the

Hendersonville High School has been planned for 4:00 p.m. Tickets have been made available. Employees desiring tickets should have seen their supervisors and requested them. Today was deadline for such requests and tickets will be issued shortly to those wishing them. If any tickets are left over, they will be turned over to the high school to be given to Junior Achievers. The program at the high school will include a talk by Mr. Reagan and a preview showing of the March 24 G. E. Theatre program.

At 6:30 p.m. Mr. Reagan will conclude his visit by attending a dinner at the Hendersonville Country Club at which he will address a group of OL personnel and key community, political, and club leaders.

Employees
On '56, O

"Ever since you becam ing Department," declared in opening the first in a s meetings, held on Wednesd keep you informed of our progr our responsibilities, and our portunities through orienta meetings, roundtable sessions, day-to-day discussions. This se of plant-wide meetings today g us a chance to discuss these sponsibilities and opportunitie a down-to-earth manner and report our business results 1956, and the outlook for future."

Four sessions were held throu out the day to accommodate the employees in the entire partment.

Mr. Bailey went on to exp how the Department tries operate in the balanced best in ests of all the claimants upon business and how each emplo contributes toward this end. pointed out that attracting keeping satisfied customers m everything and must be acc plished by combined team effo the business is to be successful. said the amount of business obtain reflects the skill, care effort put into our products. In speaking of competition Bailey declared, "Our prod must be attractive, they must

Bloodmobile Plant I

180 Empl

FIGURE 6 Ronald Reagan spent a quarter of his time—two years overall—as GE's "goodwill ambassador," touring GE's plants, talking with employees and their neighbors. *Source*: Schenectady Museum.

the writings of Ronald Reagan and his biographers give a good deal of circumstantial evidence. That evidence allows us to reconstruct the plant visit in "dotted lines." Historian-diplomat Jean Jules Jusserand once wrote, "When they publish sketches on their finds, paleontologists show by a plain line what the earth has yielded, and by a dotted one what, according to their speculations, the rest would have been like. The historian must do the same, that the reader may know what is certain and what is probable."[11]

On March 8, 1957, *The General Electric News* of the Hendersonville, N.C., Outdoor Lighting Department proclaimed: "REAGAN HERE MARCH 19."[12] The article noted that the spokesman's tours had covered fifty cities. It described the visit as "one of the highlights of the year, both for the plant and the community." The tour began at nine A.M. on March 19 with a press breakfast in Hendersonville at the Skyland Hotel. The breakfast ended at ten-thirty, and fifteen minutes later Reagan was at the plant, scheduled to talk for half an hour with the general manager and the section managers. Here he might have focused on the company's products. A year before this visit, the Reagans had built a new home on a "spectacular site" in Pacific Palisades. GE had insisted on supplying all the electrical equipment, so that Reagan ended up describing the house as having "everything electric except the chair." He could tell the outdoor lighting managers in Hendersonville about the "retracting canopy roof for indoor or outdoor dining." His command of the product line was so extensive, however, that he might go far afield of the local product, giving a sense of corporate pride in what was being accomplished elsewhere in the company's far flung empire. Hollywood columnist Sheila Graham wrote, "There was a joke about someone listening to Ronnie's spiel for the G.E. nuclear submarine, and remarking, 'I didn't really need a submarine, but I've got one now.'"[13]

Four more visits to the plant were scheduled during the remainder of the day. He met in the cafeteria in back-to-back fifteen-minute sessions, the first with hourly employees and the second with salaried employees. There was little time in the plant visits for anything but a few Hollywood anecdotes and some references to sports. The anecdotes were generally personal references, repeated often on the tour but new to the workers at a particular plant. His first mention of Jimmy Cagney, for example, began with his description of a problem Reagan had encountered in his initial meeting with the makeup crew at Warner Brothers. The makeup artists told Reagan that his head looked "too small." Then someone thought of Cagney, one of Warner's major stars. "He's got the same problem [as Cagney], a short neck."[14] The crisis was resolved by Cagney's shirt maker, who designed a special shirt for Reagan. And, Reagan could point out to his audience, the solution worked so well that he still had his shirts made by the same shirt maker.

Reagan returned to the plant after lunch. He spent an hour touring the facility and "chatting with employees." Then he went back to the cafeteria for a short session with second- and third-shift employees. By now word had spread about the earlier visits that day. The format was in large part question and answer. There might be a follow-up inquiry about Cagney, giving Reagan an opportunity to mention a part that

Cagney *didn't* get—the role of Notre Dame's legendary football coach, Knute Rockne. (Rockne's widow preferred Pat O'Brien for the part.) This in turn might lead to some sports stories based on Reagan's job, before his movie career, as a radio broadcaster of baseball games.

While workers were interested in Reagan's descriptions of Cagney and Cary Grant, they also picked up on a frequent setting for these anecdotes—meetings of the Screen Actors Guild. Cagney was a factor in recruiting Reagan for the guild.[15] Reagan's union membership was not allowed to stand by itself. Workers asked him frankly if he was accountable for his productivity, as they, his "fellow union members," were. "The first year I was hired," he responded, "management told me they wanted my TV show to get a 44 rating in the polls. Well, I drove it up to a 47. And when my contract came up for renewal, they said, 'We've re-evaluated. What we really wanted was 50.' Every year, it's the same thing. Enough is never enough. They always re-evaluate."[16] A bond was beginning to emerge. The men and women on the plant floor realized that their spokesman was also a fellow GE worker, concerned about his income, held accountable for his performance, ultimately responding to the same employer they did.

The growing candor between Reagan and his fellow employees was a two-way street. Some of the questions from the plant floor now crossed a line that Reagan felt was beyond courtesy and good taste. Someone asked "Why did you divorce Jane Wyman?"[17] to which Reagan replied, "None of your business, Buster." Not a brilliant rejoinder, but it seemed to suffice. And later in the same question period, the query was a blunt: "How much are they paying you for this shit?" Reagan's answer was equally blunt: "They haven't got enough to make me put up with you."[18] Again, not exactly as sharp as Oscar Wilde but sufficient to keep the crowd with him. Hecklers aside, he listened to the workers. Even on the nonpolitical early plant tour, he found that many of their complaints had to do with government interference in the workers' daily lives.[19]

Immediately after his talk with second- and third-shift employees in Hendersonville, Reagan went to the high school auditorium for a preview showing of the next *GE Theater* program. It was now late afternoon. GE employees and their families had tickets for this event; "any tickets not used by employees' families [would be] turned over to the high school's Junior Achievers." Reagan had his share of anecdotes about the show, particularly of the early days, when it was performed live. He recalled one program where a detective, played by Dick Powell, was about to expose the murderer. The corpse, thinking he was off camera, "walked off-stage in plain sight of twenty million viewers."[20]

Reagan had a talent for divining areas of mutual interest, particularly ones that allowed him to use his storehouse of eclectic knowledge. For example, he drew a general manager, who smiled little and was never known to speak more than a five-word sentence, into a discussion on cattle breeding. The manager, who knew a great deal about the subject, was surprised to find that the company spokesman was also knowledge-able in the arcane field. The two went on about it for some time, much to the amusement the others present. The evening ended with Ronald Reagan posing for a picture with the G.M., who couldn't stop grinning.[21]

Much of the evening at the Hendersonville country club was devoted to a reception. A lot of jokes were told, most of them by Reagan. Ed Langley made note of a comment by the wife of one of the GE execu-tives. "He was the most inventive man with a dirty joke I've ever known," she said. "He could clean up filthy stories and make them fit for old nuns. A few he told us that night, I'd heard—uncensored—from my husband. But when Ronald Reagan told them, his cover-up was funnier than the original and it was impossible to take offense."

Langley, who was not a regular traveling aide, brought a fresh per-spective of the tour, undoubtedly influenced by his experience as a for-mer actor. He "was amazed at [Reagan's] energy." Even after a full day of plant appearances and a challenging question-and-answer period, Reagan "was fresh as a daisy." Langley was intrigued by how much younger and more vigorous Reagan appeared on public occasions. One reason was the contact lenses Reagan wore in public, but Langley knew there was more to it. He commented on Reagan's "ingenious use of com-plementary colors . . . wearing a complementary blue suit . . . [which, with] his reddish hair, made a sallow fellow glow in the dark."

"I learned a trade secret," Langley went on. "I was surprised when George [Dalen] arrived in the suite with a bottle of wine. 'Best Rhine wine you can buy in Virginia, George,' Ron commented. Later I found that Ron's drink at the party was a 50–50 mix of ice water and Rhine wine, with an olive. The executives got half-sozzled, but Ron remained fresh."

Langley also reported on "the excellent relationship between Ron and George Dalen." Dalen had no reluctance to schedule speaking engagements that would occasionally alleviate the inevitable repetition of the plant tour. As Reagan later observed: "There [was] a string of highlights on the pleasure side, because of the hospitality wherever we were that provided us with wonderful experiences." These included salmon fishing on a yacht off Seattle,; deep-sea fishing in the Gulf of Mexico, and Louisville at Derby time. George "even booked us for a speech in Honolulu, and Nancy and I—as well as George and his wife Gini—made our first visit to the land of Aloha."[22]

During the early days of the tour, Reagan's routine was virtually issue-free. Although Earl Dunckel acknowledged "that this was the period that brought into being Lemuel Ricketts Boulware,"[23] he believed that the tour, at this early juncture, was not part of "Boulwarism." He felt it was being "handled at an entirely different level and in an entirely different way." [24] While Reagan himself stated that he was part of Boulware's "Employee and Community Relations Program,"[25] there is no indication that he was making any effort in those early years to put forth an economic message to the workers.

In the course of the plant tour, two things happened that changed Ronald Reagan's role as a GE communicator. First, Leonard Boulware learned that his traveling ambassador could give a speech. Second, Reagan's ideological outlook, and the content of his speeches, moved from left to right.

Earl Dunckel puts the discovery of Reagan's speech-making capacity in the first year of the tour. "We were going to stay over through Saturday," Dunckel commented in an oral-history interview.[26]

> Coincident with this there was a huge meeting of . . . high school teachers meeting at the armory. There were three or four thousand of them. At the last minute their speaker came down ill, and they came to me and said, "Can Mr. Reagan speak to us Saturday night." . . . I said, in effect, thanks a lot but no thanks. I was thinking, "My God, this is an area outside my expertise." I would have to do a lot of research to write a speech for Ron. What did I know about education?

Dunckel paused in the taped narrative, apparently enjoying the aura of mystery. "But you know what Ron said? 'Dunk, let's give it a try,' is what he said. I told him I didn't have time to write a speech, and he said 'Don't worry. Don't worry.' Now this was four o'clock Friday afternoon and he wasn't to speak till Saturday night, but we had all these things going on Saturday morning and through two o'clock Saturday afternoon."

"Saturday night," Dunckel continued, "he got up there and gave a speech on education that just dropped them in the aisles. He got a good ten-minute standing applause afterward. This is when I finally began to realize the breadth and depth of his knowledgeability . . . everything that went into that mind stayed there. He could quote it out like a computer any time you wanted. He did read widely, and he remembered what he read. He tended to mesh everything together to get a pattern out of things. It was an amazing *tour de force*. It really was."

In his second autobiography, Ronald Reagan recalls a different occasion for his departure from pure Hollywood patter in the plants.[27] This occurred "about a year or two after the tours began," when he was asked to speak to a group of GE employees who were raising funds for a local charity. He discussed how important it was for private groups to raise and spend charitable funds, for in government efforts administrative costs often ate up the money that ought to have gone to the needy. When he finished, he received a "huge ovation."

At the time of Reagan's visit to the North Carolina plant, Lemuel Boulware had changed the tour format to intersperse speeches with the assembly-line patter. Reagan felt that his "speeches were nonpartisan as far as the two major political parties were concerned."[28] He still viewed himself as a Democrat. (One report has him needling George Dalen for being a Republican—"You can tell from his black suit"—with Dalen replying in the same spirit that Reagan had been "taken in by Eleanor Roosevelt.")[29]

Nevertheless, Reagan's philosophy was changing. The transition was most apparent in the talks that he was now giving away from the plant floor, at luncheons and dinners. There were two such occasions in Hendersonville. At lunch, he addressed "the members of the Rotary, Lions and Kiwanis at the hotel." At six-thirty, he had another event, including a reception, "before a group of Outdoor Lighting personnel and key community, political and club leaders at the Hendersonville Country Club."[30]

The one P.M. talk in Hendersonville was of the "weekly luncheon club" variety, gathering the community's three major civic organizations for one event. The event was scheduled for a little over one hour, and the format probably consisted of twenty minutes of prepared remarks followed by a question period of similar duration. Writing of this period of transition, Reagan gives his audiences credit for the changing nature of his speeches. "People wanted to talk about and hear about encroaching government control, and hopefully they wanted suggestions as to what they themselves could do to turn the tide." In the course of his initial presentation and in the Q & A that followed, "The Hollywood portion of the talk shortened and disappeared."[31] The speaker now peppered his remarks with examples of government programs gone wrong and tales of government agencies, which were "tax-free, rent-free and dividend-free" competitors with private citizens.

A few early permutations of "The Speech" are filed in the Ronald Reagan Presidential Library in Simi Valley, California. They were delivered well after the "plant tour," in GE's revised format, now consisting entirely of speeches. Reagan dubbed this kind of speaking the "mashed potato circuit."[32] They carry the economic and governmental philosophy later seen in "The Speech" and in Lemuel Boulware's remarks at Harvard. In time, platforms such as the Hendersonville luncheon clubs would give way to more prestigious forums, such as the Executives Club of Chicago and annual state chamber of commerce banquets, although Reagan's basic commitments would remain cities in which GE facilities were located. When the spokesman ended his employment with General Electric in 1962, there was a three-year backlog of invitations.[33]

A further review of Earl Dunckel's oral-history interview reveals a very logical reason for the change in the speaker's ideological outlook. Dunckel puts the genesis of Reagan's *understanding* of Boulware's policies—well before his actual espousal of Boulware's principles—in the early days of the tour, when Dunckel discerned Reagan's interest in economic and governmental matters. He observed that Reagan realized that the employees in his audience were receiving a constant stream of Boulware's messages and he "didn't want to be at a loss to discuss it, if they wanted to discuss it." Reagan had no trouble mastering the material. "Everything that went into [Reagan's] mind," as Dunckel had noted after Reagan's speech to the high school teachers, "stayed there."[34]

Reagan himself states that he learned on the tour how to document "concrete examples" of the "collectivism that threatens to inundate what remains of our free economy." To do this, he had to "look up a few facts and add them together." Because he made repeated appearances before the same audiences, he had to create new versions of his speeches, "necessitating more reading and research."[35]

But where did Reagan find the "concrete examples" with which he buttressed his remarks? Why did GE workers become concerned about "encroaching government control" and develop an interest in "how to turn the tide"? And how is it that Reagan's pronouncements in the late 1950s fit so closely into the philosophy set out by Lemuel Boulware ten years before?

FIVE

===

SCHOOLS, CLASSES, AND TRAINS

In addition to the avalanche of materials—bulletins, newspapers, books, and magazines—sent to GE employees, Ronald Reagan also had access to lessons and texts specifically prepared to educate the workers and middle management of the company. Classes were held at the company's plants and in its schools. As *Time* observed, General Electric "maintains company schools with more students (32,000) than most U.S. universities."[1] The nature of these materials and the manner in which Reagan studied them is key to the understanding of his education.

Schools

The General Electric Company maintains a school. Nestled in the Hudson Valley in Ossining, New York, it was expanded in 1982 under the leadership of the then newly appointed chairman Jack Welch. It has a residence building, an education building, a learning center and a recreation building and covers fifty-three acres. Called "GE Crotonville," it was established in 1956. *Fortune* magazine described the facility as the "Harvard of Corporate America."[2]

An internally published pamphlet, "GE Crotonville," traces the establishment of the school to Ralph Cordiner, although one well-placed former GE employee gives major credit to Virgil Day, a GE executive working under the direction of Lemuel Boulware.[3] Actually, there would have been no school, nor would there have been Boulwarism or what *Time* magazine labeled "Cordinersim," had it not been for "Electric Charlie" Wilson.

The long-term studies that Wilson directed his younger colleagues to undertake—Cordiner's in corporate management and Boulware's in employee relations—became the curriculum for the education of GE employees at all levels.[4] Cordiner's "decentralization"[5] and Boulware's "job marketing" were part of the "long-range point of view," in which they both fervently believed and which would be taught at Crotonville and elsewhere.[6] General Electric's historic willingness to follow a succession of new leaders down revolutionary paths does much to explain why Cordiner and Boulware were given a broad license to pursue their unprecedented policies. The company had a tradition of constantly reinventing itself.

GE traces its origins to 1878, when a group of investors banded together to finance Thomas Edison's experiments with the incandescent lamp. In 1892, Edison's company joined with other pioneers in the field and incorporated the General Electric Company, with its headquarters in Schenectady, New York.[7] "Up until 1939," Cordiner wrote in his 1956 book *New Frontiers for Professional Managers*, "the Company was able to operate efficiently under a highly centralized form of management." He traced GE's growth from annual sales of $200 million in 1920 to $342 million in 1939. With the stimulus of war production, annual volume had increased to $1.37 billion by 1943. Continued expansion in the postwar period brought the figure to over $3 billion in the year when Cordiner's book was published. Cordiner wrote that "emphasis on innovation" was a hallmark of GE from its inception.[8]

Cordiner planned to use Crotonville to promulgate the management principles needed to carry out his plan of decentralization.[9] After a three-year study, GE purchased the Hopf Institute, with its library of thousands of texts on management, its classrooms, and its administrative buildings. The company bought further surrounding acreage, constructed other buildings, and "planted an ever-increasing variety of shrubbery and trees." Executives were brought in from all over the country to take courses such as the Professional Management Course and the Advanced Management Course. Although these were essentially Cordiner's teachings, they reveal the substantial influence of Lemuel Boulware.

In *Time* magazine's January 1959 article on General Electric,[10] Cordiner's picture was on the cover. The only other active GE executive photographed in the article was Lemuel Boulware. Physically, the two men were very different. Boulware towered over his friend by more than half a foot and was two years older than his chief. The keen attention always extended to Boulware by Cordiner, however, stemmed more from respect for his ability than deference due to age.[11]

Physical dimensions aside, Boulware and Cordiner had much in common. Both had come from small cities—Boulware from Springfield, Kentucky, and Cordiner from Walla Walla, Washington. Before ascending to their top executive positions with General Electric, they had made their mark by effective management of smaller companies. (Cordiner had left GE in 1939 to become president of Schick. *Time* credits him with putting that company "back on its feet." In 1942, he left Schick to go to the WPB, where he served with Wilson and Boulware.)

Although both Cordiner and Boulware had held distinguished positions in professional societies and commissions, Cordiner was better known by the public at large and even within the business community. In 1960, he would be named Businessman of the Year,[12] and he would receive many similar accolades. He and Boulware made a very effective team, and Cordiner's confidence in Boulware remained solid over the years. (When the company was under attack for possible antitrust criminal practices, Cordiner selected Boulware to head an intracompany task force on ethics.)[13]

Cordiner's writings and his courses at Crotonville take on historical significance because GE's model was the only example of management and leadership that Ronald Reagan had the opportunity to view over an extended period—aside from the megalomaniac methods of Jack Warner and other studio bosses in Hollywood—before he assumed executive responsibilities in government.

Reagan had great respect for Cordiner. He described Cordiner as "a remarkable and foresighted businessman" and considered himself a "fan" of the GE chief.[14] (Long after they both left GE, Reagan praised Cordiner in remarks in a 1974 Industry Week closed-circuit program. Boulware obtained a copy of the transcript and rushed it to Clearwater, Florida, where Cordiner was dying of cancer. Soon thereafter, he wrote Reagan that Cordiner's wife, Gwen, "read to him the gratifying excerpts as about the last words he understood before passing on.")[15]

New Frontiers for Professional Managers was based on a series of lectures Cordiner delivered at Columbia University's Graduate School of Business. His commitment to Boulware's program was confirmed in the book. After posing the question, "Why do people work?" he listed nine points, which were virtually identical to Boulware's 1947 "Nine-Point Job" checklist but with slightly different wording and order. Cordiner described them as a product of company research (beginning in 1948) that revealed the "qualities an employee wants to find in his position with General Electric."[16]

According to Jack Welch, who became CEO of GE in 1980, Cordiner used Crotonville "to push his decentralization idea down through the ranks."[17] The instructors used "Blue Books" containing almost 3,500 pages of "gospel," where Cordiner's POIM (Plan—Organize—Integrate—Measure) program was taught as a series of "commandments." In a process that Welch would ultimately change, "Thousands of GE managers were taught to take control of their own operations with profit-and-loss responsibility."[18]

While Cordiner recognized the obligation of the CEO to lead the company and report to the shareholders and the board of directors, he also acknowledged the impossibility of one man managing it all. "Now, the President is of course unable to do all the work himself, and so he delegates the responsibility for portions of the total work through organization channels to individuals who have the talents and knowledge required to do it."[19] The success of Cordiner's policy of delegation can be seen in GE's remarkable average annual pretax return on equity—40.49 percent—under his leadership.[20] His method was to set objectives and judge the performance of individuals and divisions by how well they met these objectives. The policy also led to some of the darkest days in the company's history. The system permitted, perhaps encouraged, the rogue.

Like Boulware, Cordiner believed that corporate responsibility went beyond the boundaries of the company's business objectives. There were "external challenges" as well. In describing them, Cordiner might have been summarizing Boulware's Harvard speech, "Salvation Is Not Free." The "four troublesome conditions that still stand as active and potential roadblocks to economic and social progress," Cordiner wrote, were "(1) excessively high taxes. . . . (2) growing, unchecked union power. . . . (3) a fantastically growing federal government. . . . and (4) the latent suspicion of 'big business,' a tempting target for demagogues who are hunting for votes regardless of the economic and social consequences."[21] The "balanced best interests," Cordiner stated (repeating one of Boulware's favorite phrases), of all groups who contributed to the company's success must be considered.[22] Accordingly, under Cordiner, the company's objectives often went beyond its workers. *Time's* comment that Boulwarism was so close to the beliefs of Ralph Cordiner that it might as well have been called "Cordinersim,"[23] was substantially true, even if somewhat backwards.

Cordiner handled many of GE's "external challenges" himself. Later in his career, he occupied a top position in the Republican Party and, working with Boulware, played a key role in Ronald Reagan's heralded political debut. Much of his work on external challenges, however— especially as they related to resolving the "troublesome conditions" affecting the country's "social and economic progress"—he delegated to Lemuel Boulware.

While Crotonville was the fount of all knowledge on Cordiner's management practices, and while his blue books spelled out his program in infinite detail, there is no record of Ronald Reagan attending any classes at the school. The classroom chaos that would have come from his celebrity status would have made any regular attendance impossible. Still, as will be seen later in this chapter, his particular methods and lifestyle made absorption of the material manageable.

CLASSES

While Lem Boulware recognized the value of having a school where executives could gather for instruction in company management policies, he preferred the plants as the sites for *his* classes. For example, HOBSO (How Our Business System Operates), a course that had originated with DuPont and that Boulware unashamedly borrowed, involved three one-and-one-half-hour sessions, offered at plant sites on company time.[24] Book clubs were conducted at the plants or in nearby homes of employees, and GE's publications were distributed at the plants or sent directly to the homes of their readers.

In the course of instructing the 12,000 foremen and 3,000 ERMs in the methods of Boulwarism, the plant sites enabled the students of these classes to observe other managers at work in their traditional fields. Of course, this was also the best place to be close to the blue-collar workers. All 15,000 supervisors had received the 120-page manual, the *Supervisor's Guide to General Electric Job Information*, but there was no substitute, Boulware felt, for observing how diligently their fellow GE managers in more traditional fields plied their trades and for witnessing the reactions of assembly line employees. "In illustrating this in our training meetings at the turbine plant," he wrote,

> we tried to picture to the foremen how thoughtfully, painstakingly, patiently and pleasantly our sales engineer went about giving a turbine customer the information and guidance that would cause the latter of his own free will to want to do what we recommended as to the selection of the equipment and the signing of the order.[25]

The *Supervisor's Guide* lists frequent worker complaints and assists foremen in dealing with these matters before they become explosive. HOBSO involved top management and the lowest-level "non-supervisory" worker in "internal sessions" at the plants. The company also offered its "discussion leaders" to "schools, churches, clubs, or other businesses in [GE's] plant cities."

Ronald Reagan toured countless plant sites over the years, but he couldn't be characterized as a student in Boulware's classes for his supervisors or for the blue-collar workers. He has written that he gained from his discussions on these visits,[26] but this doesn't begin to explain how he digested the massive amount of educational products that Cordiner produced at Crotonville and that Boulware distributed at the plants.

TRAINS

While he was not able to attend the school at Crotonville or the classes at the plants, Reagan mastered the books, articles, periodicals, pamphlets, and instruction guides as few others were able to do. The reason stemmed from a little-known idiosyncrasy: fear of flying. This seemingly unrelated phobia played a significant part in the education of Ronald Reagan. Based on an unnerving choppy flight to Catalina Island in 1937—the same trip on which he had taken his screen test at Warner's—the GE traveling spokesman refused to fly. This was memorialized in his contract with the company.[27] He traveled by train and rental car or company-furnished limousine. He used this time to read.

At the very least, Reagan had to master the material in order to avoid embarrassment. As Earl Dunckel points out, "[Reagan] was interested very much in our employee relations philosophy, Boulwarism, because we were out there talking to the people who were affected by it. He wanted to know what it was and all about it."[28] The traveling ambassador was also in frequent contact with the executives who were part of Cordiner's revolutionary system of management. He would be expected to be familiar with it. Of course, the abnormally high incidence of decentralization had been the original rationale for Reagan's tour.

Traveling aide George Dalen, a former FBI agent, fit well into the traveling ambassador's routine of study and memorization. Reagan described him as a man of "quiet efficiency."[29] If the short train and automobile trips could be regarded as prep time before a test—with Reagan reading the plant newspapers for local news and for Boulware's latest *Works News* pronouncements—the hours spent in bicoastal travel on luxury trains were study halls and homework, providing the actor with hours for reading and reflection.

When the *General Electric Theater* began in 1954, New York was still the center for television production, or, for that matter, live shows. It soon became a bicoastal enterprise. The show was among the first to film in California. Reagan loved the great transcontinental trains. "I still can't think of a more comfortable way of travel," he once commented, "than taking the Super Chief from Los Angeles to Chicago."[30] As noted earlier, Reagan loved to read. Historian Catherine Drinker Bowen has observed that "All book lovers. . . . like to ride on trains; the situation is at once soothing and conducive to reading."[31] And, as former White House aide David Gergen has commented, Reagan made a practice, formed over the Hollywood years, of "committing what he read to memory."[32]

Reagan enjoyed working into the conversation facts and figures that he thought interesting. A fellow actor commented about the pre-GE Reagan: "Ron had the dope on just about everything: this quarter's up—or down—figure on GNP growth, V. I. Lenin's grandfather's occupation, all history's baseball pitchers' ERAs, the optimistic outlook for California sugar-beet production in the year 2000, the recent diminution of rainfall level causing everything to go to hell in summer [in] Kansas and so on." He found Reagan's store of information "abundant [and] stunning in its catholicity."[33] Not surprisingly, Reagan critic Francis Fitzgerald quotes others on the set who "thought the young actor [was] naive and a memory bank without purpose."[34]

To the older Reagan, the materials from GE must have seemed like manna from heaven. The items developed by Boulware had been vetted for accuracy and were all relevant to a coherent program. As expressed by Boulware, they were not labeled "conservative"; although representing a company-oriented, free-market point of view, they were carefully couched in "non-partisan" terms. They seemed, as they were intended to be, reasonable. They were certainly not "without purpose."

Moreover, the GE materials were virtually designed for memorization. Boulware cited his Nine Points frequently, together with his three underlying principles. Hazlitt, Haney, and the other economists whose books Boulware recommended were popularizers, describing the "dismal science" in the most colorful (and memorable) manner possible. As noted earlier, Cordiner's philosophy, set out in hundreds of pages of "Blue Books," was summed up in a single word "POIM," (Plan—Organize—Integrate—Measure).[35]

The trip from the west coast was generally made on the Super Chief. The actor made notes on index cards that he would use for his talk. His use of the cards as an aid to speaking played an important part in his mastery of the materials he read. As he spoke in that age before teleprompters, Reagan would take a pack of four-by-six index cards from his jacket pocket as he approached the podium. Immediately before, as he rose from his place at the table, he would put his index finger into his mouth to moisten it, and remove one contact lens. His other (lens-enhanced) eye would allow him to see his audience, while his natural near-sightedness would permit him to read his cards. He used shorthand of his own devising on the cards. For example, if the speech read: "Never again should young Americans be asked to fight and die for their country, unless the cause is one that we intend to win," his card might read: "NEVR AGN- YAs ASKD—FITE & DIE UNLESS—CAUSE—INTEND—WIN."[36]

The GE traveling ambassador believed that "you can't hold an audience by *reading* a speech."[37] By using his index cards, he could avoid the appearance of slavishly following a text and still maintain the discipline of an address that he had thought out and written in advance. More to the point in the present context, the method also facilitated Reagan's constant development of the remarks that eventually became "The Speech." If an example did not go over well, or if a more current situation could be used for greater effectiveness, the speaker had only to discard some cards and replace them with others.

Anecdotes and examples might come from his personal reading or from Boulware's managed news. The texts undoubtedly helped to shape his basic philosophy. Initially, Reagan may have first read Hazlitt for defensive purposes. ERMs who had been to Crotonville and participants in employee book clubs studied the book. The spokesman had to be prepared to answer their questions, should any arise. Hazlitt, a writer for the *Wall Street Journal* and a nationally syndicated columnist, was a great favorite of Lemuel Boulware's. The two met and corresponded often.[38] When Boulware later retired, Hazlitt occasionally accepted Boulware's invitation to speak at a luncheon club in Boca Raton.[39] The economist was a conservative and a popularizer. Of course, he was not everyone's cup of tea. At least one critic has referred to his "extreme free-market views."[40]

If Reagan had first encountered Hazlitt's text as he traveled to a plant site, the book was more likely fare for the leisure time afforded in the longer train ride to the coast or even for his periodic breaks at his ranch. Hazlitt's preachings became an important part of Reagan's economic philosophy. The economist was the kind of a man who would appeal to Ronald Reagan. He was a well-rounded individual who had succeeded in a number of journalistic endeavors. He was an author, a literary critic, a columnist, and a practical philosopher. Biographer Llewellyn Rockwell observes that *Economics in One Lesson* "may be the most popular economics text ever written."[41] It is still in print and still read on college campuses.

Hazlitt's influence on America's move to the right is widely acknowledged. As Rockwell notes, "If you want to know where American supporters of free markets learned economics, take a look at *Economics in One Lesson*." Hazlitt may also have influenced Ronald Reagan in the view that "the art of economics consists of looking not merely at the immediate but at the longer effects of any act or policy."[42] Of course, the long-range approach was a pillar of Boulware's policies and, ultimately, of Reagan's.

Hazlitt's books were classic conservative fare. So was the text by Lewis Haney that Boulware placed on the recommended reading list. But it does a disservice to the authors and to their most famous reader to simply leave it at that. There is more to it than the generalization that the economists were conservative and therefore their readers became conservative. Consider in somewhat more depth—as an example of the education of Ronald Reagan during this period—one of the pillars of conservative economic doctrine: opposition to deficit spending. Hazlitt, Haney, Boulware, and Reagan all wrote or spoke at various times in support of the general proposition that deficit spending is anathema. Little wonder that the followers of Reaganomics were shocked in the 1980s when the president permitted what were then the largest deficits in history. How could this policy possibly square with his *conservative* education?

The preface to Lewis Haney's *How You Really Earn Your Living* stated that "this book was suggested by a keen-minded business man who is concerned about the lack of economic understanding on the part of the present generation of adults—employers, employees, and their neighbors. He is only slightly less concerned about the coming generation, I am sure; but the time is so short that progress must be made immediately with those who are now the workers, buyers, managers, and voters, if the American idea is to survive." Like Henry Hazlitt, Haney was a favorite of Lemuel Boulware.[43]

Haney published his book in 1952 and, like Hazlitt, the author was concerned about the large amounts by which the wartime spending (World War II and then Korea) exceeded government revenues. After reading and rereading the relevant sections, Reagan may well have come to the conclusion that deficit financing was often required by vigorous national defense. The amount spent and the method of repayment were essentially based on political and not economic considerations.

The book began with the problem. The first section was entitled "Defense and the Economy: Debt and Inflation." Quoting one of the country's famous battle cries—"Theirs not to reason why; theirs but to do or die"—Haney said that the armed forces had to be mobilized after Japan's unprovoked attack on Pearl Harbor. This was a matter of "liberty or death" and not "profit or loss." He pointed out that almost half of the money needed to pay for the war came from "extra taxes," but "over half, or about 60 per cent, of the government's war money was borrowed. In other words, it was added to the national debt." This, he said, was known as "'deficit financing': borrowing funds for the government to spend, and charging the amount to public debt."[44]

Haney observed that "several foreign governments" had proved that a government may refuse to live up to its promises without the fall of an administration or a revolution by simply passing a law that lowers the value of their currency. He warned against monetizing the public debt. He stressed that "experience teaches that all of us must pay for war, and do it during or soon after the war." He turned to the Cold War, comparing that period and the pre–World War II economy: "In 1950–51," he wrote, "over 70 cents out of every dollar of Federal spending was either for national defense or obligations arising out of past wars, such as veterans' services and benefits, debt service, and international arrangements. This compares with only 30 cents per dollar spent in 1939."

Other parts of Haney's text referred to the "booms and busts" of America's business cycles, noting that "America under free enterprise has been a land of surplus." This reference was to the lifestyle of individual Americans as compared to citizens of other countries, most notably the Soviet Union. The normal posture of government should be a balanced budget. As large a part of the necessary war expense as possible should be paid by direct taxes borne by all. And this should be done sooner rather than later. Haney warned against passing the debt on to the "next generation."

As he read Haney on deficit spending and the booms and busts in the economy, Ronald Reagan's mind might have focused on Lem Boulware's teaching about how the economy functioned within a democratic society. Businesses did not make these economic decisions themselves; government intervened. Haney seemed to echo this belief. "When the debt is not incurred for the ultimate production of consumer goods," Haney wrote, "the operation however necessary it may be is not a matter of *economics. It is a matter of government or *politics. It is a part of *war.*"

The *political* solution would be paying the debt out of income generated by taxes after the war was over. If there is a surplus caused by the cessation of military spending, a strong leader must see to it that it is used to reduce the debt. Franklin Roosevelt might have done this had he lived after World War II. His successor, Harry Truman, actually reported budget surpluses, until the Korean War forced him into a deficit.[45]

Hazlitt's *Economics in One Lesson*, also published after World War II and the Korean War, makes a similar point:

If the soldiers have been supported by an unbalanced budget—that is, by government borrowing and other forms of deficit financing—the case is somewhat different. But that raises a different question: we shall consider the effects of deficit financing in a later chapter. It is enough to recognize that deficit financing is irrelevant to the point that has been made; for if we assume that there is any advantage in a budget deficit, then precisely the same budget deficit could be maintained as before by simply reducing taxes by the amount previously spent in supporting the wartime army.[46]

The year-end 1957 issue of the *GE News Letter* is also important in understanding Reagan's education on the advisability of deficit spending. The cover was headlined "1957 Year-End Review of Freedom's Old But New Problem of BETTER DEFENSE or BETTER LIVING or BOTH!" At this point in history, the U.S. political crisis was generated by Russia's successful launching of *Sputnik*. The article asked the question, "Can United States citizens remain free and still make the proper decision as how much of our 'gross national product' must go for military expenditures and how much must or will remain for civilian purposes?"[47] It acknowledged that the question of how much should go for civilian purposes and how much for military spending is now "a much tougher situation than heretofore faced in any so-called time of peace."[48]

If the issue of deficit spending in time of war (including the Cold War) turned on politics rather than economics, then the solution, according to the tenets of Boulwarism, would be to educate the electorate (the legislators and the public) about the point between elections. Of course (as noted in the final chapter of this book), this is exactly the way President Reagan—some thirty years after the lessons were learned—approached the problem. For now, however, the issues were not as broad as national defense and wartime spending. But they did require that the focus of education go beyond the plant walls and GE's employees to the grass roots, lest the company lose its contest with "union officials" who were already moving on that broader terrain.

PART III

AN APPRENTICESHIP FOR PUBLIC LIFE

SIX

THE CAMPAIGN

Ronald Reagan's first national campaign began in 1958. It rose from a plan developed by Ralph Cordiner and Lemuel Boulware in June of that year. At the time of their strategy meeting, held on a small island off Florida, the two executives were among the most powerful men in the United States. It was at about this time that Cordiner was selected as Businessman of the Year in the annual economic and business review of a respected national publication. He chaired President Eisenhower's powerful Business Council. An academic observer evaluating Boulware's program concluded that "no single movement in labor relations in the past two decades has been more significant."[1] The men were prepared to use in their plan the formidable assets of the company they headed—which, after all, was the nation's fifth largest corporation, with some 250,000 employees spread over forty states.

Lemuel Boulware took GE's traveling ambassador almost entirely out of the plants and put him on the road addressing civic groups—what Reagan dubbed "the mashed potato circuit—at an increased pace. It was certainly an "apprenticeship" in public life. The campaign would not end with the fall election, like most political campaigns, but would continue through Reagan's remaining years with the company and beyond. This was consistent with the prime tenet of Boulwarism that the most effective time to move the electorate was "between elections."

Reagan's effectiveness as a campaigner was enhanced by the widespread public recognition that came from his work on television. He was more of a celebrity now than ever. Although there had been no motion pictures since he and Nancy starred in *Hellcats of the Navy* in 1957,[2] he had been featured on *GE Theater* in "Father and Son Night" in October of that year, "The Coward of Fort Bennett" in March of 1958, and three other shows later in the year.[3] Reagan was now one of the highest paid stars on television. His annual salary was raised from $125,000 to $150,000. In time, General Electric indicated that he would have the opportunity to act as producer, with the attendant greater income, for some of the shows.[4] *GE Theater* topped the Sunday prime-time ratings, and a national survey had recently named its host "one of the most recognized men in the country."[5]

A single campaigner—even if he turned out to be one of the most effective speakers of the century—was not enough, however. Ralph Cordiner and Lemuel Boulware believed that organized labor had declared war. Union support for candidates and legislation was providing the winning margin. Boulware had always advocated increased business involvement at the grass roots. Now that participation became something more than a distant goal. A campaign apparatus had to be assembled immediately. Boulware and his colleagues started too late in 1958 to turn the tide their way that year. The results of recent elections convinced them that union officials, unless vigorously opposed immediately, would win the war.

In 1956, although the head of the ticket, popular war hero and Republican president Dwight Eisenhower, was victorious, this was the first time in a century that a reelected president had failed to gain a majority for his party in either the House or the Senate.[6] In 1958, according to one observer, "political machines built overnight with union labor helped the Democrats sweep the country and to swamp the 'Right to Work' proposals in five of six states."[7] The off-year elections were regarded as "a slaughter" for the Republicans, "the worst defeat ever for a party occupying the White House."[8] The AFL-CIO Committee on Political Education had targeted sixteen U.S. senators for defeat that year. Nine of the sixteen were beaten and two others did not run for reelection. The five survivors were Byrd of Virginia and Holland of Florida, both Democrats, and Republican Senators Goldwater of Arizona, Williams of Delaware, and Beall of Maryland.[9]

George Meany, labor's chief spokesman as the president of the merged AFL and CIO, issued a statement just hours after the 1958 election. His first goal for the Eighty-sixth Congress would be to knock out the nineteen state right-to-work laws. He also called for "A complete overhaul of the federal Taft-Hartley law."[10]

Walter Reuther, now the second most powerful man in the restructured labor hierarchy, quickly demonstrated that prominent Democrats were willing to do labor's bidding. Two days after the 1958 election, a majority of the U.S. Senate Antitrust and Monopoly Subcommittee—chaired by a Reuther favorite, Senator Estes Kefauver of Tennessee—urged the Justice Department to investigate the possibility of court action to break up the United Auto Workers' major opponent, General Motors. GM was the nation's largest corporation.[11] General Electric was not far behind.

Organized labor's development of grass-roots political power had been effective, but the path to power had by no means been smooth. Walter Reuther was elected president of the CIO in 1952, within weeks of the death of his predecessor, Philip Murray, one of the founders of the organization. Reuther narrowly defeated a candidate backed by United Steelworkers president David McDonald. McDonald thought Reuther's social agenda was too broad and urged an aide to refer to the UAW leader as "that no good, red-headed socialist bastard Reuther."[12] When it appeared that McDonald might lead his union out of the CIO to form a new alliance with the International Brotherhood of Teamsters and the United Mine Workers, a move that might have destroyed the CIO, Reuther turned to a new ally, George Meany, the president of the AFL.

Meany's succession to the AFL leadership followed the death of the organization's longtime president, William Green. Green had served in that post since the demise of the legendary Samuel Gompers in 1924. Green died in 1952, within two weeks of his CIO counterpart, Philip Murray. Although Meany had been a loyal AFL officeholder for many years, his views of the need for effective political action came closer to Walter Reuther's than to William Green's. He had learned about government infighting and politics (principally Democratic) in the late 1940s as the AFL spokesman on the National War Labor Board. He led the AFL into a closer relationship with the Democrats.[13]

Meany was "an accomplished bureaucratic infighter [who] excelled in back-room politics."[14] Reuther was an out-front man. Meany, who had begun in the plumbers' union, had never participated in a strike. Reuther had no hesitation to lead his members out and to shut down plants. The men had complementary skills, and both now believed in the necessity of labor's active participation at the grass roots. Still, there was clearly a gap in how vigorously and how broadly political power should be pursued. If Reuther had any lingering reluctance to ally with the less aggressive AFL, it was offset by one compelling number: at 10,000,000 members, the AFL was twice the size of the CIO.

Reuther approached Meany in December of 1952. Differences large and small were negotiated over the next two years, until in 1955 the final issue—who would lead the new federation?—was resolved. Meany would become president of the AFL-CIO. He offered Reuther the post of secretary-treasurer (which Meany had held for decades at the AFL and which he honestly thought was the second most powerful office). Instead, Reuther chose to head a newly created Industrial Union Department, where the CIO unions, especially the UAW, would play a dominant role, with significant financial support from federation dues.[15]

The AFL-CIO had its first convention in December of 1955. Its new political clout was immediately apparent in the Democratic gains of 1956 and 1958. As Rick Perlstein points out in *Before the Storm*, "Labor was prevailing in the political war—thanks largely to Walter Reuther . . . [who] was among the first labor leaders to grasp [that] now the real battles were to be fought and won in the political arena."[16]

The announcement of the AFL-CIO's sixteen targets for defeat in the 1958 Senate elections had come from the federation's Committee on Political Education. It is useful to examine COPE's objectives, because they help one understand what Boulware had already accomplished and why he and Ralph Cordiner now planned to extend GE's program. An AFL-CIO press release states that "COPE has encouraged thousands of union members to take part in public life through programs of political education and political action whose goals are better law makers, better laws, better government, and better life for all the people." The program was not limited to getting out the vote on election day. The release continues: "Since a Democracy can only work when people are informed and vote, COPE's primary functions [include providing] year-round programs of political education for union members."[17]

COPE's overall strategy and tactics were strikingly similar to General Electric's, although a few years ahead of GE's schedule at the grass roots. Lemuel Boulware had admitted in his Harvard speech that "we businessmen" did not like politics or want to get involved in it. "But we had no choice," he said. "We have been dragged unwillingly into politics by our ideological competitors and intended executioners who were politically skilled and felt the political arena was where they would look good and we, in contrast, would put up the sorriest spectacle and thus do the most damage to people's confidence in us."[18] Now, almost ten years after his dire warning, his fears were fully realized. GE's goal could no longer be a favorable result from the Schenectady local or even a step forward in national collective bargaining. The target was now the entire community—the voters themselves. Boulware would be satisfied with nothing less than a "majority of us, as *citizens at the grass roots.*"[19]

Specific issues would be defined as GE's national campaign proceeded. But there was no question about what Boulware believed was ultimately at stake: "Our free markets and our free persons," he had proclaimed at Harvard. Nor was there any question about the identity of the opposition. "We don't like the proposals for further greatly enlarged government expenditures now being urged on the public by a combination of government and union officials."[20] The time for lofty pronouncements from academic platforms had passed. A detailed plan for the conflict must be laid out. Time lines had to be drawn. Troops had to be recruited and then trained in advertising, fund raising, canvassing, and other political skills. A mechanism as formidable as the AFL-CIO's Committee on Political Education had to be in place. As Boulware later reflected, "Our current crisis has put us in a desperate race between re-education and disaster."[21]

The political mechanism to combat COPE would, at the outset, be nothing less than the General Electric Company itself. The 1958 call to arms seemed innocuous enough: an interoffice letter from Ralph Cordiner to Lemuel Boulware confirming an earlier conversation to the effect that Cordiner would "be making hotel reservations at Boca Grande and also arranging for a chartered fishing boat." The letter suggested that Boulware bring along his golf equipment and pointed out that since there would be a full moon, the tarpon fishing would be at its best. They would fly from Westchester Airport on the morning of May 29, 1958, and return on the evening of June 2.[22]

The letter was not as mundane as it appeared. After all, the men had offices in the executive area in the same building on Lexington Avenue and could discuss most matters on a few minutes notice at their mutual convenience. The idea of meeting a thousand miles from the office suggested the special nature of the subject. Located on Gasparilla Island, sixty-five miles south of Sarasota on Florida's west coast, Boca Grande resort was a splendid example of the red-roofed stucco Spanish architecture found in the older Florida buildings. Although there were other members of the fishing party, the two men had ample opportunity over the long weekend to be alone.

While there are no minutes or notes recording their discussions, it is clear from subsequent documents and actions that they talked about Boulware's campaign to "re-educate" the workers and their neighbors. Boulware would have been positive about his program, so much so that he suggested that he be relieved of some of his corporate titles and duties, enabling him to embark on a broader national role. The two men had already put out the word that Boulware was having "headaches" and that Jack S. Parker, fresh from success in heading GE's airplane-engine plant in Ohio, would take over much of his domain. Since Parker would be assisted by two executives trained by Boulware, Phil Moore and Virgil Day, risk of any disastrous mistake was minimized.[23] In any event, Boulware was close at hand in case of an emergency and in splendid health. The only headaches anticipated were ones which he would give the opposition.

Labor was feeling its oats. The most impressive political pamphlet in circulation was the AFL-CIO's "How to Win." Boulware found an "imbalance of power" as bargaining moved from a purely economic to a political process. The union officials were simply better in the political arena. Or, as he put it, "This miscarriage is due to the customary but seldom perceived weakness of management representatives in contrast to the overwhelming but not publicly sensed strength of the union representatives involved."[24]

In the coming state, congressional, and presidential elections, there were few candidates who viewed themselves as "conservatives." If action at the

grass roots was needed to help the company—with recruitment, training, and long-range planning—Boulware and Cordiner believed it would
also help the country. To paraphrase "Engine Charlie" Wilson, former
General Motors CEO and secretary of defense in the Eisenhower administration, they felt that "What was good for General Electric was
good for the U.S.A."

After the meeting in Florida, Boulware wrote a detailed, seven-page,
single-spaced memorandum to Jack S. Parker outlining the plans for
succession and political engagement. The program was unique in American corporate history. It would do nothing less than convert the company itself into a giant political force.

Boulware's memorandum to Parker, his titular successor in the field
of General Electric's corporate and employee relations, had taken longer
to write than its author had anticipated.[25] It was dated June 18, over two
weeks after the meeting at Boca Grande. Worked and reworked, the
policy statement had to provide cover for Boulware's expanded activities
at the same time as it downplayed fresh goals and targets. The draft still
had some rough spots and was not the polished work that Boulware liked
to send out. Boulware admitted that: "This 'little' background memorandum has by this time gotten somewhat out of bounds." There was a good
deal of repetition, but Boulware wanted Parker to have a chance to review
his thoughts before they met the next day. He apologized for his inabil-
ity, due to lack of time, to thoroughly edit his work.

The supposed point of departure of the memo was a recent conversation in which Parker had revealed some of his "reorganization plans." In
fact, Boulware's message had little to do with Parker's notions of structure. The thrust was to inculcate Parker with the underlying philosophy
for his new assignment, even though his part in the new program would
be minimal when compared to the roles to be played by Boulware and
Cordiner. Parker would be expected to maintain the internal employee
program that Boulware had set in motion.

Although Ronald Reagan was never mentioned, the importance of
recognizing each GE employee as a member of the community, with
interests broader than the narrow boundaries of his or her job, coincided
with Reagan's increasing appearances before civic groups in GE communities, composed in part of GE workers and their spouses

The influence of Boulware's longstanding core beliefs in his action
memo is apparent. His "Nine Points" are present, as is his contributor-

claimant categorization. The tenets he had announced at Harvard in 1949 are restated throughout the memo. This reliance on ingrained doctrines in meeting current problems was one of the most important lessons Ronald Reagan learned from Lemuel Boulware.

Boulware may have anticipated GE's ultimate entanglement in the antitrust arena as he set out his action plan for the company. After all, GE *was* the country's fifth largest corporation. "Our bigness problem," he wrote, "is going to depend very largely for its solution on the conviction and eagerness with which vast numbers of other businessmen rise to publicly defend us when we are under attack." He listed "government regulation" as a related problem. Did he view the administrations of possible presidential candidates Kefauver and Kennedy as potentially hostile, especially if other major corporations failed to support GE and its ideas?

Boulware made no apology for moving the labor contest into the political realm. In one sense, he was simply responding to the AFL-CIO. As noted earlier, he used the term "political bargaining" interchangeably with "collective bargaining." He contended that "the union official had always seemed to me to be a politician."[26] He justified his appeal to the community at large and his direct approach to union members by the "wide and still widening gap between the *economic* interests of union members and the *political* interests of the union officials."[27]

As his June 18 memo proceeded to outline the expansion of the company's political activities, Boulware reaffirmed that the proposed course was *consistent* with existing corporate policy:

> In our union relations work we recognized right at the start that our problem could not be solved directly with the union officials. We had to start the solution with the employees. To help in getting the employees to know what we call "community relations" . . . Sooner or later we will have to get back to the employee as the focal point and recognize the union as simply the agent of the employee.

As careful and politic as Boulware had been in the wording of his memo, Parker must have been shocked on reading it to see the direction in which the company was heading. Boulware portrayed the General Electric Company—its employees, its shareholders, its neighbors in the community, and even its competitors and allies in the business world—as a political force to be mobilized to solve GE's and the country's "problems," including "those of the actual and presumed good and bad big corporations, big government, big unions, big taxes, inflation, false economic teachings, bad moral practices under freedom, and widespread naiveté in the face of demagogs."

What Boulware was proposing was a national crusade. His goals were more akin to a party platform than to a list of collective bargaining points. Boulware interpreted the term "relations" in the sphere of "public and labor relations" as a starting point whereby GE's 250,000 employees could use their "relationships" to influence their fellow citizens toward a course of right-thinking designed to frustrate and defeat the "demagogs" who normally set the agenda in matters of public policy.

The starting point was the relationship of one GE employee to another. He quickly expanded this relationship to include the contact between a GE employee and the company's shareholders, and then from the employees and shareholders to the broader community, including their neighbors, friends, and business associates. This activity, he maintained, should not be viewed as something "outside" the job. It was as much a part of employment, here using a familiar Boulware line, as "marketing, engineering, manufacturing, finance and general management." He saw GE's salesmen and servicemen making "related sales," by spreading GE's (and Boulware's) view of the nation and the economy at the same time as they spread the message about their products.

Cultivation of the employees' relationship to the "share owners" (and of the employees' frequent role as shareholders) had been part of Boulware's mission for the past eleven years. Nevertheless, he wrote that the share owner still represented the "greatest undeveloped commercial asset." Ralph Cordiner believed that he and Boulware had coined the term "investor relations." GE set up a new department to deal with stockholders. It was the first truly systematic effort to formalize a corporation's relationship with its shareholders. The mailing lists were invaluable for political activities, promoting issues such as tax reform and opposing legislation imposing regulatory restrictions.

There were certain key words and phrases in Boulware's June 18 memo that he would use again and again in defining GE's mission. People were described in their role as *citizens*. Going over the heads of politicians and government officials—whom he described as "demagogs"—had to be encouraged through "citizen relations." When he ruminated on "remaining members of the public whom we do not contact or affect other than as *citizens* [italics his]," he concluded that this left "practically nobody."

Another of Boulware's key phrases was "better business climate," by which he meant an atmosphere in which the free enterprise system could function unencumbered by oppressive taxes and intrusive government programs. In the memo, he urged that these activities should go first into the "citizens' relations" area. The phrase was probably designed to encourage grass-roots political activity while avoiding the notion that the company was favoring a particular party. The citizens still had an "undone job," Boulware wrote. He stated the mission in its broadest terms: "To go to work in their own and the rest of the public's interest in promoting economic education, proper moral conduct under freedom, and political maturity that proofs people against the demagogs."

Boulware lost no time in implementing the plan. He established a "little informal group of trade association and manufacturers' representatives."[28] Toward the end of 1958, he learned that General Hauck, who had been the Army's representative on Capitol Hill for twenty years, was retiring. He directed an aide to meet with the general and "get into the details of each Congressman's record and leanings." He also wanted the aide to explore whether Hauck might be a useful addition to the "little informal group."[29] Two months later, the same assistant was asked to seek out Guy Waterman, an employee of the Senate Republican Policy Committee, "to feed into this situation some sounder and more aggressive attack on inflation than we are now witnessing."[30]

A practical, step-by-step guide—similar to COPE's "How to Win"—was needed for corporations to enlist their personnel in grass-roots politics. J. J. Wuerthner published *The Businessman's Guide to Practical Politics* in 1959.[31] At the time, Wuerthner was manager of public affairs at GE's Electronics Park in Syracuse, New York. In the book, he describes Boulware as a pioneer in the field and quotes him for the proposition that "being politically effective . . . is now a continuing part of every manager's work and every citizen's duty to himself. It cannot be done by others. We must each do our part—and be publicly identified over our names as doing it."

A task force (chaired by Wuerthner) of the Government Affairs Committee of the Manufacturers Association of Syracuse was established. It led in time to a "Political Primer for Management," a two-day seminar on practical politics. This grew into eleven-week courses in practical politics to be held in weekly two-hour sessions at individual company offices. These activities began with a "Better Business Climate Program" (which Wuerthner describes as "pioneered by GE" and which was, in fact, headed by another GE executive). The participants in the first training seminar constituted a veritable who's who of local and national companies, including local divisions of General Motors and Chrysler and "seven departments of General Electric Company." As a result of the program, some 600 individuals in Syracuse had been exposed to "practical grass roots political affairs" by the end of 1958.

A very significant collateral benefit of this and similar programs was employment for an emerging group of conservative political consultants, who were enabled to do their candidate work because they had sustaining incomes between campaigns. In Syracuse, for example, F. Clifton White was part of Wuerthner's faculty. He was also a paid consultant of General Electric and other corporations. As Theodore White noted, "General Electric had made him an expert in the instruction of aspiring junior executives (both Democratic and Republican) who were assembled by great corporations to be taught how they should participate in public affairs."[32] Clif White was a close friend of Boulware (and later of Reagan) and played a major role in the Goldwater presidential bid of 1964 and the conservative revolution of subsequent years.

By the end of 1958, Boulware's activities had wide scope. The June 18, 1958, memorandum had been written for limited circulation within General Electric. Now there was *public* confirmation of major parts of the plan. It appeared in the *Time* magazine article referred to earlier (January 12, 1959). The lead story was about the company. As noted, the picture on the cover was Ralph Cordiner. The article contained seven pages of photographs of nuclear activities. Medical uses were portrayed, as was radioactive feeding of pigs and trout. Although the only photographs of current GE executives were of Cordiner and Boulware, there were photos of some of their illustrious predecessors.

Time made it clear that Cordiner had introduced a revolutionary management policy when he became CEO.[33] "Massive decentralization" allowed executives within the company to exercise their responsibilities absent the shackles of bureaucracy found in most large corporations. The company was split into 27 autonomous divisions containing 110 small companies just the size "for one man to get his arms around." The "ad-

FIGURE 7 GE president Ralph Cordiner's unusual system of governance was one that Ronald Reagan had a chance to observe at length. It brought Cordiner to the cover of *Time*, to one of the highest points in the company's history, and later to the lowest.
Source: *Time* Magazine, © 1959 Time, Inc. Reprinted by permission.

vanced management center" at Crotonville was portrayed as the instrumentality of instruction for executives to learn the "demands and duties of the management revolution." *Time* described the great size of the company and its role as a community force in these terms: "GE spreads its influence beyond industry and finance. It employs more people (about 260,000) than the population of all but 40 U.S. cities, [and] is the economic and often social center of dozens of 'company towns' where 'the GE' is more important than city hall."

GE's labor policy, *Time* reported, is referred to as "Boulwarism," but it is so central to GE policy that it might just as well be called "Cordinerism." Some of Boulware's tactics—"a steady barrage of propaganda aimed at winning the worker . . . speeches, plant publications, [and] community relations to attack overweening union power"—are mentioned. The caption under Boulware's picture reads: "Over the union's head to the workers."

The article notes that Cordiner "has brought his weight to bear on local and national politics, recently [visiting] several states to support right-to-work laws." It observes that GE maintains one of the "biggest and most aggressive lobbying offices" in the nation's capital and "encourages" company executives to enter politics and community life. It concludes with Cordiner's view that "civilization is moved forward by restless people, not by those who are satisfied by things as they are."

There were federal and state statutes prohibiting corporate involvement in politics, and Cordiner and Boulware were scrupulous in fashioning their program to avoid these strictures. Boulware spelled out this policy in a letter to A. C. Nielsen Jr., CEO of the polling company. Nielsen wanted guidance in establishing "an educational program with its employees" similar to GE's program. He stated frankly, "We are convinced that the Republican Party has a better program and would like to promote its virtues as opposed to the Democratic Party."[34]

In reply, Boulware pointed out that "for reasons of both law and policy, we carefully refrain from using any company time, money or influence on straight-out partisan political activities" or activities having that appearance.[35] He was quick to point out, however, that occupants of GE's Executive Office encouraged associates to exercise their "own good citizenship" and support the party and candidates of their individual choice. He enclosed a guide to "Non-Partisan Political Activity," which he had set out in a speech.[36]

Perhaps the Nielsen Company would discover, as GE had, that the constant dissemination of Boulware's message would tend to create conservative conversions and that middle managers, once given nonpartisan instruction in grass-roots politics would, as a matter of individual choice, overwhelmingly support Republican candidates. The litmus test for prohibited activity was the backing by a corporation of a candidate or a party. That was *partisan political* action and it was condemned by law. GE's expanded, community-oriented approach to establishing a "better business climate" was always carefully presented as a nonpartisan civic program. In fact, it was honored as such. The *Works News* proudly ran the headline, "GE Gets Freedoms Foundation Award for Aid to Economic Understanding."[37]

There is a certain irony in the recognition GE received for its "non-partisan" program to establish a "better business climate." The phrase was virtually a code for the variety of grass-roots corporate efforts that led inevitably to conservative, generally Republican activity. J. J. Wuerthner's 1958 Syracuse operation, for example, introduced its eleven-week course in "Practical Politics" as the "Better Business Climate Program." Wuerthner made it clear that the program would extend to all of GE's "decentralized operations in more than thirty states . . . in each of the more than 125 communities where the company maintains manufacturing or research operations." He reaffirmed that the company had "recently embarked on an accelerated program toward building a *better business climate*" (italics added).[38]

The term came from Boulware's Harvard speech, where he urged businessmen to get involved in politics "immediately." Specifically, he said that "we [businessmen] have maybe got to get something like the Better Business Bureau after our office holders and politicians—low and high—in all parties."[39] A statement from Boulware's public relations department later reaffirmed the point that this was not just a casual effort. It involved big issues, with GE's efforts directed at "the community's public servants" in "such areas as the courts, taxes, and law enforcement."[40] If anyone wondered about the kind of climate the campaign sought to achieve—whether it was liberal or conservative—they had only to read the transcript of "Salvation Is Not Free".

Ronald Reagan's public involvement in the program increased significantly. The September 1958 issue of *Monogram* carried an article about the *General Electric Theater*, which was "poised and polished for its fifth season." The magazine's cover was a photo of Reagan, standing next to an easel listing three "Key Subjects Ahead." The center subject, to which he was pointing, was "Better Business Climate."[41]

Boulware was quick to use Ronald Reagan's heightened name recognition in GE's political program. When Reagan was asked after a speech on the "mashed potato circuit" in Schenectady (a frequent site because of the large GE plant and independent local situated there), what "the average guy" could do about federal budget deficits he said (in a response which may seem ironic to some readers): "Every organization can pass resolutions asking an end to deficit spending. Give the resolution to the press, send it to your congressman."[42] Even more effective, he believed, were letters to congressmen. "Fifty letters from a group such as this," he would say, "means more than a resolution or a petition. Demand immediate tax reform which will reduce the percentage of the national income taken by government."[43] With practical political insight, he would point out that "a congressman doesn't read all his mail, but he does know whether it's running for or against a bill."[44]

The most significant role Ronald Reagan could play in the campaign to establish a better business (i.e., political) climate was as a communicator. Convincing GE employees and their neighbors of the Cordiner-Boulware message could have a highly significant impact at the grass roots. While Boulware felt that the nine-point job "was to be an *intimate* relationship between the employee and his immediate supervisor" (italics added),[45] his calculation of the cumulative effect of the employees as "communicators" reveals the foundation for his confidence in the extensive political potential of the company.

Boulware's math is important to recognize. He wanted to move M— the majority, and not some handful of marginal voters. In short, if each of the company's 15,000 supervisors and managers ("communicators") reached 5 to 50 employees, this cadre (75,000 to 750,000) would actually exceed the total size of the company's work force. As more GE employees became "mass communicators," and as other companies from Boulware's group joined the effort, the numbers at the grass roots would be further increased.[46] Since many of the targets were the smaller states, the South, and the localities where GE had facilities, the total might be enough to carry the electoral day. And now that the Reagan was on the "mashed potato circuit," speaking directly to civic forums, the impact could be even greater.

The high esteem in which Reagan, Boulware, Cordiner, and the General Electric Company were held was a platform that could be used effectively to defeat union officials at the grass roots. Nevertheless, with all its power and its forty-state range, GE still did not command sufficient terrain on its own to carry a national contest or to elect enough senators, congressmen, and state officials to assure a favorable legislative context. To prevail, Boulware needed allies.

SEVEN

ALLIES

Each month a group of corporate executives met in a conference room on the seventh floor of New York's University Club. The membership list was maintained by Boulware's secretary.[1] Although the attendees wielded tremendous power, no public mention of the group or its meetings ever appeared. They modestly referred to themselves as "The Wise Men."

Virgil Day was the regular attendee for GE, but Lem Boulware set the agenda and often attended personally. Not all of the members of this ad hoc group could make each meeting, but twenty to thirty was the usual number. They were the executives in charge of their corporations' public affairs and government-relations programs. Their companies were at the top of the *Fortune* 500 list. They represented a cumulative net worth in excess of that of most nations. They were an important part of a powerful alliance.

While no minutes exist, the group's activities can be reconstructed from surrounding events. A meeting in, say, mid-1959 would probably focus on two agenda items: First, Virgil Day would cover what GE was doing in-house with the IUE. Although all of the participants would present information on their respective programs, there was special interest in the current materials and components of Boulwarism. The second item would likely be Boulware's analysis of the previous fall's elections, with particular attention to the effect they had on candidates and issues of concern to the group.

Day's review would involve the "managed news" promulgated by GE and the critical path the company was following in its labor program. Because all of the materials were going to ERMs and directly to employees, it was clear that the union would have most of the information anyway and that there was relatively little risk in its further distribution, especially to this group. Malcolm Denise of Ford, Louis Seaton of General Motors, and other corporate members shared their ideas, but it was clear that the lead company was General Electric. Day would not go into highly confidential or sensitive areas, nor would Ronald Reagan ever be mentioned as part of the program.

All of the men were familiar with the corridors of power in Washington, D.C., and in state capitals throughout the nation. Through their lawyers and lobbyists, they had an impact on legislation. For all their money and sophistication, however, they lacked power at the one place where it was most strongly felt by the officeholders who would make and enforce the laws. They were losing the contest at the grass roots. There were young men and women in their companies who believed as they did, who might play an effective part in politics, but they simply didn't know how.

The Wise Men, especially GE and GM executives, found ample stimulus for increased political involvement in the contemporaneous national scene. Soon after the 1958 elections, Senator Kefauver's Antitrust and Monopoly Subcommittee requested the Department of Justice to explore the possibility of court action to dismantle General Motors, the nation's largest corporation.[2] A GE spokesman appeared on television to meet the serious charges that had been leveled at American business. This time, it was not Ronald Reagan but a man selected to represent not only General Electric but the entire business establishment—Ralph Cordiner. He was joined in this undertaking by another corporate leader, Roger Blough, the chairman of United States Steel.[3]

The two executives had been invited to speak at a hearing of the very same Senate Subcommittee on Antitrust and Monopoly. Senator Kevauver, who planned to run for president, presided over the hearing. The subcommittee was considering a bill, S. 215, proposed by Senator Joseph O'Mahoney of Wyoming.

In the course of introducing the legislation, Senator O'Mahoney stressed the need to promote competition in a number of industries in which he felt that there was excessive concentration. The senator quoted a newspaper article that stated, "This concentration presents a great temptation to rig prices. How many executives have been sent to jail up to this time for violation of the Sherman Act? Practically none." Jail sentences, indeed! In his testimony, Cordiner made the following categorical defense of American business: "Is it assumed that companies in industries affected by this bill have the ability to 'administer' prices in a manner not responsive to market supply and demand? If so, the assumption is false, because these companies are just as much subject to competitive market conditions as any other."

But the industry giants were facing pressure in the press as well as from Congress. On May 13, 1959, Julian Granger, a reporter for the *Knoxville News-Sentinel*, wrote, "Some American manufacturers, primarily in the electric field, have regularly submitted identical bids on TVA purchases of equipment and materials, the Authority revealed today. For the first time, TVA cited three instances of identical bidding in announcing new contract awards."[4] In a second article, Granger named names.[5] The two biggest manufacturers of electrical equipment came up more frequently than any others in the bidding—General Electric and Westinghouse. Senator Kefauver placed Granger's second article in the *Congressional Record* and turned the subcommittee's attention to GE. He announced hearings that would pinpoint GE's dealings with the Tennessee Valley Authority, one of the largest employers in Kefauver's home state.[6]

General Electric's extensive news-management operation moved into action. It unleashed a barrage of specific responses to the claims that GE had conspired to fix prices. A press release issued from GE's "Public Relations Department" in Schenectady quoted William Ginn to the effect that 1960 would be an excellent year.[7]

Ginn was vice president of the GE Turbine Operation in Schenectady. He was generally regarded within the company as an executive who had the potential to become GE's president in time.[8] A number of people in the executive suite called Ginn "the toughest competitor they'd ever met." The promise of intense competition was supported by further

GE announcements in three contemporaneous articles in the *New York Times*.

GE's press releases were not allowed to stand. Testimony before Senator Kefauver's subcommittee gave an entirely different picture of competition in the heavy-electrical-equipment industry. Senator Kefauver announced that the Knoxville hearings were set up to discover whether the present antitrust laws were adequate to keep free competition thriving. If the identical bids submitted to TVA were found to be the result of conspiracy or agreement among competitors, then they would be referred to the enforcement agencies: The Antitrust Division of the Department of Justice and the Federal Trade Commission.[9]

Lemuel Boulware had to weigh the possible impact on his strategic plan of an antitrust prosecution against General Electric. Time was running out. Walter Reuther had the ear and the full cooperation of powerful men in the U.S. Senate.[10] The unions had fashioned a political engine of considerable effectiveness. Now Cordiner, Boulware, and their colleagues had to meet the challenge.

One would have to go back to the days of Mark Hanna and William McKinley to find corporate political activity as vigorous and effective as GE's. But the laws had changed since those free-wheeling times. Federal and state statutes now prohibited using corporate resources for *partisan political* purposes, and many companies feared being charged with crimes.

As noted earlier, Boulware was very sensitive to this issue. When Clarence Manion, the dean of Notre Dame Law School and a famous figure on the far right of the American political scene, urged corporations to purchase and distribute *The Conscience of a Conservative*, by Senator Barry Goldwater, a conservative Republican, Boulware found such activity "inappropriate." He wrote that a corporation had to be "lily white." It should not "as a Company, circulate a book written by a prominent public servant who is so actively mentioned as both a Presidential and Vice Presidential candidate."

More modest than the record called for, Boulware stated that he had "been erroneously credited with inventing the whole idea of non-partisan political activity by corporations and partisan political activity by businessmen as individuals." *Partisan political* activity must be carried out by individuals on their "own time and [with their own] after-tax money." The company "leans over backwards in making very sure our case is airtight in that we have in practice followed absolutely our stated intentions that the Company's educational and other political activities will be truly non-partisan in letter and in spirit."[11]

In spite of the strictures, the number of allies increased. Some followed the lead of the GE executives, and some proceeded on their own. J. J. Wuerthner's instructional guide for politically minded corporate personnel mentions a number of successful company-inspired political programs independent of GE's efforts: the Ohio Plan, Philadelphia's Committee of 70, the Pennsylvania Manufacturers Association's Keystone Plan, the Citizen Responsibility Council of the Missouri State Chamber of Commerce, and programs by industrial associations in seven other states.[12] The major automobile companies were members of both Wuerthner's seminal task force and of the Wise Men.

Corporate political operatives chafed at what they felt was a statutory imbalance in their grass-roots contests against organized labor. The companies had to toe the line of civic nonpartisanship, while unions existed as national entities or federations with funding and salaried personnel specifically dedicated to backing legislation and candidates of particular parties. But the companies had a huge advantage on their side, which they did not publicize. General Electric provides a classic example.

The rationale for Ronald Reagan's plant tour was to give a sense of corporate identity to the far-flung GE empire, located in some forty states. In the thousands of pages issued at Crotonville and in his book explaining this decentralization, Ralph Cordiner explained the *administrative* advantages of his management system. There was another reason for this dispersion, however. GE and other companies were moving the battle to more favorable terrain.

Significant plant movement away from New England and mid-America to states located primarily in the South, most of which had passed "right-to-work" laws, was part of Boulware's program. Plants and other facilities were now located in Alabama, Arkansas, Georgia, Kentucky, Maryland, North Carolina, Texas, and Virginia.[13] This was essentially more favorable ground for NLRB contests, contract negotiations, and the inevitable paving the way for moving the majority of voters. The longer-range grass-roots effect was important. To pursue the war analogy, it was like creating higher ground for supporting fire before beginning an assault on an outpost.

A conservative disposition on many domestic issues had existed in these southern states for some time. A vigorous Republican Party had not. Now a genuine two-party system was set in motion. The difference would be seen initially in the election of congressional and local candidates and, later, in the electoral vote for president. In today's parlance, the states were turning from blue to red.

Cordiner and Boulware stepped up their own "nonpartisan" activities to marshal the political efforts of corporate America. During the Eisenhower administration, Cordiner became chairman of the Business Council. This was a younger organization than the National Association of Manufacturers and the U.S. Chamber of Commerce. It is described by one business historian as "tiny and elite," composed largely of CEOs of the country's largest corporations.[14]

The two men, enthusiastic about the effectiveness of the work they had pioneered at GE in energizing stockholders, urged other companies to follow suit. With other Wise Men, they founded the National Investor Relations Institute. NIRI, following the GE model, sought to get companies to engage in lobbying and to use their shareholder mailing lists to promote important corporate issues such as tax and regulatory reform.

After his retirement from GE, Boulware maintained an active political agenda. When he found kindred spirits among the wealthy and powerful (e.g., Joe Coors, John Olin), he enlisted their support and occasionally placed operatives he had trained within the upper levels of their corporations. GE's John McCarty, a Boulware protégé who became director of public relations at Coors Brewing and a significant operative in conservative causes, is one example.

Boulware went on his own "mashed potato circuit." His typical audience was not composed of blue-collar employees or middle management personnel as was Reagan's; instead, he might use a platform provided by the NAM or the American Management Association to urge corporate executives to disseminate his message to their own workers. His listeners included personnel managers, labor vice presidents, and other corporate executives from the nation's leading companies. As noted above, Boulware delivered "Salvation Is Not Free" to the Chicago and Detroit Economic Clubs and seventeen other forums. His listeners admired his efforts, even if most of them had not yet gone down a similar road.[15]

Boulware often spoke to very small groups that he thought could broaden the scope of the conservative movement. It was never his intention to limit his audiences to fellow retirees. Sometimes he would talk to a handful of students, encouraging them to be part of the burgeoning student enthusiasm for the right. He utilized his status as a distinguished alumnus to help to establish an undergraduate group at his alma mater, the University of Wisconsin. He supported their magazine, *Insight and Outlook*, as he later helped to finance another conservative student publication, *The Dartmouth Review*.[16]

Boulware would often give a small contribution (which could enable a club such as the International Society of Individualists to meet its annual budget) to accompany his words. In time, he stepped up his giving to ISI and other conservative college clubs. One of ISI's founders, now in his seventies, recalled in a recent interview that Boulware told the students, "If you think right, you'll vote right."[17] The youth movement thrived. America's youngest voters later supported Ronald Reagan by a "nearly two-to-one margin."[18]

Many articles and two books were written about Lemuel Boulware. Regrettably, the great bulk of this writing was addressed to Boulwarism in its narrowest aspect, the combat with organized labor within General Electric. The broader Cordiner-Boulware program of citizen "education" went virtually unnoticed by political commentators. Boulware's own books were essentially how-to guides for blue-collar suasion, on the one hand, and grass-roots involvement by businessmen, on the other. They were widely read and acted upon but failed to register on the radar screens of historians and contemporaneous pundits.

Some insight as to Boulware's role may be gathered from his influence on better known leaders of the conservative revolution such as William F. Buckley Jr. and F. Clifton White. Buckley's *National Review* included Boulware as one of its founding backers. The magazine gave greater respectability and exposure to conservative movers and shakers than they had ever had before. White had lectured at schools of politics in which the General Electric Company sought to establish a "better business climate." His Draft Goldwater Movement would capture a presidential nomination in 1964 and, in the words of one of its participants, "was the incubator for the successful careers of at least a score of present [1981] United States Senators, several dozen governors, and probably more than a hundred members of the House of Representatives, as well as untold numbers of state legislators, county and local officials."[19] Boulware was the lineal predecessor and sometime mentor of both Buckley and White.

Before there was a *National Review*, there was Boulware's weekly *Employee Relations News Letter*. The GE publication was initially mailed to the company's 15,000 supervisors and managers. By the late 1950s, it had been requested by enough "columnists, teachers, clergymen, politicians, and other businessmen" that circulation, as noted earlier, rose to "several times the original 15,000."[20] While this didn't compare to *Time* or *Newsweek*, it was huge for a political publication.

The *News Letter* was no puff piece or intracompany product-promotion mailing. Under Boulware, "only controversial issues of acute current interest from a material or emotional standpoint, or both, were treated." The object was to provide information which would "supply power . . . the power to help the supervisor and his employees to avoid the wrong course and take the right one . . . power to overcome the otherwise damaging power of anti-business forces seeking to cut down the usefulness of business while claiming to increase it." Boulware gauged the letter's effectiveness in part by the "public anguish" that it caused the "knowing and unknowing charlatans" who promoted contrary views.[21] It was years before *National Review* and like-minded publications would produce cumulatively as many pages or engage as many readers as Boulware's publications. But after Boulware's retirement, his publications and GE's program diminished in scope and effect. A replacement was needed. And an expanding *National Review* phased in at almost exactly that time.

Bill Rusher was an active member of the Draft Goldwater Movement. But his "day job" was publisher of the *National Review*. It is no surprise that Rusher liked to say that the founding of that conservative journal in 1955 was "arguably the most important" of the developments in the conservative resurgence. Certainly the emergence of Bill Buckley, the author of the best-selling *God and Man at Yale*, as an intelligent and highly articulate voice for the new movement was a key factor in the mobilization of the right. Buckley was founder and editor-in-chief of the magazine. He took on all comers in debate, established a popular television program, and added an aura of intellectual credibility on the ideological right. His campaign for mayor of New York City in 1965 did much to publicize conservative principles, even though he made it clear that "if elected, I'll demand a recount."[22]

Buckley was in touch with Lemuel Boulware from the time of the *National Review*'s founding. Boulware was still five years away from retirement. He was an early financial supporter of the magazine. He personally purchased subscriptions for dozens of friends, many of them in high places. He also forwarded ideas from time to time for inclusion in the publication. He suggested, for example, that the *Review* publish a "round-up on the progress conservatives are making." Buckley liked the idea and turned it over to his editorial right hand, John Chamberlain.

Bill Buckley was impressed with the older man's effectiveness in the burgeoning movement. It was at this point that Buckley wrote Boulware, "Incidentally, you are unquestionably one of the people most responsible for that significant turn of events [the development of the *National Review* and the progress conservatives were making]. We aren't out of the woods, but when we are, boy, if it's the last thing I do, I'll build a statue with your name on it."[23]

Just as Boulware began his retirement, Clif White's Draft Goldwater Movement began with a meeting of twenty-two people in the Avenue Motel in Chicago in October 1961 The group was tiny in comparison to Boulware's cadre at GE. Boulware's grass-roots efforts started with 3,000 employee relations managers and 12,000 other supervisory personnel spread through 135 locations in twenty-nine (Ronald Reagan put the number at forty) states. To be entirely accurate, these troops were not specifically engaged in electing a president, but they were concerned with legislation and positions that were later described as "conservative." Pursuant to Boulware's canon, much of the work had to be done between elections. The converted—largely blue-collar workers and members of the middle class—became the "mass communicators" of the early conservative wave.

The Draft Goldwater Movement's first office was located just seven blocks south of GE's headquarters in Manhattan. Suite 3505 of the Chanin Building comprised two rooms spartanly furnished with two desks, some chairs, file cabinets, and a rented watercooler. Directed from this cramped space, a handful of operatives moved throughout the country to organize Republican delegates to support the Arizona senator. The directory in the lobby read simply: "F. Clifton White and Associates, Inc."[24]

Clif White and his colleagues realized that trying to wrest control of a state political organization at its annual meeting was bound to fail. The insiders and old timers had it locked up. But if you sent your troops to a local district meeting, where the expected attendance was, say, ten people, then you could prevail with a dozen of your own faithful. If you had a majority of the districts when the county committees met, then you could elect the delegates to the state conventions, who, in turn, would send the delegates to the national convention. Following one of Boulware's cardinal principles, the draft movement was "going over the heads" of the state party leaders. It was going directly to the voters at the grass roots.

At the outset, White had an advantage because his organization was virtually unknown. His opponents were often defeated at the grass-roots level before they realized that they were in a contest. This stealth approach to capturing Republican delegates would only last so long, however. In addition, there would be primaries to contest, advertisements to buy, and phone banks to maintain, all of which required more troops and more money. The draft movement's early successes encouraged others to come forward. These were new Republicans, who were pleased to see the hacks who had led the party deposed. The old guard had often been put in place by Democrats to give the *appearance* of opposition. The new group wanted to defeat their adversaries.

Conservatism had long been a major thread in the American political fabric. As *Forbes* magazine pointed out in another context, Senator Sherman, the legendary author of the nation's first antitrust laws, was a *conservative* Republican. But the right wing of the party had diminished in strength in the three decades after the triumph of the New Deal and Dwight Eisenhower's wresting the Republican nomination from Senator Robert Taft, a conservative. Now, however, the long somnolent movement was showing signs of life. As Bill Rusher put it, "For the first time in living memory, individuals and groups called themselves 'conservatives' in public forums, representing a new current in public opinion."[25]

Even so, newly minted conservatives needed support—most crucially, they needed money and advice. Now fully in retirement, Boulware supplied both, in abundance. He had given up his Fifth Avenue apartment but continued to rent a summer home in Greenwich, Connecticut. His principal base of operation became Delray Beach, Florida, where he maintained a "lovely, gracious home with large picture windows overlooking the Atlantic Ocean."[26] He had been well compensated during his GE years and had apparently invested well. Some of his friends thought that his wife Norma had brought considerable money to their marriage.[27] A gracious woman, well regarded as a hostess, she saw as her mission in life to support her husband in his business and in his other pursuits. They were an affectionate, formidable team.

Boulware contributed extensively to "conservative Congressional and Senatorial candidates of both parties in the states with small populations."[28] (To get some measure of the extent of his personal giving, during the 1960 election year, as he was winding down with GE, he contributed "over 20 percent of his income" to political candidates and "allied economic education and political sophistication activities." These were personal, not corporate, funds.) He also aggressively solicited further contributions from "conservative friends." The money was directed to select candidates. He did not give to either political party's national committee.

At the other end of the political spectrum stood Walter Reuther, who had learned long ago, as Boulware had, "the limits of collective bargaining as a tool for sociological change."[29] The UAW was an active force in the Leadership Conference on Civil Rights, and Reuther had been an organizer of the Coalition of Conscience, which, in Reuther's words, "through the 1963 Washington Rally for Jobs and Freedom, mobilized the national conscience in behalf of enactment of the civil rights and voting rights laws."[30] Reuther stood beside Martin Luther King Jr. as Dr. King gave his famous "I have a dream" speech. The union leader had weekly meetings with President Johnson to discuss legislative and political initiatives.[31] Walter Reuther was at the apex of his political power.

Reuther, Vice President Hubert Humphrey, and other leaders of the civil rights movement swelled with pride when Lyndon Johnson signed the Civil Rights Act of 1964 on July 2. But Johnson was enough of a political realist to comment at the time, "I think we just gave the South to the Republicans for your lifetime and mine."[32] LBJ's "Great Society," packed with new and large programs of federal assistance, gave conservatives even more targets to shoot at. Still, President Johnson was riding high. His approval rating was over 70 percent, even in the South.[33]

Lem Boulware was not deterred. While he personally concentrated on the small states, Boulware did not give up on the big ones. He advised conservative fund raisers in states such as Illinois and Texas that "the time has come when they must do the solicitation the hard way and get small amounts of money from lots of people who can also become politically active through attendance at political workshops." He did not claim huge success in this enterprise, but he was "able to awaken some considerable few to new habits of contributing money and legwork in this important field."[34]

Boulware continued to be in demand as a speaker. Soon after retirement, he spoke at Columbia Business School, at Harvard, and at a meeting of the Economic Policy Committee of the Chamber of Commerce in Washington, D.C.[35] The intensity of his schedule may have slackened somewhat after he retired, but he continued to speak to many groups over the years. In 1964, for example, he participated in a panel sponsored by the Industrial Relations Division of the National Association of Manufacturers. His topic was "Statesmanship in Industrial Relations." His remarks were published by the NAM and quoted in a book coauthored by Harvard University president Derek Bok, an expert on labor law.[36] In 1981, he was selected to introduce John Olin at a tribute to Olin—the event was virtually a national conservative folk rite—in St. Louis.[37]

As he grew older, he became a regular at the weekly luncheon of the Scuttlebutt Club in Boca Raton, Florida, close to his home in Delray Beach. Here he renewed his acquaintanceship with Ray Livingstone, who had first heard him speak in Cleveland in the late 1940s. Livingstone taught at Florida Atlantic University's School of Business and brought the former GE executive there to lecture. Other "Scuttlebutters" included nationally known economist Murray Shields and Edward Warren, former president of Cities Service. Warren, one of Boulware's closest friends, had also headed the Petroleum Institute, providing Boulware with extensive contacts among the oil men. Boulware's friend Henry Hazlitt was a favorite of the group.[38]

Not all of Boulware's endeavors were successful. When he and Livingstone discovered that there was a Florida statute requiring the teaching of "free enterprise" in grades K-12 of the public schools, they developed a curriculum. They made it available to all schools within a 300-mile radius of their homes and offered to travel to schools to help implement the course. There were few takers.[39]

Boulware's collected papers reveal that toward the end of this period, he was at work on a third book. Extensive notes, most of them in his then somewhat shaky hand, are devoted to the new book. It was intended to be a guide to enable others to accomplish what he had achieved in mobilizing a usually somnolent majority of voters. His working title was *The Citizen's Undone Job*.[40] One draft of his introduction reads, in part, "This book is about every citizen's job. It is about our glorious opportunities. It is about what should be *welcome* as our corresponding *obligation* to serve our own best interests. It is certainly about me and my undone job."[41] There are many references to the Reagan administration in Boulware's notes. His comments on citizen involvement touch on both Reagan's efforts to gain the presidency and on events that occurred *during* the Reagan presidency. Boulware refers to the "Shining City on the Hill" and to the role of Gorbachev in the end of the Soviet empire.

While Boulware never completed *The Citizen's Undone Job*, his notes indicate his awareness of new issues to be dealt with in modern America. While his core doctrines remained the same, he recognized the need to turn to the problems that the nation now faced. Even in his nineties, he was not content to rest on the record that he and his protégé had achieved. After cataloguing a "Summary of Our Failures"—largely social issues that had not been featured in Boulwarism, such as drugs, drunken driving, TV influence, violence—Boulware turned to possible solutions.

Throughout this array of activities, Boulware's continuing contact with his former GE protégé is apparent. The shoe is on the other foot, however. Now it is Boulware who is concerned as to whether his work is consistent with Reagan's program. He follows a reference in one of his papers to "government practices" with a note to himself in the margin to "Get Prex RR's OK."[42]

EIGHT

THE SPEECH

Ronald Reagan acknowledges that he "wasn't unaware" that during his first couple of years on the road "GE sometimes had to sell a few groups on taking on a Hollywood actor as a speaker."[1] Reagan was plagued with such doubters throughout his career. If he was delivering a polished or moving address, they asked who wrote the script. After all, his critics and opponents would point out, he *was* an actor. While virtually all of Reagan's biographers acknowledge that early versions of "The Speech" were delivered in his GE years, very little has been written about how the content developed. Reagan's own recollection is clear: "Although GE gave me a platform, it left me to decide what to say. As a liberal in my younger days I'd had an inherent suspicion of big business and couldn't believe there wouldn't come a day when the company would begin trying to write my speeches for me. Never once did that happen."[2]

In fact, there *was* one incident on record where Ralph Cordiner's comments led to a change in Reagan's remarks on the stump. But in that case, it was Reagan who called Cordiner, and the CEO made it clear that "General Electric would not tell any individual what he could not say."[3] The traveling ambassador had learned through George Dalen that a government official had complained to Cordiner that Reagan was using TVA as an example of how government programs grow beyond their original purpose. The official had apparently suggested that the $50 million business on which GE was bidding could go to others. Actually, this situation was far more complex than the rendering it receives from the aforementioned accounts of Cordiner, Dalen, and Reagan. TVA was becoming the focal point of U.S. Senate and Justice Department antitrust investigations of General Electric. In any event, Reagan told Cordiner that he could easily drop TVA from his remarks, because "you can reach out blindfolded and grab a hundred examples of overgrown government."

What was the source for Reagan's "hundreds of examples of over-grown government?" Reagan's change in philosophy developed over the entire eight years that he was in the Employee and Community Relations program, but "The Speech" itself was honed primarily during the latter part of his tenure when he addressed civic forums. Only President Eisenhower was more sought after as a public speaker.[4]

"The Speech" would focus on issues rather than candidates. As noted, there was a need for GE, as a legal matter, to maintain a "non-partisan" posture. Reagan would live by the guidelines set out in the company's *Guide to Non-Partisan Political Activity*. Paradoxically, these supposed restraints actually enhanced the spokesman's message. In his later writings about this period, Reagan confirms that his "speeches were non-partisan as far as the two major political parties were concerned."[5] Even his calls for political action were addressed to "the Average Guy" or to "Joe Taxpayer," rather than to any particular political party.

When he first turned to the mashed potato circuit, Reagan's speeches still focused on his Hollywood experience. He spoke about confiscatory taxation—during his greatest earnings years in films he was in the 90 percent bracket—and learned in the Q & A or in the informal conversations after his talk that GE's blue-collar workers and middle management and their neighbors also had problems with taxes. "No matter where I was," Reagan recalled, "I'd find people from the audience waiting to talk to me after the speech and they'd all say, 'Hey, if you think things are bad in your business, let me tell you what is happening in my business.'"[6]

As Reagan heard "from hundreds of people in every part of the country" of the encroachment of the "ever-expanding federal government" on traditional individual liberties, he would "make a note of what people told me, do some research when I got home, and then include some of the examples in my next speech." As a result, the Hollywood stories began to disappear from his remarks and his speeches "became a warning to people about the threat of government." He became troubled by his support of Democratic candidates, the habit of a lifetime up to this point. As he wrote in *An American Life*, "One day I came home and said to Nancy, 'You know, something just dawned on me: All these things I've been saying about government in my speeches (I wasn't just making speeches—I was preaching a sermon), all these things I've been criticizing about government being too big, well, it just dawned on me that every four years when an election comes along, I go out and support the people who are responsible for the things I'm criticizing.'" He added: "I remained a Democrat for another two years, but by 1960, I had completed the process of self-conversion."[7]

The actor occasionally received feedback from sources other than his typical audiences. For example, he sent a lengthy report of another early version of "The Speech"—which he entitled "Business, Ballots, and Bureaus"—to Richard Nixon, who was then vice president. Nixon replied, "You have done an excellent job of analyzing our present tax situation and the attitudes that have contributed to it. . . . Speeches such as yours should do much to cause some solid thinking about the inherent dangers in this philosophy with the final result being a nationwide demand for reform." If Nixon was puzzled as to why an actor was giving speeches about the national economy, he made no comment. In fact, he said: "I hope you will have many opportunities to repeat your wise words."[8]

Reagan had established a rapport with General Electric's employees. They remained a part of his audiences when he spoke at civic functions in their communities. As he shifted to the mashed potato circuit, they were curious about the change in format. When asked if he missed going to the plants, Reagan later wrote that "I reached all of the 135 plants and personally met the 250,000 employees . . . two of the eight years were spent traveling, and with speeches sometimes running at fourteen a day, I was on my feet in front of a 'mike' for almost 250,000 minutes." Still, he continued, "*I enjoyed every whizzing minute of it.* It was one of the most rewarding experiences of my life."

Reagan was also frank to admit that not all of the plants wanted him. He described a plant in Owensboro, Kentucky, where GE employed

5,000 "ladies in white," attired in sterile nylon dresses and caps, who worked in a dust-free environment making electronic tubes. One of the women shouted out, "How do you-all like Owensboro?" He answered that he certainly couldn't complain about being in the midst of 5,000 women, especially since he was on his way to Pittsfield, Massachusetts, where there were 13,000 men. At that point, his questioner shouted back, "You stay here and we'll go to Pittsfield."[9]

While the Hollywood patter was now missing from his remarks, Reagan still used his background as a movie actor as his point of departure with civic audiences. It was, after all, his best-known credential. "It must seem presumptuous to some of you for a member of my profession to stand here and attempt to talk on problems of the nation," Reagan would begin. "However, a few years ago a 'funny thing happened to us on the way to the theater.' Ugly reality came to our town on direct orders from the Kremlin. Hard core party organizers infiltrated our business." He was off and running. He pointed out that 70 percent of the playing time of "all the screens in the world" emanated from Hollywood. Having established a credential that few in the room could match, he went from the attempted communist infiltration of the film industry to the internal deterioration of America.

The Ronald Reagan Library—the presidential library in Simi Valley, California—has no transcripts of Reagan speeches given between 1958 and 1960. (The earliest speech the library had in its files is "Encroaching Government Control," also occasionally referred to as "Encroaching Controls.") However, contemporaneous media coverage and biographies, including his autobiographies, show that his earlier speeches on the mashed potato circuit were variations on the themes set out above.[10] He was constantly revising, updating, and polishing "The Speech."

He learned from his listeners. When a member of his audience mentioned the federal government's seemingly inconsistent policies on egg production, for example, he did "some research when he got home," and his next speech cited the government's six programs to help poultry growers increase egg production, and a seventh, costing as much as the first six combined, to buy surplus eggs.[11] His basic subjects remained the same, even as examples changed. In 1959, the GE traveling ambassador appeared in Los Angeles, discussing "Tax Curbs"; in Des Moines, attacking federal bloat in the speech that he sent to Vice President Nixon, "Business, Ballots, and Bureaus"; and in Schenectady (again), talking about "Professional Patriots" (who feared that teaching the Bill of Rights in public schools might bring on a revolution).[12]

An excellent example of Boulwarism in action can be seen in Reagan's speech to the Schenectady YMCA in early 1959. The ground was prepared for the speaker long before his appearance on the local platform and validated by subsequent publications as well. A representative sampling of articles from the *GE Schenectady News* from 1958 through 1960 bear the following headlines:[13] "Kennedy-Ives: A Bad Bill" (Boulware felt that the Senate proposal didn't really protect union members from abusive leaders as it was supposed to]; "A Right to Sue and A Right to Work"; "Fifth in Sales, Ninth in Profits"; "Inflation: An Illusion of Wealth"; "Who Shares in America's Billions"; "Two Firms Seek Better Business Climate"; "The No-raising-hog Business"; "GE Takes Stand on Taxes, Asks NO New Spending"; "U.S. Gold Moving Abroad"; "Talking About Taxes . . ." (complaining about the confiscatory federal tax structure); "Capsule Economics" (complaining of the communist/socialist approach that government should decide how capital is distributed); "U.S.-Soviet Gap" (referring to the great weakness of the Soviet economy compared to the United States); "Social Security Taxes Triple"; and "Taxes Harm Economic Growth."

In the midst of this outpouring of Boulwarism came Reagan's speech. It was closely integrated into the overall program. The January 23, 1959, issue of the *GE Schenectady News* reported that "Hollywood and Schenectady met on equal ground yesterday with the personal appearance of popular film star Ronald Reagan." The host of the *GE Theater* and "unofficial 'ambassador of good will'" spoke before 350 guests at the tenth annual YMCA dinner at the State Street headquarters.

The *Works News* interview with the company spokesman, which appeared a week after the local civic speech, was most likely distributed to every plant in the country in the local newspapers. It provides an excellent example of what Chief Judge Irving Kaufman described in his judicial opinion on Boulwarism as GE's "coordinated, massive campaign" of messages to its employees.[14] The article was headlined: "Reagan Sees a Loss of Freedom Through Steady Increase in Taxes." It began by asking, "Everybody talks about taxes, but what can the average guy do about them (other than cough up more tax money each year)?"[15] Reagan observes in the interview that 34 percent of the phone bill, 27 percent of gas and oil use, and "more than a fourth of the cost of the automobile you drive is in direct and indirect taxes." Why are taxes so high? Because Americans are paying for three million federal employees ("more than there are farmers in the U.S.") and for a number of businesses the government is in "which private groups or citizens could do more efficiently under the spur of competition."

The *Works News* report of the 1959 Schenectady speech reveals the striking similarity to "The Speech" Reagan would deliver on national television five years later. The themes were identical: the danger lurking in a system of confiscatory taxation, the threat to freedom inherent in big government, and the insidious influence of international communism. Key points were closely matched in the two speeches: YMCA remarks: "We have been told by economists down through the years that if the total tax burden ever reaches 25 percent, we are in danger of undermining our private enterprise system. . . . more [federal employees] than there are farmers in the U.S." "The Speech": "No nation in history has ever survived a tax burden that reached a third of its national income. . . . one-fourth of farming [is] regulated and controlled by the federal government. . . . There is now one [Department of Agriculture employee] for every 30 farms in the U.S."[16]

Reagan's lawyer, Laurence Beilenson, also made major contributions to "The Speech." More than Boulware, more than anyone else in fact, Beilenson helped shape Reagan's views on foreign policy. Ultimately, this input led to the end of America's policy of containment with the Soviet Union, the establishment of the Reagan Doctrine, and endorsement of a nuclear-defense shield. Many of these initiatives first appeared on the mashed potato circuit in early versions of "The Speech."

Beilenson did not work for GE; nor did he represent the company. The lawyer first came to Reagan's attention through the legal work he had done for the Screen Actors Guild and, before that, for the Screen Writers Guild. His contacts with Ronald Reagan would have been frequent if SAG counsel were the only part he played. But in time he became counsel for MCA, Reagan's agent, and for Revue, the producer of the *GE Theater*. Along the way, he was also one of the attorneys who represented Reagan in his divorce from actress Jane Wyman.

A short, bald man who wore wire-rimmed glasses and conservative three-piece suits, Beilenson was not a typical Hollywood lawyer by any

FIGURE 8 Laurence Beilenson was a master of conflict (as a foreign policy advisor) and conflicts (as a lawyer). His constant was Ronald Reagan. Here he is pictured in 1949 receiving his SAG "Gold Honorary Membership Card," flanked by SAG president Reagan and former and future presidents (*left to right*) Edward Arnold and Dana Andrews. In his career he represented SAG, Reagan, Reagan's agent MCA, and Revue productions.
Source: Screen Actors Guild Archives, Los Angeles, California.

standard. Born in 1899 and raised in Helena, Arkansas, he was a graduate of Phillips Andover Academy, Harvard College, and Harvard Law School. He advised Ronald Reagan at various points in his acting career, but his major impact—on Reagan and on the world—was in the field of foreign policy.

Larry Beilenson, who enjoyed one of the most lucrative and active law practices in California, still had time for an avocation. He was interested in foreign affairs. His articles appeared in *American Bar Journal*, *Modern Age*, and the *National Review*.[17] He wrote three books on the subject, the most recent in 1980.[18] Governor Reagan, after he left Sacramento, had a weekly radio program on which he referred to Beilenson by name four times.[19] As president, he referred to one of the lawyer's books in a speech at West Point and recommended the book to a key White House aide.[20]

V. I. Lenin was a prime source for Larry Beilenson, even though he did his threshold research—in the field and through intensive study—in China. Beilenson's views were most likely conveyed to Reagan in conversation, before they were published in detail in his three books. A reference to Lenin can be found in Reagan speeches delivered on the road for GE in 1961. Since his civic addresses for the company were a work in progress, it is likely that Lenin appeared years earlier.

U.S. policy on the Soviet Union at the time was based on coexistence. Reagan believed that "the ideological struggle with Russia is the number one problem in the world" and that the Soviets were fundamentally opposed to peaceful coexistence. In his remarks, he quoted the following from Lenin: "It is inconceivable that the Soviet Republic should continue to exist for a long period side by side with imperialistic states. Ultimately, one or the other must conquer."[21]

Beilenson had a distinguished military record. Rising to the rank of colonel, he served as an American commanding liaison officer in the United States Army in China in World War II. He was awarded the Silver Star, the Bronze Star with Oak Leaf Cluster, a Commendation, and the Combat Infantry Badge. An intelligence officer, he had the opportunity to observe the communists firsthand and to study the teachings under which they operated.

Beilenson was attached to the Chinese nationalists, not the communists. The nationalists had a powerful lobby in Washington and in the press during the war. Madame Chiang Kai-Shek, the wife of the nationalist leader, was a graduate of Wellesley and was especially popular with the American public as she toured this country seeking funds and support for her government. Although Chiang's forces were America's allies in fighting the Japanese, they also fought the communists. It was *this* enemy, especially their leader, Mao Zedong, whom Beilenson studied on one of the world's great stages.

When Beilenson first got to China in 1943, he became intrigued with Mao, who was a poet and military strategist as well as a political leader. Unlike Chiang—or for that matter, most of America's leaders—Mao had written extensively. As might be expected, the nationalists had collected extensive material on Mao, including his own writings. While the Kuomintang (nationalists) did not make these available to the Chinese public or even to their own troops, Beilenson had no trouble as an intelligence officer in obtaining the materials, many of which had been trans-

lated into English. In a very real sense, he felt that his education truly
began when he started this reading program.

From the outset, he found that there was nothing original about
Mao's guerrilla tactics, successful though they may have been. Mao himself frequently quoted Sun Tzu's *Art of War*, which was written about
500 B.C. Actually, a more recent work—von Clausewitz's classic *On War*
(1874)—and Mao's use of it were far more instructive to Beilenson. Mao
studied *On War* after reading the works of Lenin. *On War* was one of
two books that Lenin took with him into hiding in July 1917. It had a
strong influence on him, and Mao admitted frequently that his own
policies were derived from Lenin. In fact, in order to understand the
policies of China or Russia or any other nation formed by communists,
Beilenson believed, one had to read Lenin carefully. Lenin said it all.[22]

It may be hard to conceive of Beilenson passing on to a friend or pupil
tracts on military history and politics that were written 50 or 150 or 500
years ago, especially during occasional meetings, sometimes while con-
suming a meal. The process is more understandable if we consider the
form of Beilenson's findings. He had developed a series of "guides" or
rules to govern foreign policy decisions, which he later published. It was
the application of these guides to current international problems that
was most likely the gist of his periodic discussions with Ronald Reagan.
The guides were also ideal fare for memorization.

Beilenson's guides were expressed as absolutes, as he believed any rule
had to be. They could be readily absorbed, especially by someone with a
good memory and a good ear. They may have occasionally have been
accompanied by memoranda or drafts of his works in progress. Most of
them were set out in his first book, *The Treaty Trap*, which appeared in
1969. A selection follows:[23]

> **Guide.** Lenin taught that the Communist end always justifies the
> means. No subsequent ruler of Russia has forsworn him.
> **Guide.** If a treaty is made, the Soviet Union will probably violate it.
> **Guide.** In relying on treaties, the short guide is simply don't.
> **Guide.** If nuclear weapons are not destroyed, they will be used,
> sooner or later.

But what can a nation do when it has relied on a treaty with Russia that
that country later chooses to ignore? After tracing the record under the

leadership of Lenin, Stalin, and Krushchev, Colonel Beilenson sets out his ultimate "Guide": "The Soviet Union retreats when faced with strength."[24]

Beilenson's distrust of treaties stems in part from his background as a lawyer. "Men have always been astute," he writes, "in violating the prohibition of words, whether in law or treaties."[25] The reluctance to rely on "mere words" and the refusal to be bound or deterred by treaties became core beliefs of Ronald Reagan. Stating his policy decisions simply and sticking to them was a familiar Reagan approach, commented on by many observers of his foreign policy, as well as those involved in crafting its details.[26] Beilenson gives two other authorities in *The Treaty Trap* for the point that silence is often preferable to a profusion of treaty words: Genesis, chapter 34; and comedian Jack Benny, a friend of both Reagan and Beilenson, who was renowned for his skillful use of the dramatic pause.[27]

Some of the more controversial components of Reagan's views on foreign policy emerge from Beilenson. In the 1961 version of "The Speech" (at that point called "Encroaching Government Controls") delivered to the Business Institute of New Jersey, Reagan uses the phrase "subversion and treason." The GE ambassador observes that in November of the previous year, communist parties of eighty-one countries met in Moscow and on December 6 issued the following principle of war to the death: "In a 20,000-word manifesto, they called on Communists in countries where there are non-Communist governments to be traitors and work for the destruction of their own governments by subversion and treason."

It is not difficult to find the source for this hard-hitting language. Beilenson's second book was entitled *Power Through Subversion* (1972). In it he explores this pillar of Lenin's legacy at length. He also urges a corollary of the policy: "In turning Lenin's preferred tool against his heirs," Beilenson writes, "the United States should give to the dissidents against all Communist governments protracted sustained aid—initially money for propaganda—agitation with supplies and arms added where feasible and warranted by the developing situation."[28] It is the assumption here that Beilenson and Reagan used these phrases and concepts for years. Beilenson had first encountered the communist dogma before 1945. Reagan mentioned the concepts while traveling for GE and, twenty years later, in the course of his presidency, in the Reagan Doctrine.

In his third book, *Survival and Peace in the Nuclear Age* (1980), Beilenson cites the Declaration of Independence for the proposition that it is the right and duty of people living under absolute despotism to "throw off such Government."[29] He rejects the Soviet policy that "all non-Communist governments are fair game, but Communist regimes are irreversible . . . [which] we have tacitly acknowledged by containment and our actions." He asks that the president "announce that we have rescinded the old rule."[30] Of course, the president at the time was Jimmy Carter. Ronald Reagan, speaking before the Fargo, North Dakota, Chamber of Commerce at an annual meeting, had rejected containment as a policy almost twenty years before in still another precursor of "The Speech."[31]

Beilenson's most controversial proposal was probably the nuclear shield, a defensive cover which came to be known in the Reagan administration as the Strategic Defense Initiative or, when referred to by its critics, "Star Wars." Many sources for this policy are pointed to in biographies and articles, including Reagan's early reading of fiction involving outer space—such as Edgar Rice Burroughs's *Carson of Venus*—and his movie role as flying Secret Service agent Brass Bancroft.[32] More serious observers pinpoint a visit with scientist Edward Teller. In fact, there is evidence that Reagan became interested in a nuclear defense shield while working for General Electric. The shield as such does not appear in "The Speech." But its beginnings are present in GE publications and in the work of the company as a defense contractor. And references by Beilenson in his first writing on the subject (before the Reagan administration) fit well within the framework of that information.

Beilenson introduces the concept of a nuclear shield in his third book with a quotation from a favorite authority, von Clausewitz, pointing out that one-third of *On War* is devoted to defense: "The defensive is the stronger form of making war. . . . What is the conception of defense? The warding off of a blow. . . . What is the object of defense? To preserve."[33] In *Survival and Peace in the Nuclear Age*, Beilenson translates von Clausewitz into a proposal for a twentieth-century policy: "To ward off the nuclear blow, active defense seeks to stop, deflect, or destroy the incoming missiles. To be totally effective it must neutralize all of them; to be partially effective, some of them."[34]

The genesis of the nuclear-defense concept may be found in the evidence Beilenson cites in support of the idea. He points out that "the idea of hitting a bullet with a bullet" had been accomplished by an anti-ballistic-missile intercept of an ICBM over Kwajalen in 1962 and cites a report of Charles Benson from 1971 that states that "the technology is either available

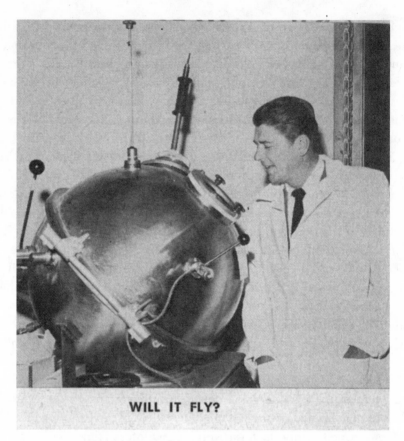

WILL IT FLY?

FIGURE 9 It was part of Ronald Reagan's job to meet with GE employees at every level—including the company's scientists—and to familiarize himself with their publications. These procedures marked his first exposure to antimissile defense programs, the forerunners of SDI. Here, as pictured in the November 1957 issue of *The Monogram*, he inspects a vacuum melting unit at GE's Vallecitos Laboratory.
Source: Schenectady Museum.

or on the verge of becoming available . . . if the resources are committed to them."[35]

It is entirely possible that Reagan's lifelong interest in space may have inspired a discussion with the General Electric TEMPO organization in Santa Barbara, which "had studied the ballistic-missile defense (BMD)" during Reagan's years with the company. A planning meeting on BMD was held in Syracuse in 1958 that ultimately led to GE's entry into the BMD radar business.[36] GE radar was tested over the Pacific Missile Range, which included the Kwajalen Atoll, referred to by Beilenson.

While missile defense was not a major subject of public debate before the Reagan administration, GE's role in the defense industry may have created an especial awareness in the company spokesman. As noted briefly above, *The General Electric Forum*—a magazine that the company described as its "Defense Quarterly"—published an article entitled "Military Defense: Free World Strategy in the 60's" by Dr. Robert Strausz-Hupé and Dr. William R. Kintner.[37] The article, which appeared shortly before Reagan left GE, called for a basic U.S. deterrent posture, which included "space systems for reconnaissance, warning, communication, and possibly defense." The authors then called specifically for "an active defense system against manned aircraft and missiles."[38]

One further point from the *Forum* article should be mentioned, in light of the continuing role of the SDI issue throughout the four Reagan-Gorbachev summits. The authors observe that "the Soviet Union is devoting a far greater percentage of its total R & D effort toward achieving an effective defense than the U.S."[39] Of course, the economic burden of nuclear-shield defense played a significant part in bringing the USSR to agreement in the negotiations at the summits.

How likely is it that Ronald Reagan read the *Forum* article that presaged such key elements in Beilenson's writings and Reagan administration foreign policy? Reagan's practice of reading GE publications has already been commented upon. In the case of this article, there is additional compelling evidence. The coauthors were professors of political science at the University of Pennsylvania and founder-director (Strausz-Hupé) and deputy director of the Foreign Policy Research Institute. The institute and its quarterly journal, *Orbis*, represented the vigorous, proactive anti-Soviet policy that Reagan favored.

Kintner wrote the foreword to *The Treaty Trap*, and one of his books is listed in the bibliography. Six books authored or coauthored by Strausz-Hupé are included in that bibliography. Strausz-Hupé was described by Reagan's first secretary of state, Alexander Haig, as "a brilliant geo-strategic thinker and writer," and was appointed ambassador to Turkey by Reagan.[40]

Anticipating criticism that the nuclear-shield proposal lacked scientific validation, Beilenson provides an analogy. He points out that "on the eve of the ICBM," President Eisenhower's science advisor, a former president of MIT, advised Ike that the weapon was "technically impossible."[41]

Beilenson's guides set out above about the unreliability of treaties and the attendant need for a strong military; the financing of forces against communist regimes; and the nuclear-shield initiative became major parts of the Reagan foreign policy. In seeking to go beyond containment and to reverse detente, Reagan established an agenda that created a new, far more aggressive U.S. policy toward the Soviet Union. The premise for these sweeping changes, Beilenson points out, is found in the United States Constitution.

After examining modern concepts such as containment and detente, he says that "the founding fathers were more modest and simple about our foreign aims, which our Constitution twice states as 'the common Defense and general welfare of the United States.'" He underlines this point by adding: "The best foreign policy is not to have one; our two aims are sufficient guides."[42]

The focus on the "evil" nature of the Soviet empire—the point of departure for Reagan, Boulware, and Beilenson—is not a frivolous or transitory thing. In explaining the two constitutional aims set out above, Beilenson cites James Madison in *The Federalist* (no. 51) for the rationale of government itself. "If men were angels," Madison writes, "no government would be necessary. If angels were to govern men neither external nor internal controls on government would be necessary." To make sure his point is hitting home, Beilenson then adds a fundamental truth: "As the Bible and all literature teach, man has a dual nature torn between good and evil."[43] This premise coincides with Ronald Reagan's view of international communism and provides a key to understanding his foreign policy.[44]

What to do when faced with the "general amorality that has marked the actions of governments abroad?" As we face the Soviet empire, Beilenson answers, we must understand that "Communist ethics, as formulated by V. I. Lenin, and as they have been practiced ever since, are simply a lack of ethics as we understand them." Beilenson urges "vigilance against evildoers," concluding that "for the foreseeable future, even though the *evil* ones are in the minority, they still will require us to keep up our guard" (emphasis added).

Beilenson and Reagan shared an experience that ensured that the lawyer's "guides" would fall on receptive ears. Both had dealt directly with communists, and their respective experiences led them to believe in the fundamental evil of the Soviet masters. Beilenson had studied Mao and the rest of the Chinese Communist leaders at a time when he actually faced them as an enemy. At least that's the way they were regarded by the nationalists to whom Beilenson was attached, ostensibly to fight the Japanese. Reagan, in his brief membership with the Communist-front HICCASP and in the CSU/SAG contest, also had direct experience with communists.

While Lemuel Boulware's writings were directed primarily to domestic concerns, he felt, as noted briefly above, that there was an "inescapable *moral* requirement for our continued freedom and the enjoyment of the rest of the material and non-material well-being open to us."[45] Communism, on the other hand, was a "win by any means" ideology. He certainly perceived this in the communist-dominated United Electrical Workers. To prevail at the bargaining table and elsewhere, he believed in doing the right thing, "no matter what outwardly attractive but essentially *evil* blandishments are offered to the contrary" (emphasis added).[46]

Beilenson, Reagan, and Boulware all had a deep-seated distrust of communism. Their contempt for what they saw as a foreign ideology dedicated to the destruction of their domestic economic system was pronounced. They had each encountered communists within the continental United States, and the experience had only confirmed their hatred. They made it a point—especially Beilenson, who had also witnessed the theories of Lenin and Mao embodied in international military action—to understand where and how the communist theory and practice had developed and where it had taken hold. They talked about how the threat posed by the Soviet government might some day affect their lives.

"The Speech," at this point, was a stunning work in progress. What had developed on the mashed potato circuit was a coherent message on domestic and foreign matters that GE's traveling ambassador could use effectively in both the contest with the IUE and in the Cordiner-Boulware national grass-roots campaign. There was no inconsistency in Reagan's mind about these twin targets. The objective of Boulwarism was always to capture the minds and hearts of the workers by going over the heads of their leaders. As Reagan delivered early versions of "The Speech" on GE's campaign trail, he never lost sight of Boulware's lifelong focus on the "widening gap between the *economic* interests of union members and the *political* interests of union officials."[47]

NINE

TWO UNIONS

In March 1960, AFL-CIO president George Meany telegraphed Ronald Reagan that Reagan had "the full sympathy and support of the AFL-CIO in your fight for fair treatment." He commended Reagan for his "long record of peaceful collective bargaining."[1]

Of course, Meany's endorsement had been offered to Reagan in his capacity as president of the Screen Actors Guild. The full text of the telegram, along with strong expressions of support from other union leaders, is set out later in this chapter. Presidential biographer Garry Wills writes, "The New Deal prepared the way for Reagan in Hollywood," and quotes Reagan's appraisal of his SAG experience: "I turned really eager and I have considered myself a rabid union man ever since."[2]

In 1959, friends in Hollywood had approached Reagan to run, again, for president of SAG. Although he had been elected to the guild presidency five times in the past, his last term having expired in 1952, something more was expected of him this time. Wills finds Reagan's motivation in his guild work to be inspired by a sense of "altruism" rather than the economic interdependence found in more traditional union solidarity.[3] In any event, the actor was back at the helm at a crucial time in his profession as the new medium of television intersected with the production of feature films.

The account that follows is about two unions: the Screen Actors Guild, with the most visible membership of any union in the nation, and the IUE, one of the largest and most powerful units in the AFL-CIO. Their respective managements were the moguls who ruled Hollywood and the executives at General Electric, the country's fifth largest corporation. The players involved in these contests—Cordiner, Boulware, Reagan, Jim Carey, George Meany, Jack Warner, Spyros Skouras, and Lew Wasserman, to name only a few—were among the most powerful and best known people in America.

It was a compliment to Ronald Reagan that his professional peers sought his leadership at this crucial time. But there was a possibility that the actors would go out on strike against the movie producers—for the first time in history—on the issue of the uncompensated showing of their films on television. The SAG contract was set to expire on January 31, 1960, eleven months before the expiration of the GE/IUE contract, which therefore would be in collective bargaining negotiations within the same year as the SAG contract.

This aspect of Reagan's education—dealing with the intersection of long-range goals and immediate, unexpected crises occurring on a number of independent fronts—presented a unique opportunity to learn, one that few men and women who ultimately hold public office ever have. Nevertheless, it must have been a massive headache for Lemuel Boulware to contemplate the GE spokesman leading the guild membership out on strike at the same time as he was urging IUE members—GE employees—*not* to strike.

THE GUILD

The Screen Actors Guild was founded in the early 1930s. A group of stage-trained actors and actresses retained attorney Larry Beilenson to assist them in establishing an organization to represent them in their negotiations with the studios, which at the time had absolute control of the movie industry. Beilenson had just written the charter and bylaws for the Screen Writers Guild. He had a commanding credential in a very narrow field.

Beilenson found that many of the actors were opposed to joining a "union." Like the screenwriters whom Beilenson had represented at their organization's creation, the actors thought a union was demeaning and unprofessional, even though the producers were running roughshod over them. So Beilenson came up with the notion of a "guild," much like the guilds that stage professionals had belonged to in the Middle Ages. He pointed out that actor-writer William Shakespeare was a member of a guild. The issue was turned around, and the formation of a guild suddenly seemed consistent with the oldest traditions of the profession. The actors still didn't warm up to the idea of going out on strike, however. Beilenson dealt with that by making it necessary to get the approval of three-quarters of the membership before the actors would go out.[4]

The Screen Actors Guild was officially established in 1933 and set up office in a fifteen-by-twenty-foot room with one window at the corner of Cherokee Avenue and Hollywood Boulevard. It was recognized by the AFL in 1935, and the studios accepted SAG jurisdiction in 1937.[5] An attempt by IATSE, the "Set Erectors'" union, to create a rival actors' group when many of the SAG leaders were in the service during World War II was defeated.[6]

"Before our first contract in 1937, we had to meet in secret," longtime guild secretary Midge Farrell later wrote. "We never knew who was spying on us and keeping an eye on this young, upstart union. Some of the companies had goon squads." In 1933, salaries were cut in half for actors who were already working six-day weeks for $65.

The group that led Ronald Reagan to become active in SAG was not itself a union or even an official organization of any kind. The "Emerald Isles Class" was the informal tag adopted by actors of Irish heritage at Warner Brothers. Most of them, like Ronald Reagan, had been born into a Roman Catholic family although some, like Reagan, no longer followed their Catholic faith. But they were all Irish and proud of it. Pat O'Brien was a "member." He had moved Reagan's career up to a new plateau when, as star of *Knute Rockne—All American*, he had shown studio head Jack Warner a photo of Reagan in his Eureka College football uniform. It convinced Warner that the young actor could play George Gipp, the tragic Notre Dame gridiron hero. Another Emerald Isles member, Byron Foy (who played vaudeville in his youth as one of the "Seven Little Foys") produced five of Reagan's pictures. Character actor James Gleason was one of the founders of the Screen Actors Guild. And senior members Jimmy Cagney and song-and-dance man George Murphy had each served as guild president. It is not surprising that when the guild sought some new faces for its board, Reagan, early in his career, was happy to respond to the invitation of his Emerald Isles colleagues.

But why, in 1959, would Reagan take on this second tour of SAG leadership? He felt an especially strong bond with the actors' union. The guild gave him credentials in his speeches before both blue-collar workers and civic groups. It also gave him a wife. In 1949, Nancy Davis, as she was then known, saw her name listed in a newspaper as one of Hollywood's communist sympathizers. Apparently, the list described another film actress with the same name. When Nancy saw the list, she was concerned about her career, but she also feared what her beloved stepfather, Dr. Loyal Davis, would think. She wrote: "My parents would die if they heard about this."[7]

Nancy took steps to clear up the confusion, and her studio managed to get a mention in Louella Parsons's gossip column to the effect that the person listed as a communist sympathizer was not the Nancy Davis under contract to MGM. This helped but did not fully resolve the matter. At the suggestion of producer-director Mervyn Leroy, she arranged a meeting with the president of the Screen Actors Guild, Ronald Reagan.[8] Soon after they met, they started going out with each other exclusively. In March of 1952, they were married.

Nancy's interest in the guild went beyond the origin of her romance with its president. In 1959, she was in the middle of a three-year term on its board. She undoubtedly urged her husband to once again undertake the presidency. It was not that she was unaware of his expanding role with GE; she made it a point to keep informed, and actively engaged when appropriate, on her husband's activities in every aspect, not just in the acting profession which they shared.

The Screen Actors Guild is an important institution in Hollywood. The three-story headquarters on Sunset Boulevard had been built especially for the guild in 1956. To enter, you walked up a "Ramp to the Stars" through a large flagstone arch to a glass-walled reception area. Eduardo Samaniegos was the architect. By 1959, the guild had 14,000 members and was already outgrowing these quarters. Jack Dales, the executive secretary, and Midge Farrell, the secretary, had both been with the guild for decades and provided an institutional memory. At the beginning, Midge Farrell was the entire staff. Her desk was a large orange crate and the typewriter was rented. Her salary was twenty dollars per week, which she felt was "pretty good" for 1933 and higher than most screen actors, even when they were working in their chosen field.

The founding board had about twenty members. Probably the only one who would be remembered today would be horror-movie star Boris Karloff. Most of the men belonged to a private club known as the Masquers, and many of the women belonged to a sister group called the Dominoes. The theater background was important because Actors Equity, the stage actors' union, had tried unsuccessfully to organize the film actors in 1929.

It may be hard to understand militant unionism in an industry in which salaries for some members were among the highest in the country. But the stars remembered their own beginnings, often at meager salaries and extremely unsatisfactory working conditions. Guild literature is filled with these recollections: Douglas Fairbanks Jr. recalled that "Jack Warner was a loudmouth bully" who insisted on a six- or seven-day work week and placement in another film on the day after the current one was finished. Robert Young said that the organization meetings were like communist cells, with small numbers gathered late at night in private homes lest they be fired for their union activities. Anthony Quinn remembered that his first job paid eight dollars per day. But even after he had established himself, the studios of the 1940s, influenced by the reigning star, Van Johnson, were looking for blue-eyed actors with light brown hair to play the American leads. Darker people like Quinn were relegated to play the villains. Quinn sought relief from the tyrannical, whimsical rule of the moguls.

Maureen O'Sullivan described "working until we dropped and then we'd have an early call." Jimmy Stewart commented that when he first came to Hollywood in 1935, working conditions were not favorable to actors. They often worked until midnight and reported back to the set at six the next morning. Stewart interrupted his career with four years of highly distinguished military service. When he returned to Hollywood, much had changed due to a lawsuit brought by guild member Olivia de Havilland. De Havilland was personally familiar with Jack Warner's highhanded ways. When David Selznick wanted her for the part of Melanie in *Gone With the Wind*, Warner let her do it only when Selznick gave him a one-picture commitment from Jimmy Stewart in exchange. De Havilland sums up her lawsuit: "I was very proud of that decision [in

1945] for it corrected a serious abuse of the contract system—the forced extension of a contract beyond its legal term. Among those who benefited by the decision were the actors who fought in World War II."

And so the stars were just as militant as the journeymen members when they called Reagan back to action. In 1960, the key issues were the pension fund and TV compensation and residuals.[9] These issues defined as well as anything could the polar elements of SAG membership. The pension was crucial to the journeymen members; compensation for TV showing of films and residuals, while of concern to actors at every level, was of especial interest to the stars.

The pension was needed because most members of the union did not work steadily for one employer. In fact, for long periods, many of them didn't work at all. They needed some kind of industry-supported pension and welfare plan. Stage actors had received just such a program through AFTRA, their union, five years before, but the film industry had no such employee benefit plans. Many of the stars didn't even see the pension as a big issue, but they were adamant about getting paid if any of their films were shown on television. Interest had focused on films made from 1948 on, and the studios would not budge. When asked about their policy on films released in 1960 and afterward, they still would not budge. Spyros Skouras, the head of 20th Century Fox, actually cried when the issue was brought up and said that payment of residuals would bankrupt the studios.

In addition to the possibility of a strike, there were other time bombs that could explode in Hollywood and embarrass General Electric in its bargaining on the East Coast. In 1960, there were two situations that could fall into this category. The first was the way the guild leaders acted in the House hearings in the 1940s and early 1950s on communists in the industry. This was still a very sensitive subject ten years later. Ronald Reagan was SAG president at the height of that matter.[10] This point was difficult to assess. It might possibly be used to discredit Reagan—now that he was front and center once again at SAG—in the eyes of GE workers.

The second potentially explosive issue was referred to in the entertainment industry as the "blanket waiver." This was virtually unknown outside of TV and movie circles. During Reagan's prior tour as SAG president, a rule was established that no company could act as an agent representing talent at the same time as that company was producing films for television. Of course, MCA was the largest talent agency in town and, through its wholly owned subsidiary Revue, the largest producer of television shows, as well. It was anticipated that companies from time to time might get waivers for individual actors or specific productions, but MCA applied for and obtained a blanket waiver. It was the only company granted such an exemption.

There were rumors at the time that Reagan had received a "sweetheart deal" in return for gaining favorable treatment for his agent, MCA. In his defense, Jack Dales and others pointed that Reagan was out of town (on his honeymoon, in fact) at the time and that SAG vice president Walter Pidgeon signed the agreement. Moreover, Dales also pointed out, the deal created thousands of jobs and an increased membership for SAG. If Reagan were involved in a union battle on the West Coast, the issue might again come to the fore and complicate GE's union contest in the east.[11]

On January 18, 1960, the president of the Screen Actors Guild and his fellow negotiators had their first face-to-face meeting with the producers. The first formal bargaining session had actually taken place a month earlier, soon after Reagan had again assumed the SAG presidency. At that time, management sent two nameless representatives. Nothing happened, and the guild questioned whether these negotiators had any real authority to bargain. Not so at this second session, where Spryros Skouras, Barney Balaban, Joe Vogel, and Jack Warner, the men who actually headed the major studios, were at the bargaining table.[12] The moguls themselves had never appeared in full complement at any other negotiations over the years.

The union demands were placed directly on the table: The actors wanted higher base pay; a pension and welfare plan; and payment and residuals when pictures produced between 1948 and 1960, as well as pictures made after 1960, were sold to television. In the December meeting, the so-called negotiating committee had said that they were under orders from the presidents of their companies not even to discuss the post-1948 pictures or any compensation for showing on television of the post-1960 films. It was this intransigence that had led Reagan to request direct confrontation with the studio heads themselves. But one after another, the producers said, "We won't discuss it."

How often did Ronald Reagan and Lemuel Boulware discuss the strategic problems that confronted them in the course of the two almost simultaneous, independent negotiations taking place on opposite coasts? We can only guess, but the impasse in California fell within one of the cardinal principles of Boulware's approach to what he described as "political bargaining." It is a rule he taught to his staff and his ERMs and set out in his writings both during his active years and in retirement. Whether over the phone, over a meal, or in his office, it is likely that he talked to his protégé about the fundamental precept that would apply to the situation. "Any bargaining to be worthy of the name," Boulware wrote, "[has] to involve equals."[13]

If Reagan complained about the producers' united front, Boulware could point out that no one of them was really in charge of the elements on his own side of the table. Each controlled only one part of the producers' alliance. They had a well-documented record of unimpeded ego within their respective domains, hatred of one another, and cutthroat competition. Reagan, on the other hand, was in charge of his forces. He appeared to have the overwhelming support of his membership. He believed that he would soon have a vote to prove it. While he was authorized to make decisions, not one of the producers could act for the industry as a whole.

Ronald Reagan—on his own initiative or pursuant to the counsel of his mentor—knew that if he was to prevail in his negotiations, he must deal with the real power in this changing industry. He must seek out an *equal* in bargaining rather than attempt to work with these relics of a now outmoded studio system. In time, he would find the appropriate power center. For now, he needed the formal support of his membership. He also had to bear in mind that in his other life he was the spokesman (i.e., on the management side) for a giant company that itself might be faced with a strike.

On February 18, the Screen Actors Guild issued the following statement to the press:

RESULTS OF GUILD STRIKE REFERENDUM

In the largest vote ever polled by an actors' union in the United States, the Screen Actors Guild membership voted by a majority of better than 83 percent to authorize the Board to call a strike in theatrical motion pictures if it became necessary to obtain a fair and equitable collective bargaining contract. . . . A total of 7,245 ballots were received. Of these, 5,899 voted "Yes" and 1,199 voted "No." There were 147 ballots ruled invalid for various reasons.

The result had been expected, but the margin was higher than anticipated. A March strike deadline was set by the SAG board. If there was any doubt as to whether Ronald Reagan was regarded as a bona fide union leader, it was dispelled by the affirmation he now received from leaders of other unions. Expressions of support came from Ed S. Miller, general president of the Hotel and Restaurant Employees and Bartenders; Morris Weisberger, secretary-treasurer of the Sailors Union of the Pacific; James S. Suffridge, president of the Retail Clerks International Association; and about fifteen others. David McDonald, president of the United Steelworkers of America, assured SAG not only of the "moral sustenance" of his union, but also of his "personal support." The most powerful pledge of support was contained in a Western Union telegram:

> *Ronald Reagan, president, screen actors guild*
> *7750 Sunset Blvd., Hollywood, Calif.*
> Please be assured that the Screen Actors Guild has the full sympathy and support of the AFL-CIO in your fight for fair treatment. Your long record of peaceful collective bargaining, spanning more than a generation, indicates without question that this strike was forced upon your union by the stubborn refusal of the employers to negotiate reasonable terms. Like workers in other American industries, you are asking to share in the benefits of technological progress—a share to which you have both a moral and economic right. You can rely upon the cooperation and assistance of all your fellow unionists in the united labor movement in this struggle.
>
> George Meany, President, AFL-CIO

The IUE

The AFL-CIO was actively involved at this time in labor matters at GE. Its Industrial Union Department (created by Walter Reuther) had estab-

FIGURE 10 At the AFL-CIO convention in Bal Harbour, Florida, in 1961, Eleanor Roosevelt is flanked by "union officials." To her immediate left is Walter Reuther, head of the CIO and one of the most powerful men in America. To his left is the flamboyant James Carey, president of the IUE, GE's principal union opponent.
Source: Franklin D. Roosevelt Library.

lished a coalition of unions for the purpose of exchanging information and coordinating other activities related to the 1960 General Electric negotiations.[14] The lead union in the coalition, the designated representative for collective bargaining, was the International Union of Electrical, Radio, and Machine Workers—the IUE.

In the decade he had faced the IUE, Boulware had suffered few defeats. He was invariably generous in victory. As the *Berkshire Eagle* reported at the conclusion of one bargaining session, "Boulware, a master of showmanship, gave his expensive Countess Mara necktie to [the business agent of IUE Local 255 John] Callahan, saying, 'You may as well take this—you've taken everything else I have.' As the press cameras clicked, Callahan gave his North Street bargain cravat to Boulware." The event took place in Pittsfield, Massachusetts, in 1955. In fact, the union's victory was not quite what it seemed.

The *Eagle* described the incident again in 1988 when the General Electric Company gained another significant victory in the labor wars. The latter article was sent to Boulware by GE CEO Jack Welch, who observed in his covering letter that "the employees really gave a message to their local leaders who opposed it. Our plant people did a terrific job in communicating the fairness of the package." Since communicating the fairness of an offer was what Boulware was all about, Welch thought he "would get a kick out of the coverage."[15]

In spite of his public remarks to the contrary, Boulware had also done well with Callahan at the bargaining table in 1955. In exchange for a cost-of-living escalator, he obtained a rare five-year contract. And he built into it a reopening provision that contained a time bomb that the union would ultimately come to regret. He knew that a good labor negotiator must not only develop a satisfactory package and educate his employees on its merits, he must plan ahead—often for years—and prepare for any contingency.

In 1958, the IUE sought to reopen the contract on the issue of job security. This was Boulware's "time bomb." He had, with seeming reluctance, allowed the union to include it as the sole basis on which the contract could be reopened prior to its expiration in 1960. He knew he could win on the issue because GE had plenty of jobs. The company's victory on this point in 1958 would give it the momentum it wanted for the major contract negotiation of 1960. IUE president James B. Carey, infuriated at the result, used it to convince his membership to lower the requirement for a strike vote from two-thirds to a simple majority. Carey's new weapon of greater access to the strike alternative would also, in time, prove a boon to the resourceful Boulware.[16]

In 1959 Carey was even more famous than Boulware. While the GE vice president was well known in executive suites throughout the country, the colorful Carey had long been quoted on the front pages or in the business sections of the nation's newspapers. Although only forty-seven years old, Carey had been on the national labor scene for twenty-five years. He had been president of the IUE since 1949, when the CIO expelled the UE and created a new union, the International Union of Electrical, Radio, and Machine Workers. The IUE succeeded the communist-dominated UE as the major bargaining unit with the General Electric Company.

Herbert Northrup, who had served as employee relations consultant at GE before he became professor of industry and chairman of the Department of Industry at Penn's Wharton School of Finance and Commerce, had ample opportunity to study Carey at close hand. He described the early Carey as "an attractive young man and good speaker . . . capable at moving crowds and at debate. But these same qualities, combined with his lack of restraint in controlling his emotions and in dealing with people, made Carey neither a good administrator nor an effective bargainer."[17]

Although Carey's public demeanor had grown smoother over the years, he had never learned how to control his temper. Boulware played on this and other Carey shortcomings to defeat him again and again in the labor wars. In 1950, for example, when GE convinced the workers at their huge Schenectady plant not to confer bargaining rights on the IUE, Boulware had gone over the heads of the union representatives to the members themselves. (Ironically, this move left the communist-dominated UE Local 301 as the plant representative.) In that same year, Boulware persuaded IUE Local 255 in Pittsfield to reject Carey's entreaty for a strike authorization. Carey came out of that session "boiling mad," telling reporters that "those SOBs [union officials who voted against the strike] would have treated Charlie Wilson [then still GE's president] better than they treated me!"[18]

The failure of the IUE to present a united front of workers was not the result of accident or inertia. Lemuel Boulware was mindful of the venerable tactic of divide and conquer. Although the IUE (either individually or as a member of the IUD or another bargaining vehicle, the GE Conference Board) had emerged as the certified representative for bargaining, the stark fact of the matter was that of the company's 250,000 employees, only 120,000 were in organized bargaining units. The IUE represented about 70,000 employees; the UE was (in spite of its expulsion from the AFL-CIO) the second largest union; and there were one hundred other odd unions under contract with GE.

GE bested the IUE at the bargaining table throughout the 1950s. The years 1955 (when John Callahan was deputized to head the negotiating team) and 1958 have been touched on briefly above. The 1952 agreement—which Carey described as "unconditional surrender" by his union—and the 1954 agreement were both accepted by the IUE-GE Conference Board, which was then the central organization of local unions certified as representatives of GE workers. Carey refused to sign both contracts.[19]

On the crucial strike issue, Carey may have given Boulware a trump card. The July 1959 issue of *Steel* magazine quoted Jim Carey as saying, "I owe GE a strike."[20] Although Carey denied making the threat, the magazine stuck to its guns. The very independent Schenectady IUE Local 301 had already chided Carey on the point, saying that he was probably recalling 1958, when he should have called a strike on the job security issue but failed to do so.

In any event, Boulware planned to make the threat an issue. He recalled that Carey had convinced his membership to lower the strike vote requirement in 1958. Boulware would put the strike issue in the context of one man's ego precluding the acceptance of a solid offer by the company. But wouldn't the impact of this issue be reduced, perhaps eliminated if GE's goodwill ambassador was pursuing a strike as the only legitimate way to get management's attention in his own industry on the West Coast?

TEN

THE ART OF NEGOTIATION

Ronald Reagan is the only U.S. president to have served as a union president. His secretary of state, George Shultz, commented on that before Reagan's first summit with Mikhail Gorbachev. "Reagan saw himself as an experienced negotiator," Shultz observed, "going back to his days as president of the Screen Actors Guild."[1] Shultz felt the experience made the president more "self-confident." Reagan himself commented that "after the studios, Gorbachev was a snap."[2] Moreover, during his GE years, Reagan had the opportunity to observe Lemuel Boulware, the acknowledged master of union-management negotiations, and to participate in his program. The development of skill in negotiation is certainly a key element in the education of Ronald Reagan.

The issues in labor-management contests often determine the manner in which individual lives are lived. This was certainly true for the GE workers in 1960 and for the great majority of screen actors at that time. The outcome of the negotiations determines whether one can afford to send children to college, the kind of a house one lives in, the kind of a car one drives, how the medical bills will be paid, and how one will exist in old age. These are the most important issues the average citizen ever faces.

In the 1960s, when the power of organized labor was near its peak, negotiations could often affect more people than municipal or state elections. Consider the confrontation in which GE and the IUE were involved in 1960. It was national in scope, and the employee base of 250,000 was larger than the population of all but forty American cities. If the extended base, including the families of the workers, is considered, there are few political contests in this country with larger constituencies. In U.S. elections, only half of the voters have enough interest to turn out to vote for president, and local and state elections get an even less enthusiastic response. In contests between labor and management, virtually every employee is a voter. Positions are strongly held. Public protests, violence, and arrests are often involved. The voters care passionately about the issues they are called upon to decide.

The negotiations of SAG and the producers overlapped those of the IUE and GE's management, each having consequences that related to the other. While the GE/IUE battle was massive, more newspaper readers and television viewers would probably follow the SAG situation closely because the most famous people in America were involved. The screen actors' contract with the producers expired first, at the beginning of 1960, with the General Electric contract terminating toward the end of the year. Of course, negotiations in each case began well before the expiration dates.

The Screen Actors Guild vs. the Producers

The marquee of the Hollywood Palladium has announced many dramatic productions over the years, but the credits on Sunday evening, March 13, 1960, were without precedent: "SAG STRIKE MEETING," the sign proclaimed boldly. Almost 4,000 people filled the theater in what the press described as "the largest membership meeting ever held by an actors' union in the United States."[3] SAG board members sat on the stage accompanied by leaders of other theatrical unions, including Actors Equity, AFTRA, AGMA, and AGVA. This was one of those rare assemblages, however, where the faces of the audience were more recognizable than many of those who appeared on the stage.

Still, the group facing the audience was not too shabby. Although the leaders of other unions were virtually unknown to the public, the members of the SAG Negotiating Committee included Leon Ames, Dana Andrews, Rosemary DeCamp, James Garner, and Charlton Heston. Reagan began by introducing the other union leaders on stage and then made the current position clear: "We are now in the first and only strike we have ever had against the major motion picture producers." The giant audience rocked with laughter, shouts, and applause when their president said, "This is the first time in our history that we have ever found ourselves negotiating for the right to negotiate."

The SAG board of directors had voted to recommend a strike as a prelude to this meeting of the membership. The union president's next words reassured the audience that the current situation was not quite the unbreakable impasse suggested by the producers' refusal to negotiate. Reagan said, "In the meantime, one studio came to us—Milton Rackmil of Universal-International. He came to us and he said, 'I want to tell you something. I never agreed with the producers' stand. From 1952 on, in every negotiation, I have been overruled and outvoted when I urged the Producers' Association to make a deal before this problem becomes as big as it has become.'" This time, Rackmil had entered into a deal with SAG, as did some 400 independent producers.

Although the details of the agreement were still being worked out, the major provisions, which were approved by the SAG board and Universal's board of directors, were incorporated into a memorandum that made provision for wage increases; pension payments consisting of a percentage of gross television receipts from films produced between 1948 and 1960; and, most important, an understanding that post-1960 "photoplays released on pay television will be considered as theatrical releases." The concession on the post-1960 films, which the other studio heads would not even consider as being on the table in negotiations, was a huge breakthrough.

At this point, one can see a number of negotiating tactics coming into play. They may have developed from Reagan's natural instincts and his previous terms as SAG president, but they also reflect Lemuel Boulware's cardinal principles of negotiation, which Ronald Reagan had observed for the six years in which he had been part of Boulware's program. Prior to the SAG membership meeting, Reagan had "paved the way," preparing his followers and his adversaries for the choices they would have to make. He had made it a point to "know his adversaries," realizing before they themselves did that the ego-centered studio heads no longer dominated the movie business. He knew that he had certain "trump cards" or "bargaining chips" that, if played at the proper moment, could turn the tide of the bargaining. He sought to "divide and conquer" his adversaries. He knew that he must "deal with equals," even if it meant going "over the heads" of the Producers Association to meet "directly" with the real decision makers in the industry. In the GE/IUE bargaining, Boulware believed that the real power resided in the employees, not the union leaders. Reagan knew that in Hollywood the power resided in one man.

Lew Wasserman, Ronald Reagan's great friend and agent, was at this time described by the cognoscenti as "the most powerful man in entertainment." The *New York Times* introduced its readers to the MCA CEO in these terms: "The name 'Lew R. Wasserman' on a movie marquee would mean nothing to moviegoers. But in Hollywood—and in the nation's entertainment industry—he is regarded with a mixture of admiration, fear and animosity that suggests Richelieu during the reign of King Louis XIII." Three years before the SAG-Universal agreement, MCA with Wasserman at the helm had acquired the Universal back lot, Hollywood's largest. There were rumors in the Hollywood winds about MCA acquiring Universal and its corporate parent, Decca Records, a transaction which later took place. Milton Rackmil, in effect, reported to Lew Wasserman.[4]

Reagan recognized that the dynamics of the entertainment industry had changed. It was no longer dominated by the studios, with actors held under long-term contracts by the major producers. The decision in de Havilland's court case and earlier efforts by SAG had changed that, even though the megalomaniac studio heads—the likes of Barney Balaban, Jack Warner, and Spyros Skouras—stubbornly refused to acknowledge the change.

Through its talent agency, MCA represented many of the top actors in Hollywood. Some of them, like Reagan, wore "two hats now and we are the bosses ourselves in some of the pictures we make." But, Reagan stressed in his Palladium speech, "at this particular moment we are actors and we are on the actors' side." MCA facilitated many of these arrangements. Through its Revue subsidiary, headed by Taft Schreiber, the company also played a major role in television production. This was the power. Acquiring a film studio and record company would be the icing on the cake. It was the longtime vision of Lew Wasserman and his men-

FIGURE 11 President Reagan and MCA chairman Lew Wasserman are pictured in the Oval Office in May 1983. Wasserman played a major part in Reagan's career as his agent, as the producer of *GE Theater* (through MCA's subsidiary, Revue), and, in the SAG negotiations with the movie moguls, when Wasserman was viewed as "the most powerful man in entertainment." *Source*: Ronald Reagan Library.

tor, the venerable MCA chairman, Jules Stein. For all its elaborate corporate structure, the decisions of this entertainment empire were made by one man, Wasserman.

Reagan's announcement of the agreements with Universal and the independents filled the Palladium with tumultuous applause. After it died down, actor Cornel Wilde and others made short speeches in support of the strike. Although the vote was a formality, the board having resolved a week before that SAG should go on strike, some prominent actors—Mickey Rooney and Bob Hope among them—had condemned the board's decision.[5] Public disagreement at this point by prominent members could take the teeth out of the action. But when Warner Anderson called for a vote of confidence on the strike, the place went wild. Guild secretary Midge Farrell, who sat on stage at a separate table off to one side taking the official minutes of the meeting, made no attempt to count the vote. She entered into her minutes that the support was "unanimous."

Five weeks later, Reagan again stood before his membership. The strike had brought agreement from the recalcitrant moguls. The SAG president made this announcement: "I think that the benefits down through the years to performers will be actually greater than all of the previous contracts we have negotiated put together."[6] Waves of applause from the thousands gathered at the Palladium confirmed the feeling of victory that filled the air. The board had recommended the settlement at its meeting of April 8, and the membership was now balloting by mail overwhelmingly in support of the board's vote (the eventual tally was 6,399 to 259).

The guild had won on television payments for films made after 1960 and on the producers' contributions to the pension and welfare fund. There would be a payment into the pension fund, but no further compensation for the movies released between 1948 to 1960. But the producers had previously been adamant that there would be no payment for sale of *any* pictures to television, including the post-1960 films, and the SAG membership was exultant with the victory. Not everyone was satisfied. Mickey Rooney said, "SAG screwed us and I am mad about it." Of course, he had been making movies since he was four years old. He was one of the 259 dissenters.

At the conclusion of the meeting, Jack Dales proclaimed: "I doubt if you will ever realize the debt of gratitude we all owe Ronald Reagan." His words were greeted with a prolonged standing ovation.

GENERAL ELECTRIC VS. THE INTERNATIONAL UNION OF ELECTRICAL WORKERS

One of Lemuel Boulware's precepts was to "know your adversary," and Boulware knew Jim Carey well. Negotiations were still months off, but Boulware knew that Carey's threat—"I owe GE a strike"—if properly used, might be the trump card or bargaining chip that would win the day for the company.

There were many steps to be undertaken in the course of paving the way before negotiations began. But how could Boulware possibly exploit Carey's threat when GE's spokesman had led his SAG members out on strike, garnering an unprecedented victory in the process? Less than two months after the SAG strike, just before GE/IUE negotiations were scheduled to commence, an article appeared in one of GE's publications that dealt with the issue head on. The June 1 *Monogram* stated, "Ronald

Reagan spends a lot of time in the public eye as host of the General Electric Theater. He is also making headlines with the Screen Actors Guild, which has just concluded a strike against the movie industry." The GE magazine republished portions of a recent column by Charles Denton of the *Los Angeles Examiner* that addressed *Monogram*'s question, "How has Reagan the entertainment figure, Reagan the union chief, Reagan the public speaker viewed his various roles?"[7] While most IUE members had undoubtedly read about the SAG strike, this was General Electric itself bringing the news to them and not mincing words.

The Denton article pointed out that "his bosses at General Electric . . . said nothing to him about his prominent and sometimes beleaguered position as a labor leader, even though he often represents the firm as a touring speechmaker." Reagan confirmed the company's refusal to place shackles on him, even on labor issues on which it had taken a diametrically opposite stand. The *Los Angeles Examiner* quoted him as saying, "Even when the right-to-work issue was a hot one between labor and management, the company knew I was an official of a union that opposed right-to-work bills and never said a word to me about it."

How did Boulware use the *Monogram* article to help him in his campaign against the IUE? The answer is found in a key observation by Hollywood columnist Denton. He points out that the "only [SAG] union demand which would have benefited [Reagan] directly was for residual payments on the sale of films made between 1949 and 1960 to television. That was dropped in the final settlement—and Reagan was one of those who argued in favor of compromising on the issue." Denton concludes that "the ironic thing is that because he seldom works in movies any longer, Reagan gained almost nothing from the strike."

How refreshingly different was Reagan's selfless position from that of the IUE leader who said that he owes the company a strike before even seeing the company's offer. Still, a statesmanlike and modest Jim Carey might do much to disarm this issue by maintaining that he had been misquoted—his first reaction to the *Steel* magazine article—and moving on to more substantive matters. In later negotiations, however, he made it clear that his enlarged ego would not permit him to let the matter go. As negotiations proceeded to the bargaining table two months later, Carey told Phil Moore that if Moore continued to "misrepresent my attitude . . . Hell will break loose, physically and violently. You ever speak for me and see what happens. I'll break you apart."[8] The next day, he expanded on this message. "I'll break every bone in your body," he told Moore. "Damn it, I'll come over there and bust you right in the mouth."

Phil Moore was part of GE's negotiating team, as were Jack Parker and Virgil Day. Boulware was not. As the National Labor Relations Board observed in the course of its "Boulwarism" proceedings, "During the 1960 negotiations Boulware no longer occupied [the position of vice president for labor relations] having been succeeded by Jack S. Parker, but still participated in a consultant capacity in some of management's deliberations relating to such negotiations."[9] GE's key representatives had been trained by Boulware over the years, however, and there can be little doubt, as the NLRB suggests, that he was involved.

In fact, Boulware had invited Parker, Moore, and Day to meet with him in January of 1960 in Florida at the Hillsboro Club.[10] There, without interruption by anyone within or without the company, marching orders were put in place. At the top of the list were the issues of compensation and benefits that would constitute management's offer and, ultimately, the contract that would emerge from collective bargaining. Boulware and Reagan had "paved the way" for consideration of these issues in the broader context of employees' role of "contributor claimants" for years. Of course, General Electric was not the only party trying to win the minds and hearts of the workers in the coming negotiations. The way being paved was a two-way street.

On September 1, 1959, the union had published the following survey results in its monthly newsletter:[11]

IUE MEMBERSHIP SURVEY

IN SUPPORT OF IUE POSITION ON GE PROPOSALS
96%–4%
IN SUPPORT OF STRIKE
87%–13%

Boulware would place little credence in the IUE figures. The union's head-to-head survey on single issues would not impress him. Survey methods had changed in significant ways. While the union was examining the percentage of its membership who favored a strike, Boulware was determining the *depth* of their commitment. He acknowledged the use of "formal surveys" in testing employee attitudes toward job-related issues covered in *Works News.*

Works News articles covered subjects such as: "How Big Are General Electric Profits—Are They Too Big?"; "Who told You These Fairy Tales—Do You Still Believe Any of Them?"; "Should Wages Go Up—And Down—With Profits?"; "What's Your Extra Pay? What Are the Hidden 'Extras' in Your GE Pay? How Much Extra Can Be Added to Your Regular Earnings?"; and "Whose Promises Were Kept—and Whose Charges Were Wrong?"[12] A worker who learned that GE's profit margin was much smaller than he had been led to believe or that union officials had not been truthful with him in the past was less likely to stay out, even if he had agreed to strike in the first place.

The answers to all of these questions were useful to Ronald Reagan as he addressed GE employees who were present in his audiences on the mashed potato circuit. They also gave him more intimate and accurate insights into blue-collar workers than his future political opponents were likely to possess. The survey results were a primer on worker attitudes. Other issues tested came even closer to the communicator's frequent remarks: "Let's Learn from Britain"; "Two Cars in Every Garage"; "Is Opportunity Dead?"; "Why Are You Paying High Prices? Who's Responsible? What's the Cure?"; and "What Is Communism? What Is Capitalism? What Is the Difference to you?"

But why, if Reagan was familiar with the various labor issues and the broader political landscape, was he taken out of the plants? Most likely, Boulware was responding to a union initiative based on a court decision involving sausages. The NLRB had established long ago the principle that "on the part of the employer, [there is] a minimum recognition that the statutory representative [i.e. the union] is the one with whom it must deal in conducting bargaining negotiations, and that it can no longer bargain directly or indirectly with the employees." The board was now expanding the window to include activities well before the commencement of negotiations. Having the company's spokesman in the plants could create a target for an unfair labor-practice charge.

Boulware's prescience was later confirmed. The NLRB in the Boulwarism case cited *Herman Sausage*, which had been decided at about the time Reagan was moved out of the plants, for the proposition that it was inconsistent with the obligation not to bargain directly or indirectly with the employees for the employer to mount a campaign disparaging the union "both *before* and during negotiations" (emphasis added).[13] Reagan was not mentioned in the Boulwarism decision or in the later Second Circuit opinion affirming the board's order.

Even though removed from the plants and on the mashed potato circuit, Reagan still had to toe another important line. As Boulware had carefully spelled out in his policies at GE and his advice to other corporations, it was a crime for corporations to participate in partisan politics. Accordingly, there was no endorsement of Republican or Democratic issues as such. In fact, Reagan (and Boulware in the extensive job-marketing campaign that included the traveling ambassador) avoided party labels and even the words "conservative" and "liberal," speaking instead in terms of pocketbooks and patriotism. The methodology served Reagan well before blue-collar audiences years later, even after he entered partisan politics.

Reagan was not the only one traveling beyond the plants and to the neighboring communities. An "IUE Caravan" had already visited GE locations "for the purpose of dramatizing to the employees and communities the nature, need and reasonableness of the IUE bargaining objectives."[14] Moreover, labor's efforts now went beyond the IUE. That union and four other members of Walter Reuther's creation—the AFL-CIO's Industrial Union Department—announced a loose coalition "for the purpose of exchanging information and coordinating certain other activities related to the 1960 negotiations."[15]

Boulware made sure his leaders in the field were current on the company's positions on the narrower job issues on which the IUD caravan was sure to focus. GE came out with a new handbook entitled *Building Employee Understanding in 1960*.[16] The twenty-eight topics included: "How automation makes more and better jobs . . . The role of profits in providing jobs . . . The why and how of curbing inflationary settlements . . . [and] . . . Why employees could not gain and would lose by striking." A national management tour was scheduled, when the thousands of plant supervisors and ERMs could be briefed.[17] Ronald Reagan would undoubtedly be questioned on these points by blue-collar members of his audiences. His understanding of them was an important part of his education.

As most casual observers—readers of daily newspapers and television viewers—track the progress of labor negotiations, they focus on how far apart the parties are on the bread-and-butter issues. The general assumption is that management starts low and labor starts high and eventually the two meet on a figure approaching what each may really have had in mind from the outset. Boulware abhorred this kind of bargaining. He felt that management's use of "trick offers," with a "wink at the union leader" made management look like "liars and thieves" when they finally put forward a package the union could accept.[18]

Rather, it was GE's strategy to put a "full and fair offer" on the table at the outset, changing only if new facts were brought to management's attention that warranted a change. This was by no means a static process, however, and the company's basic strategy subsumed *tactical* elements— trump cards and bargaining chips—which, even though they carried the day, may have escaped the notice of casual observers or latter-day historians. Consider how GE used Carey's strike threat in the course of discussing the overall bargaining process as it began to pave the way at its giant Schenectady plant. At the first meeting of supervisors and ERMs, Boulware's longtime assistant Phil Moore said:

> Now whether we have a strike next fall depends not alone, however, on whether employees believe they have an appropriate offer from General Electric Company and have received satisfactory day-to-day treatment from their bosses. It also depends on whether employees believe they can gain anything further by a strike. And, lastly, it also depends on whether employees understand that they will be asked to strike in any case to support the political ambitions of some union officials.[19]

In a later visit to the Schenectady, Jack Parker and Phil Moore were pictured on the front page of the *Works News* with Schenectady executives Bill Ginn and A.C. Stevens. Moore commented on their "nationwide" visits, observing that they had "met with every employee relations manager in the company and asked each of them to give . . . his best analysis of employee needs and his suggestions as to how any company proposal might meet them."[20]

In the fall, when GE extended its offer, an article in the *Works News* explained in detail how the company arrived at the package: "The offer General Electric made this week in New York is the result of thousands of hours of work by GE people who are experts in a number of fields."

There were photographs of these experts at work, giving their names and credentials, with captions that began: "Proposal of Higher Pay . . . Scientific Inquiry Into Human Needs . . . Benefits for Employees are Constantly 'Up Front' . . . Study of Employee Sentiment . . . Company Proposal Based on Solid Economic Facts."[21]

As Chief Judge Kaufman noted in his *Boulwarism* opinion, when proposals were exchanged, "the Boulware approach moved into high gear." But the company's "avalanche of publicity" was met as the *IUE News Letter* unleashed its own avalanche, though it was significantly smaller. A number of unfair labor-practice charges were exchanged. This was the nitty-gritty, the clustered background, on which the more significant moves were made.[22]

Refusing to allow hundreds of ongoing details to distract from matters of substance is a major skill in negotiating. A prime example was Boulware's use of the personal-accident insurance issue, which he broached a month before formal negotiations began. A letter to all GE employees announced that the company had arranged with an insurance company to offer an accidental death or dismemberment group insurance policy. The decision to make it available, the letter said, had "resulted from intensified employee interest in additional coverage of this type."

The offer supplemented the plan already provided for in the contract in effect from 1955 to 1960. The letter made it clear that if the IUE didn't want the plan offered to its members, the nonunion employees would still have the opportunity to participate. GE maintained that it did "not regard the new insurance as related to the forthcoming negotiations, but simply as an opportunity for personally interested employees to secure additional insurance at a lower cost than would normally be available to them as individuals."

GE had created a bargaining chip where none had existed before. Jim Carey's venomous attack on the plan contained implicit references to Boulwarism. "The company," he said, "in offering the insurance at this time on a *take-it-or-leave-it basis* is attempting to discredit the union and 'undermine' collective bargaining by making it appear that the union, if it defers action, is depriving employees of a benefit they could have had during their vacations" (italics added). Boulware knew that it didn't make any difference how Carey reacted. In the unlikely instance that he accepted the company's plan, GE could take full credit for it. But that is not what happened. Carey gave GE even more than it bargained for. On behalf of his members, Carey rejected the plan.

A seed was thus planted that might lead to a result similar to what SAG had achieved by splitting off Universal in the guild's contract negotiations. GE's nonunion employees and locals not represented in bargaining by the IUE might find the plan attractive. IUE members might regret the unavailability of the plan. This was a strategy that Ronald Reagan had observed many times in the course of his years with Boulware: Divide and conquer.

Just before formal negotiations began, a four-page *Employee Relations News Letter*, entitled "Another Round of Astronomical Union Demands Versus 1960 Problems," was mailed out. ERMs and other supervisors were instructed by teletype that "supervisors should be able to discuss this subject [IUE demands] with employees on the basis of the July 1 *Employee Relations Newsletter* and the interest generated [by] the news stories."[23]

Two of Boulware's cardinal principles now came vigorously into play. First, the move to the bargaining table did not diminish GE's continuing direct communication with its employees. The NLRB decision on Boulwarism introduced the relevant portion of its report with a separate heading: "GE presents its offer directly to employees." Second, contrary to the mythology surrounding Boulwarism, the offer reflected, in its original form and as later amended due to the emergence of "new facts," information from employees—including feedback and surveys—that contributed to GE's position.

When the company's offer was formally put on the table, Jim Carey promptly described it as a "declaration of war."[24] There were some surprises. One example: Income Extension Aid was new. It had never been discussed with the union, and the only thing vaguely resembling it in the union proposal was in the Supplemental Unemployment Benefits section, which the company treated as a separate issue. IEA gave employees with three or more years of service benefits to enable them to move into other jobs. This move could occur because of a layoff but could also come into play in the instance of a plant closing. Among other things, it provided for tuition at a "recognized school" to train for another job. A second revision in the offer was the inclusion of a holiday-vacation option.

While GE gave credit to "several members of the Union's negotiating committee from the old-line plants" for reshaping the offer in part, the

NLRB decision pointed to other sources, as well. One was "feedbacks" of employee reactions to the offer, which came to the company from its "two-way employee communications channel." Another factor that the board acknowledged as part of GE's ability to gather information on employee needs was the company's "independent employee attitude surveys."[25]

The rest of the company's offer was pretty much as expected: a three-year contract; wage increases without cost-of-living adjustments; pension and insurance-plan improvements (some of which the union had not asked for); and certain provisions that could be changed locally to reflect local conditions.

The IUE representatives took a one-week break from negotiations to attend the union's annual convention, where Carey and others recommended rejecting GE's offer.[26] When they returned to the bargaining table, GE told them, "Our whole offer is on the table."[27] Unsurprisingly, IUE representative Leo Jandreau disparaged this stand as "Boulwarism."[28] But while the conferees were sitting around, calling one another names, the local managers put into effect for unrepresented employees the wages and benefits contained in GE's basic offer to the IUE. In another alleged end run, the company made offers to IUE's Schenectady and Pittsfield locals on strike-truce terms. The IUE claimed that the terms were more favorable than those put to the IUE in the national negotiations and called a strike.[29] The workers' willingness to go out was based largely on Carey's dramatic presentation of the union's position. Boulware, in New York, observed that Carey was "one hell of an actor."

The members of Local 301, the workers in the giant Schenectady plant, returned to work. Jim Carey called them "a pack of Benedict Arnolds who have betrayed the strike."[30] The *Wall Street Journal* saw it differently: "Actually, the workers in Schenectady have simply turned things around. In the interest of their own welfare, they have struck against an autocratic union boss." Lem Boulware spread the press reaction across the pages of the *Works News*, published in every GE plant in the country. The *New York Daily News* quoted "several top AFL-CIO leaders" as saying that Carey's call to strike "was the dumbest stunt of the age." The *New York World Telegram* observed in an editorial that "really competent union leaders should be able to drive a good bargain with management without a strike. . . . Strikes punish companies, but they also punish the customers, the public and, most of all, the strikers." *New York Journal- American* columnist Leslie Gould called it a "strike that should never have been called." And the *Chicago Sun-Times*, citing Carey's "I owe GE a strike" pledge, wrote that "if ever a major strike carried the earmarks of a one-man job, this one does."

Still, Carey was unrepentant. He said that "the struggle against General Electric will not be decided by the timidity of a handful of leaders at Schenectady." One of those leaders concluded that Carey was determined to "fight to the end."

The strike ended at about the expiration date of the original contract term. A new three-year agreement was concluded and signed.[31] Lemuel Boulware believed that it was a fair deal, based on the best offer the company could make. The executives and managers at the General Electric Company were extremely pleased. The *New York Times* described the GE/IUE agreement as "the worst setback any union has received in a nationwide strike since World War II."[32]

PART IV

ENCOURAGING AN INCREASING
MAJORITY OF CITIZENS

ELEVEN

THE CAMPAIGN CONTINUES

The campaign that Ronald Reagan began in 1958 did not end until he removed himself from public life, due to the anticipated disabling effect of Alzheimer's disease on November 5, 1994. Then, as he said in his poignant letter to his "Fellow Americans," he would soon "begin the journey that will lead me into the sunset of my life."[1]

Although GE had scored a significant victory over the IUE in its new labor contract, union power throughout the country was at its zenith as the 1960s began. Statutory changes at the state level in supplemental-unemployment benefits and right-to-work laws could tilt the balance in favor of "government and union officials" opposed to GE, undoing the recent accomplishments. But Lemuel Boulware's retirement was imminent, and Ralph Cordiner's was not far off. Not everyone in the executive suite agreed with them. Would the company continue its aggressive efforts at the grass roots?

This was certainly Reagan's preferred course of action. He had a backlog of years of invitations on the mashed potato circuit. He was carrying out Boulware's strategy of paving the way between elections. He was now a self-proclaimed "convert," not just giving speeches, but "preaching sermons."[2] And although he was not ready to admit it publicly, there may have been stirrings within his breast of personal political ambitions.

For a third of a century, Ronald Reagan campaigned continuously, starting in the towns and villages where GE plants were located, and, after leaving the company, in small and large cities, from civic and political platforms, throughout the country. The objectives of the campaign were set out in some detail by Boulware in his "Salvation Is Not Free" speech at Harvard in 1949. They did not change: "Our free markets and our free persons are at stake." The opponents were also constant: "A combination of government and union officials."

Ronald Reagan has only one parallel in American history—William Jennings Bryan. Of course, Bryan's influence came from the left, not the right. Today, plays such as *Inherit the Wind* focus on the end of Bryan's life, picturing him as a pompous old windbag. But in his prime, he was the Democrat candidate for president three times and later served as Wilson's secretary of state; he resigned from the cabinet on principle because he opposed Wilson's decision to enter World War I. He championed a handful of ideas that grew stronger through his endorsement and eventually became law: trust-busting, railroad and bank regulation, the popular election of U.S. senators, a graduated income tax, and suffrage for women. Bryan brought the Populists, the free silverists, and advocates of big government into the Democrat fold. He captured the party from the more conservative side, the followers of Grover Cleveland. Woodrow Wilson and Franklin Delano Roosevelt emerged from the Bryan wing.[3]

At almost exactly the time that the new GE/IUE three-year contract was signed, the nation went to the polls. The results gave the company a scorecard in state elections and a measurement of the effectiveness of its grassroots efforts at the national level in its continuing campaign to place a government in Washington in accord with its essentially conservative principles. The outcome gave the political right little encouragement. The immediate consequences to the General Electric Company were especially grave.

1960

Two prominent figures tried to influence Reagan's thinking on presidential candidate Richard Nixon before the election of 1960. He received a call from Joseph Kennedy, an old Hollywood hand who was the father of John Fitzgerald Kennedy, Nixon's opponent, and who insisted on coming to see Reagan in California. Joe Kennedy wanted Reagan to support his son Jack for president. Reagan turned him down. Ralph Cordiner, after hearing Nixon address a group of businessmen, told Reagan, who was still not a Nixon enthusiast, "I think you might be wrong about Nixon," and Cordiner's view, ultimately, carried the day. Reagan campaigned as a "Democrat for Nixon."[4]

Although Nixon's tough anticommunist stance might have provided some weight with conservatives, he had campaigned as a moderate, hoping to capitalize on Eisenhower's popularity with that constituency. Ironically, if Nixon had possessed Reagan's television skills—or even his knowledge of proper makeup techniques—he might have won the crucial first televised debate with Jack Kennedy. As it was, Nixon's pasty pancake appearance (contrasted with Kennedy's tan, a look Reagan also favored) was given by most commentators as a major cause for Nixon's defeat in that turning-point encounter.[5]

Organized labor's influence flourished in the Kennedy administration. Walter Reuther claimed that his union had given Jack Kennedy his margin of victory. Union official Jack Conway commented that "Bob [Kennedy] used to say flatly that the UAW was the spine" of the whole election.[6] Two acts soon occurred under the incoming administration that had a significant effect on the General Electric Company, with the potential to damage the political career of Ronald Reagan. They involved the National Labor Relations Board and the Justice Department.

The Unfair Labor Practice Charges

In 1960 and 1961, the IUE filed charges against the General Electric Company alleging unfair labor practices. The National Labor Relations Board's statement of the case observed that "GE's present approach to employee and union relations was first conceived in 1947 and developed under the guidance of Lemuel R. Boulware, then and for many years later GE's vice president for relations service. The approach has often been referred to as 'Boulwareism.'"[7]

Although Reagan had been an "integral component" of Boulware's program, there was no mention of him in the complaint filed by the NLRB.[8] This confirmed Boulware's wisdom in taking the spokesman out of the plants and putting him on the mashed potato circuit. The union's failure to mention him in the charges may also have been attributable to the AFL-CIO's support for Reagan during the recent SAG strike, which was still fresh in the minds of the public and the union members.

The ensuing litigation on Boulwarism (or "Boulwareism," as it was spelled by the board and later by the court) would take years. It would continue through the beginning of Reagan's California governorship and his first attempt to capture the Republican presidential nomination. On October 28, 1969, almost ten years after the charges were first filed, the United States Court of Appeals for the Second Judicial Circuit handed down its decision in *National Labor Relations Board v. General Electric*.[9] It covered thirty pages. The U.S. Supreme Court refused to grant an appeal, so this was the final judicial word on the matter. In time, Chief Judge Irving Kaufman's opinion on "Boulwareism" would be commented on in hundreds of law review articles and labor-law texts. The lengthy NLRB decision that GE had appealed was already the subject of thousands of pages of commentary. Labor lawyers would follow or misconstrue the Second Circuit's decision for generations.

The Court of Appeals for the Second Judicial Circuit had one of the most prestigious benches any court could muster. Two of the judges on the panel—Sterry Waterman and Henry Friendly—had already served as chief judges. Irving Kaufman, who wrote the court's opinion, was now the chief. Friendly dissented with the following observation: "I believe the majority's decision to be deeply mistaken—the familiar instance of a hard case producing bad law." He went on to point out that in his view, there was no evidence to support a finding of "single offer bargaining." He wrote: "The lead opinion does not do this, and the concurring opinion [of Waterman] expressly disclaims any such view." (An internal UAW document describes the dissent as "Friendly's not-too-subtle bid for a Nixon Supreme Court appointment.")[10]

Even Kaufman's opinion seemed equivocal on the IUE's main charge: "We do not today hold that an employer may not communicate with his employees during negotiations. Nor are we deciding that the 'best offer first' bargaining technique [often referred to as Boulwarism] is forbidden. Moreover, we do not require an employer to engage in 'auction bargaining,' or, as the dissent seems to suggest, compel him to make concessions, 'minor' or otherwise." Nevertheless, Chief Judge Kaufman eventually wrote that the company's "take-it-or-leave-it approach," its failure to furnish information, and its direct bargaining with locals provide sufficient basis to grant enforcement of the NLRB order. But the contract GE negotiated was not retroactively modified on any substantive point. One of the best labor agreements the company ever made, was, in effect, upheld.

Lemuel Boulware's publication of his defense of his program later in 1969, *The Truth About Boulwarism*, did not to mention his famous protégé. In fact, other than the dedication to one George Pfeif, his "oldest surviving associate," Boulware omits the names of all GE coworkers, "even those prized former associates who were so helpful but whom I might thus inadvertently appear to be involving in responsibility for the inevitable imperfections of the recollections here recorded."[11]

The Antitrust Actions Against General Electric

In 1961, the newly appointed U.S. attorney general, Robert Kennedy, announced in a television interview, "I regard the price fixing in the electrical industry as a major threat to democracy. These men were not gangsters. They were respectable and highly regarded members of their communities, yet they got together in secret and cheated the Army, Navy, the Government, and the public."[12]

Ronald Reagan had absolutely no connection with the acts of GE executives that later led to unprecedented criminal convictions and substantial civil damages. The litigation is described in the next few pages because the situation occurred under Ralph Cordiner's administration of GE, the only system of executive governance that Reagan observed at close hand and studied in some detail.

The antitrust prosecution commenced toward the end of the Eisenhower administration, when five grand juries in Philadelphia handed down twenty-one indictments involving twenty-nine manufacturers and forty-five individuals.[13] During the four years covered by the indictments, the conspirators, allegedly led by GE executives, controlled business worth $1.6 billion. As one account pointed out, "if the forty percent damages alleged by the Justice Department were true, the money involved could establish two universities with the resources of Yale, with a lot left over."[14]

The antitrust criminal litigation concluded with two unusual steps. The first involved Cordiner. General Electric emphasized that the "conspiratorial practices" violated company policy and "secured a statement from the government which in effect absolved its chairman, president and board of directors of knowledge and involvement." The *New York Herald Tribune* asked, "If they didn't know what was going on, why didn't they?"[15]

The second step was a highly unusual move by Chief Judge Gainey. He sentenced seven of the price-rigging conspirators to jail. Bill Ginn, George Burens, and Lew Burger of General Electric were included. At the time, Ginn was a respected GE vice president and general manager of the company's turbine division. While the fines imposed on the companies were in the millions, it was the "Unlucky Seven" who drew major media attention. Jail sentences were severe, almost unprecedented. Still, not everyone thought that justice had been done. Senator Estes Kefauver, in the limelight again, commented, "A man can get a year in jail for making a gallon of moonshine. I think the electrical machinery manufacturers are getting off mighty light."

The media coverage of the case was ratcheted up when the equipment involved in the price-rigging conspiracy gained dramatic national attention from an otherwise unrelated event. On June 13, 1961, there was a "blackout" in New York City. The press reported that "two circuit breakers went out of kilter." The city was "paralyzed for hours." It was noted that "nothing could emphasize so clearly the importance to the public of the equipment which was being cartelized by [GE, Westinghouse, and the other corporate] conspirators." The criminal antitrust issue was still current, and there was little sympathy for the companies involved.[16]

The penalties and economic consequences to GE were extreme. Capital Gains Research Bureau reported at the time that the drop of GE stock from a high of 99 7/8 to a low of 61 1/8 represented an estimated loss to shareholders in market value (in 1960s dollars) of $3.5 billion.[17] Fear of further severe economic damage to the company led one close observer to comment, "We do not want to see these corporations injured or damaged economically any more than their officers have already damaged them. On the contrary, for the economic health, reputation and prestige of these enterprises, we want to see mismanagement, corruption and criminal activity in executive echelons suppressed so strenuously that they can never again be revived."[18] This entreaty for a measure of financial stability was issued by none other than union leader James B. Carey, in his finest corporate statesman mode.

Civil antitrust actions now commenced. Within a decade, the General Electric Legal Department would count over 4,000 civil antitrust suits filed against the company by public utilities and other customers of GE's heavy-equipment division. Brought under section 4 of the Clayton Act, which had supplanted the Sherman Act in this area, the suits sought treble damages, court costs, and attorneys' fees.[19] The company, through outside counsel, fought each case with every legal weapon at its command. Nevertheless, plaintiffs recovered hundreds of millions of dollars of damages.

Lem Boulware had retired, and Ralph Cordiner was winding down. General Electric's new high command—battered and bruised from its antitrust problems and the attack on Boulwarism—decided that Reagan's road tour should be confined to pitching the company's products. When Reagan balked at this suggestion, he left GE, and the television program was terminated.[20] The *General Electric Theater* had been highly successful but had recently been replaced by *Bonanza* as top-rated show in the Sunday evening television lineup. Reagan signed on as host of another show, *Death Valley Days*, but soon gave that up, as well.[21] In the course of Reagan's continuing campaign for conservative principles, his election as governor and president and beyond, the charges that had been directed at the company and some of its key executives were never used in any meaningful way against him

1962

While the AFL-CIO had embraced Reagan's efforts as SAG president, by 1962 the union included him on their list of "dangerous anti-Communists" and referred to him as "a right-wing zealot."[22] A Minnesota high school cancelled a Reagan speech because they thought he was "too controversial." Controversial or not, there was no paucity of forums at which Reagan could speak. As he left television and made his last movie, he was in "wide demand as a speaker."[23] As his objectives changed—for the first time in eight years, GE was no longer his sponsor on the trail—so did his geographic focus. Now he concentrated primarily on the west.

When he first went on the hustings in California, he preached to the choir. He appeared before groups in Southern California that needed no warning about the communist menace; in fact, their existence was based on that premise. Reagan addressed Frederick Schwartz's extremist Christian Anti-Communist Crusade and was invited to deliver the keynote at a fund raiser for Congressman John Rousselot, a self-proclaimed member of the John Birch Society. Although Rousselot tried to walk a fine line about his endorsement of the society's program, the press had picked up the assertion in founder Welch's *Blue Book* that Dwight Eisenhower was a "Soviet agent." Press commentary on the society was almost universally negative.[24]

Friends urged Reagan to oppose liberal incumbent Thomas Kuchel for the Republican nomination for senator from California in 1962, a suggestion he rejected. For one thing, he was still a Democrat. The official act of conversion to the Republican Party occurred in the course of his campaigning for Nixon for governor of California later in the year. A woman in the audience stood up in the middle of Reagan's speech and demanded to know whether he had registered as a Republican. "Well, no, I haven't yet," Reagan replied, "but I intend to." "I'm a registrar," the woman said, and proceeded immediately to the front of the room and poked a registration form at the speaker. As Reagan later described the incident, "I signed it and became a Republican, then said to the audience, 'Now where was I?' "[25]

1964

In 1964, Ronald Reagan made his last movie. Revue was the producer. The movie was part of Project 120, where a film originally shown on television would later be released for theatrical distribution. It was a new idea, one which never did come to full fruition. But Revue put together a first-rate cast, remade a movie that had been successful twenty years before, and assigned Don Siegel to direct. The cast included John Cassavetes, Lee Marvin, Clu Galager, Angie Dickinson, and Reagan.

If this was a bold innovative move for Revue, it was for Reagan as well. He was willing to accept fifth billing. Based on Ernest Hemingway's famous short story, *The Killers* was the tough, violent kind of film for which director Siegel later became famous. In the earlier version, Burt Lancaster had made a spectacular screen debut. Cassavetes played that role in the new release. Bill Meikeljohn, Reagan's original agent and still with MCA, was the first one to come up with the idea that Regan be cast as Browning, the sadistic, unrepentant villain. In a scene that had the audience gasping, tough guy Reagan slapped Angie Dickinson hard in the face.[26]

The film bombed. The public simply refused to accept Ronald Reagan in such an unfavorable role. At liberty for the first time in years, the actor was financially well off. He spent time chopping wood, mending fences, and riding the trails at Yearling Row, his ranch in the Malibu Hills. His favorite horse was a dapple gray named Nancy D.[27] Recalling his years on *GE Theater*, he wrote that he "chose to continue speaking [on conservative principles] even when to continue meant the loss of my television show."[28] Now when he appeared on the mashed potato circuit, it was as a private citizen.

Well before delivering "The Speech" on national television, Reagan attempted to enlist in the Goldwater's California campaign organization, but first he had to gain acceptance as a Republican. He had been in the party for less than two years. A pivotal moment occurred at a meeting of the California Citizens for Goldwater-Miller on August 21, 1964, in San Diego. The noisy partisan audience had just heard a blistering attack on Reagan by one of their own. Phil Davis, a southern California businessman, appeared to be the choice of most of those present—certainly the most vocal part of the crowd—to serve as statewide chairman of the organization. He had the credentials. He was a leader in Goldwater's spectacular victory over Nelson Rockefeller in the California Republican presidential primary. He was the glue that helped to keep together the largest single state delegation pledged to Senator Goldwater at the party's national convention.

Phil Davis and the others in the room had been soldiers in the front line of these battles. While Reagan had been giving early versions of "The Speech" in hotel ballrooms throughout the state, these citizens had been in the trenches. They were not going to have a Johnny-come-lately shoved down their throats by the Arizona gang who ran the national campaign. Davis had just finished saying as much, concluding with a finger-pointing diatribe that was greeted by tumultuous applause.

Clif White, who was seated next to Reagan at the meeting, rose to defend him. But Reagan reached over and grasped his arm. "No, Clif," he said quietly. "This is my fight. Let me handle it." He made no effort to conceal his lack of partisan grass-roots experience, going right to the issue that Davis had exposed. He began: "Folks, I'm the new boy on the block. I haven't been involved in a campaign like this in the past. But I can see that there's trouble here and there ought not to be trouble here." The actor focused more on the need for unity behind Senator Goldwater than on his own candidacy for leadership of the group. He finished to resounding applause. He and Phil Davis were then photographed in the midst of a warm handshake. They were elected cochairmen on the spot.[29]

At about this time, an election took place involving another player from the Cordiner-Boulware-Reagan era at General Electric. Jim Carey had led the IUE for over a decade. During those years, he had been in the vanguard of the civil rights movement. But his relationship with AFL-CIO president George Meany had often been as turbulent as with his adversaries from GE. In 1964, he ran again for reelection as IUE president. What seemed like still another victory turned out not to be so. The U.S. Labor Department investigated charges of "fraudulent voting proce-dures," and Carey resigned. He was never again a significant factor in the labor movement or in politics.

While Lem Boulware and Ralph Cordiner had both retired and were no longer active with GE, they were thriving politically. Boulware was working many vineyards, and Ralph Cordiner had accepted Barry Gold-water's invitation to become chair of the Republican Finance Commit-tee. Goldwater's brain trust regarded Cordiner's acceptance as a coup. As a result, Cordiner felt that he was in a position to negotiate the condi-tions of his employment. He wanted to run the campaign as an example of how the candidate, if successful, would run the government. Cordiner insisted on a balanced budget, something unheard of in the political wars. This meant raising campaign funds before they were spent, an idea that appealed to Goldwater, if not to the few political pros who advised him. The immediate consequence of the policy was the cancellation of television time previously reserved by the Republican National Commit-tee (since the campaign lacked money in hand to pay for the time.) One journalist referred to this move and Cordiner's policy as a "greenhorn mistake."[30]

Goldwater suffered a resounding defeat in 1964. Lyndon Johnson won the popular vote by 43 million to 27 million. This gave Johnson the high-est percentage of the vote (61.1) of any presidential candidate in modern history. The electoral vote was 486 to 52.[31] One of Goldwater's support-ers blamed the result in part on the assassination of President Kennedy, whose candidacy would supposedly have presented a more vulnerable liberal stance.[32]

Commentators predicted a woeful future for the Republicans if the party continued on this course. Presidential chronicler Theodore White said that "the elections of 1964 had left the Republican Party in desperate condition." Historian Arthur Schlesinger Jr. observed, "The election results of 1964 seem to demonstrate [moderate Republican New York Governor] Thomas Dewey's prediction about what would happen if the parties were realigned on an ideological basis: 'The Democrats would win every election and the Republicans would lose every election.'"[33]

The pundits were wrong on two fronts. First, they missed the local consequences of the vote. Even with the shattering loss at the top of the ticket, Republicans made significant gains at the grass roots, particularly in the South. Goldwater carried only six states. One was his home state of Arizona. In the other states Goldwater won, all in the South, the margin was impressive: Mississippi (87 percent); Alabama (70 percent); South Carolina (59 percent); Louisiana (57 percent); and Georgia (55 percent). Local election contests reflected these gains in a Republican Party that was rising to new prominence. Further, as journalist Rick Perlstein notes, "In every Southern state [Goldwater] lost—Texas, Tennessee, North Carolina, Arkansas, Florida [with 49 percent], Virginia and Kentucky—Republicans were elected to statewide office in unprecedented numbers."[34]

Just what effect, if any, the efforts of Lemuel Boulware or Ronald Reagan had on the respectable conservative vote attained in these states is beyond precise proof. It should be noted in passing, however, that almost all of them were sites of General Electric plants or distribution centers.[35] All were stops on Ronald Reagan's mashed potato circuit. Some were also locales of operations of companies run by The Wise Men. Boulware's program of "educating" the workers and their families and utilizing them in the move of "M" to the right was fully operative in these areas. In his retirement, Boulware was concentrating on small states in his extensive fund-raising efforts, but he had counseled conservative operatives in states like Texas to go for small contributions and aggressive recruitment at the grass roots.[36]

The second result of the 1964 election that most pundits missed at the time was the emergence of Ronald Reagan. Theodore White did not even mention Reagan in *The Making of the President, 1964*.[37] The statement about Reagan's highly successful political debut appeared three years after the election in a book by columnist David Broder and political scientist Stephen Hess.[38] With the wisdom of hindsight, the importance of Reagan's delivery of "The Speech" on national television toward the end of the 1964 campaign becomes clear.

In August, Reagan had given the latest version of "The Speech," which he had honed over his GE years, to 800 of the party faithful at the Coconut Grove, a night club in the Ambassador Hotel in Los Angeles. Afterward, Holmes Tuttle and other friends who had been in the audience suggested that he give "The Speech" on national television. Reagan agreed, but when the idea was broached to Goldwater, the senator's brain trust ("the Arizona mafia") vetoed the idea.[39]

Goldwater's advisors criticized "The Speech" because they thought it unfairly attacked Social Security, a stance that had caused Goldwater problems earlier in the campaign. When Goldwater saw a video of the speech, he found this criticism without merit. (In fact, Goldwater had apparently heard an earlier version of "The Speech" on the mashed potato circuit in Phoenix in 1961, including the supposedly controversial reference to Social Security. Reagan's father-in-law, Loyal Davis was also in attendance.)[40] But there was still the problem of how to finance the telecast. It was here that Ralph Cordiner's "balanced budget" approach came into play as the Arizona brain trust's last resort. No money had been set aside for a telecast at this point. It would have to be raised from supporters who had already been squeezed to the limit.[41]

John Wayne came to the rescue. But now, instead of John Ford, who often directed Wayne's screen heroics, the man behind the scenes was Lemuel Boulware. The men who went on to form Governor Reagan's "Kitchen Cabinet" are generally credited with supplying the necessary financing for the event. But Lemuel Boulware's collected papers reveal a different source. Less than two weeks before the proposed telecast, an organization called "Brothers for Goldwater" presented a giant mock-up of check for $60,000 to the presidential candidate at his Madison Square Garden rally. The chairman of the group was John Wayne, who, like Goldwater, was a member of the Sigma Chi fraternity. So was former Texas congressman Livingstone Wingate, who was secretary-treasurer of the committee. And so was GE employee J.J. Wuerthner, who came up with the idea and acted as director and chief operating officer of the fund-raising effort.

When the Arizona gang announced that there were no funds for the Reagan telecast, Boulware spoke to Wuerthner and to Cordiner. The $60,000 had not been allocated for any other purpose. This was cash on the barrelhead and Cordiner, as Republican finance chairman, enthusiastically endorsed the use of these funds for the national telecast.[42] The event was scheduled for October 27, just one week before election day.

"The Speech" took as its point of departure the speaker's well-established role as a television performer. "Thank you very much. Thank you, and good evening," Ronald Reagan began. "The sponsor has been identified, but unlike most television programs, the performer hasn't been provided with a script. As a matter of fact, I have been permitted to choose my own words and discuss my own ideas regarding the choice that we face in the next few weeks."[43]

Toward the end of his remarks, in a stirring peroration, Ronald Reagan asked, "Should Moses have told the children of Israel to live in slavery under the Pharaohs? Should Christ have refused the cross?" Of course, these words were part of a Reagan pep talk—as was the "rendezvous with destiny" phrase (also in "The Speech") that Franklin Roosevelt had made famous—to a group of school children visiting a state house five years before.[44]

Just before he went to sleep that night, Ronald Reagan said to his wife, "I hope I haven't let Barry down." Two hours later, just after midnight, the phone rang. The call was from the Goldwater for President headquarters in Washington. "The switchboard has been lit up ever since you signed off," said the caller. "It's three a.m. and there's been no let up. Thousands of people have called pledging support and saying that they're sending checks. Some of the old hands who are on the staff of the Republican Finance Committee say they've never seen anything like it. I'm sorry to call so late, but I thought you'd like to know. Of course, you probably expected this reaction all along."[45] Within a few days, the committee received $500,000 in the mail. It is estimated that "The Speech" raised $8 million overall, not counting all of the places that later rebroadcast it locally, with their own solicitations at the end. The results exceeded any previous campaign-fund-raising event.[46]

Ronald Reagan was now a national political voice. His postgraduate education in political science had taken years and had borne fruit in a most spectacular fashion. His apprenticeship was also largely behind him, but he would be the first to admit that there were still lessons to be learned. He would be directing his efforts at the grass roots, which he and his mentors had already done much to change. Now—as a candidate, as governor, as a citizen-politician—he proceeded on his path to the presidency.

1966

Most candidates evolve from the local to the national stage. Reagan reversed this process. He had spent the better part of a decade traveling the country, addressing audiences in forty states. As he admitted privately, he had devoted so much time to "overall philosophy, national and international policy, that [he] did not know anything about the organization of state government, the problems and what would be the issues in state government."[47] He and Cordiner and Boulware had sought to change the business climate—moving M to the right—throughout the South and in the smaller states, primarily in locales in which General Electric had facilities. Now the focus would be on one state, Reagan's home state.

In California, two results of the 1964 elections had a direct impact on Ronald Reagan's nascent political career. An actor, George Murphy, was elected to the United States Senate. A longtime worker in the state's Republican vineyards, he had the steadfast financial support of conservative multimillionaire Patrick Frawley. Goldwater's efforts in the state undoubtedly helped Murphy. His opponent, Pierre Salinger, John Kennedy's former White House press secretary, turned out to be a terrible campaigner. Nevertheless, the lesson was there: a veteran of the silver screen—a former SAG president, in fact—had prevailed in a statewide contest.

The other 1964 California election result did not appear at first to be a portent of success for Ronald Reagan. New York's liberal/moderate governor, Nelson Rockefeller, after a late start, had come within an eyelash of defeating Goldwater for the Republican nomination in the state's presidential primary. Goldwater's commanding lead of 30 percent had been reduced to 3 percent. Rockefeller's campaign had been managed by the team of Stu Spencer and Bill Roberts. These young professionals demonstrated in the primary what knowledgeable observers of the California political scene had already recognized: They were the best. Their California political savvy could be the next chapter in the education of

Ronald Reagan. But there was a hitch. Spencer-Roberts had managed Tom Kuchel's successful 1962 reelection effort. In 1964, they managed Rockefeller. Their clients came from the moderate or liberal wing of the party. Ronald Reagan had heard that they felt that "conservatives made poor political candidates."

Much of Reagan's background information on the team came from Clif White. The three men had been in the Young Republican National Federation together, though in very different camps. The Californians shared the liberal views of their governor at the time, Earl Warren. Still, as much as White had disagreed with their ideological orientation, he admired their political skills. Their firm was relatively new but followed in the California tradition of Whitaker-Baxter and Baus and Ross, who had for some time managed lobbying efforts and campaigns for a fee. It was less than a decade since Spencer had quit his post as director of parks for the city of Alhambra and Roberts had left his job as a television sales-man. For a time they worked for the Los Angeles County Republican Central Committee, but in 1960, they formed Spencer-Roberts. They en-joyed immediate success.

One of the things that Reagan liked about them, right off the bat, was their candor. No words were minced when Reagan invited them to a lunch to get acquainted. The young managers expressed many reserva-tions about taking Reagan on as a client. They had heard he was "a real right-winger" and a "martinet" to boot. Roberts told him bluntly that his firm would not work for "dogmatists or prima donnas. A candidate can-not be a star and treat his staff like dirt," he said.[48] And they did not like what they had read about Reagan's supposedly Birch-like, unthinking anticommunism.

There would undoubtedly be a primary in 1966 for the Republican nomination for governor. Spencer-Roberts could pretty much pick their candidate. Their participation might be enough in itself to ensure vic-tory for their client. Reagan, if he entered the contest, would face op-position from established politicians, most likely centrists, who regarded the actor—in spite of his vaunted speaking ability—as little more than an entertainer. Why get involved with someone who had no governmen-tal experience and who seemed to enjoy appearances before some of the state's most outspoken right-wingers?

If they had to make a decision at this point, Spencer and Roberts would most likely have turned down this engaging, surprisingly bright man who had invited them to an introductory lunch. This was nothing new for Reagan. Throughout his entire career he had been underestimated, especially at those times when he had moved from one kind of job to another. He had decided in the course of lunch that he liked these men and needed them. At the end, when the young pros agreed to another meeting, Reagan knew that it was just a matter of time.

Soon after the lunch, Reagan invited the managers to dinner at his home. As the principals later recalled the evening, the deal was closed because of a pair of socks. Reagan believed Spencer and Roberts were inclined to take him on, but they were still hesitating. They were afraid that the actor was so wrapped up in an anticommunist mindset that he might pop off at some point in the campaign and overturn an otherwise well orchestrated effort. He told them that he *was* concerned with communism but that he could deal with it as one issue in panoply of issues. When they sat down for drinks in the living room, the young men noticed that Reagan was wearing a pair of bright red socks. They apparently felt that if he had a sense of humor on the "red" issue, then he probably had a sense of balance, too. They laughed, but soon they shook hands on a deal. At the end of the night, Roberts came out with a line that, to Reagan, if not consciously to Roberts himself, had two meanings. He said, on behalf of the firm that "they were prepared to go all the way if things went right."[49]

Spencer and Roberts were subjected to immediate attack for taking on their new client. Two telephone messages, of the dozens received after the news broke, are representative of the range of criticism. The first was from a San Francisco political reporter, who said that they were "absolutely crazy" to take on a "long shot" like Reagan. The second message used the word that most of their friends and clients had used in their calls: "turncoats."[50] Many of the calls came from political leaders and potential clients who said that their business would shrink to nothing if they stuck with Reagan—all of which only served to strengthen their resolve.

They felt that if they were willing to change, however, their candidate must change as well. An abandonment of his firmly held ideological positions was not something that Ronald Reagan could do. But a muting of how some of these points would be expressed—particularly on the communist issue—was imperative. Moreover, if Reagan was going to oppose a popular career politician now in his second term as governor, he had to have a complete understanding of state and local issues. Their notion of how to bring their new client up to speed took some time to develop and was unorthodox, to say the least.

The firm's recommendation on this point must have been a bitter pill for Reagan to swallow. Spencer and Roberts wanted him to spend some concentrated time with behavioral psychologists who were going to teach him how to perform before an audience. He must have wondered what they thought he'd been doing for the past ten years. Weren't they listening on October 27? Why go back to school? Hadn't he already undergone a thorough "postgraduate education" in politics?

This was true, but he had not yet had his course in *California* politics. Had he been asked where he stood on the redwood controversy or the Bay Bridge problem, Ronald Reagan would not have had a clue. The continuation of his postgraduate work was a concentrated process, but because of the subject matter and the way it was taught, it was by no means arduous. At the outset, the two teachers selected by Spencer and Roberts set aside three days for concentrated work with the candidate. To make the work as comfortable as possible, they chose to meet Reagan in Malibu, rather than their own office in Van Nuys.

Professors Kenneth Holden of UCLA and Stanley Plog of San Fernando Valley State were behavioral psychologists who had established a company, BASICO (Behavioral Science Corporation of Van Nuys, California). As the weekend at Malibu began, Holden and Plog "liked what they saw."[51] Plog observed that Reagan had a well-developed ideology and a set of fundamental beliefs rooted in the Constitution. He felt that "Reagan knows who he is and what he stands for. His library is stacked with books on political philosophy. He can take information and he can assimilate it and can use it appropriately in his own words."

Still, Holden and Plog felt that Reagan knew "zero" about California issues. They lamented his lack of a secretary and felt that his practice of clipping articles from newspapers was not sufficient for the rigors of a statewide campaign. Accordingly, they worked with the candidate's ability to ingest and articulate information and prepared black binders filled with "5x8 inch index cards" on each California issue. The behavioral scientists undoubtedly deserve credit for schooling Reagan on state issues and, with their considerable staff, for working with him throughout the campaign to ensure that his statements were factually correct.

The psychologists did not fully understand, however, that their candidate had been part of a similar educational enterprise at an earlier point in his career. They may not have explored the source for many of the economic and political tracts they observed in his library, and it was not in Reagan's nature to volunteer insights into his personal background and the formation of his beliefs. But surely they must have realized that his strong ideological base had not simply sprung full-grown at some miraculous instant one day as he waited on a set for his cue. In some measure, they suffered from the misapprehension experienced by almost all of Reagan's adversaries and even a few members of his staff. They knew he had been an actor and, accordingly, did not expect very much.

When the role played by Holden and Plog in Reagan's campaign later surfaced, one observer described it as "intellectual baby-sitting." He went on to say that Barry Goldwater would never have submitted to such a process.[52] The behavioral scientists themselves didn't realize the extent of Reagan's prior knowledge. Stanley Plog, for example, gave credit to his colleague Holden for inserting into Reagan's speeches quotations from prominent figures out of history. "You should have seen those newspapermen jump when Ron first quoted Jefferson to them," he remembered with pride.[53]

Lem Boulware must have gotten a kick out of this when Reagan passed on the comment. The GE traveling ambassador had been using such quotations for years and had, in fact, included quotations from Jefferson in a forerunner of "The Speech" that he gave before the Business Educational Institute of New Jersey five years before and in a public statement as SAG president in 1947.[54]

Still, when he was later on the campaign trail, Reagan felt that his crash course with Holden and Plog was serving him well. He was armed to the teeth on local issues. The behavioral psychologists had divided the issues into seventeen major categories, such as transportation, education, water, and the economy. They kept some thirty-one staff members, including statisticians, sociologists, political scientists, and other psychologists, busy much of the time. They had blunted the extremist charge by convincing the candidate not to use phrases like "totalitarian ant heap." They believed he would come across as a "reasonable guy" offering a "positive program."

While Spencer and Roberts supplied professional management, the fledgling Reagan campaign had in place from the outset the other key ingredient to a successful campaign—the capacity to raise funds. Many would-be candidates drop out before they even start because they cannot achieve that requirement. In Reagan's case, a group that later gained fame as his "Kitchen Cabinet," supplied that necessary element. In fact, two of its members, Holmes Tuttle and Henry Salvatori, had agreed to pay for BASICO. Certainly Spencer and Roberts were aware of this financial clout before they signed on. Management could be hired. Fund raising was the most difficult component to recruit for a campaign organization.[55]

For years before the gubernatorial campaign, the core group could be found meeting at Walter Annenberg's lush desert estate, as it did every New Year's Eve, or, at other times of the year, in Betsy Bloomingdale's dining room in Bel Air (later, in Holmby Hills) or around a barbecue grill in Nancy Reagan's back yard in Pacific Palisades.[56] They were, at heart, a group of friends—a moveable feast, enjoying one another's company at their various homes and ranches. They occasionally added a few other close friends, like Jack Benny and his wife, Mary Livingstone, and George Burns and his wife, Gracie Allen. Taft Schreiber and Lew Wasserman of MCA and their wives also joined the feast from time to time.[57] The group had no political raison d'être, although Jack Benny, the legendary radio comedian, had been addressing Reagan as "Governor" for some time. No one was quite sure why.[58]

A few other members were from the acting community. Bill Holden and his wife, Ardis (who once appeared in westerns under the name of Brenda Marshall) were old friends of the Reagans. They were best man and matron of honor at the Reagans' wedding. Bonita Granville appeared as a teenager in the Nancy Drew, girl detective, movies of the 1930s. These days she was known as Mrs. Jack Wrather. Her husband had made a fortune in real estate and was getting interested in television properties. In fact, he was more representative of the group than she was.

The members had a few things in common. First of all, they were all rich. Holmes Tuttle was the major automobile dealer in Los Angeles. William French Smith was a corporate lawyer whose firm represented many of the country's top companies. Henry Salvatori owned an oil company. Earle Jorgensen owned a steel company. Alfred Bloomingdale headed Diner's Club. Charles Wick was an entertainment lawyer at one point, but now he owned a chain of nursing homes. Justin Dart chaired a chain of drugstores and, later, an industrial conglomerate. The richest member of the group, Walter Annenberg, owned *TV Guide* and a number of other profitable publications. He lived in Philadelphia about half the year but would always be at his estate in Palm Springs when the group made the pilgrimage for its annual New Year's Eve party.

Although their get-togethers were purely social, many of them played a role in Republican politics. Justin Dart, a latecomer to the group, was a top fund raiser in Dwight Eisenhower's 1952 campaign and finance chairman of the president's 1956 reelection campaign.[59] And Dart wasn't the only one who raised a lot of money. Tuttle and some of the others were the financial backbone of the party in California. Because they played such an indispensable part, they often had something to say about state policy and party candidates.

Rich and Republican—but this was not their strongest bond. The common thread can be found in the wives. They were the glue that held the group together. They were very strong women. They had a lot to say about what went on in their town. They were at the heart of many of the charitable events that established the pecking order in the Hollywood community almost as much as movie stardom.

Nancy Reagan was the key. In the months after the Reagans were married (in 1952), Nancy was somewhat at sea. Her own movie career was going no place, and she turned to some of the local charitable activities. These committees are as tough to crack as the Mayflower Society. But Betsy Bloomingdale befriended Nancy. They hit it off, and Nancy found that she was part of the in-group and that she enjoyed their company. As their families grew older, the members often settled on the same schools and summer camps for their children.

The men got along well, too, and the couples tended more and more to be the center of one another's social lives. Like just about everyone else in town, the men liked Ron. He brought a touch of glamour to their number but was also able to discuss civic issues and political questions, something that not all of the stars could do. In fact, they were more impressed now than ever. Henry Hazlitt's column in the *Wall Street Journal* was daily fare for America's business leaders. Ron had apparently met Hazlitt through Boulware and could discuss economics with the best of them. Some had undoubtedly seen the laudatory letter that Vice President Nixon had sent Ron about one of his GE tour offerings and had probably received copies of the speeches, as well.[60]

On January 4, 1966, Ronald Reagan appeared on statewide television and officially announced his candidacy. As with most of his speeches, he had written this one himself. If his official announcement of his intention to run for governor sounded little like the extremism which had marked Barry Goldwater's campaign rhetoric, it also bore little resemblance to the Ronald Reagan who had addressed the Christian Anti-Communist Crusade and the rally for John Birch Society member John Rousselot. This was "The Speech," West Coast version.

He expressed his concern over the spread of crime. There was nothing new about this; only now it was focused on his home state. Disorder, he felt, had descended on California. His state compared unfavorably with others: "Our streets are jungle paths after dark, with more crimes of violence than New York, Pennsylvania, and Massachusetts combined. Will we meet [the Berkeley students'] neurotic vulgarities with vacillation and weakness; or will we tell those entrusted with administering the university we expect them to enforce a code based on decency, common sense, and dedication to the noble purpose of the university? That they will have full support of all of us as long as they do this, but we'll settle for nothing less."[61] The overall tone of the announcement was positive. It focused (in very general terms) on problems but promised solutions: "It won't matter if the sky is bigger and bluer out there if you can't see it for smog, and all our elbow room and open space won't mean much if the unsolved problems are higher than the hills. Our problems are many, but our capacity for solving them is limitless."

There was no grace period for the new candidate. Reactions were immediate and often savage or patronizing. California Democratic Party Chairman Robert Coate accused Reagan of "hiding his right-wing bonafides and trying to fool voters into thinking he was a moderate." Incumbent governor Pat Brown commented that "The thought of Ronald Reagan sitting in the governor's chair moves me to great lengths." Bumper stickers advocating "Elizabeth Taylor for H.E.W." began to appear. The *Sacramento Bee* editorialized: "The latest innovation in political life is the acceptance of actors as creditable political figures, even though they lack the background and experience in government which are prerequisites to success in public office." The most quoted remark came from Reagan's former boss Jack Warner: "Reagan for Governor? No, Jimmy Stewart for Governor, Ronnie Reagan for his best friend."[62]

The points that would constitute the challenges of the campaign were all there: a reputation for right-wing extremism, the shallowness often attached to the acting profession, and the candidate's lack of familiarity with the local issues and the details of government. Reagan had anticipated the challenges. Like Cordiner and Boulware and *their* mentor, "Electric Charlie" Wilson, Reagan believed in advanced, even long-range, planning. Two steps in particular shaped his gubernatorial campaign.

The attacks based on Reagan's profession became more pointed and vicious as the campaign progressed. The *Sacramento Bee* opined, "There is something scary, about the idea of actors in politics." The most scathing attack came later, from Governor Brown. In a campaign film, he told two elementary school students, "You know I'm running against an actor. Remember this. You know who shot Abraham Lincoln, don't you?. . . . An actor shot Lincoln."[63] The premise of these attacks was that Reagan might be effective in a speech (presumably written by someone else), but what did he really know? How could he convince the voters that he actually had a grasp of these issues? That he was not just parroting the information.

Ronald Reagan proposed a solution to his managers: "I've got a suggestion," he said. "From now on, why don't I just say a few words to whatever group I'm with, no matter how big it is, and then just open it up to questions and answers? People might think somebody had written my opening remarks for me, but they'll know it would be impossible for somebody to feed me answers to questions I didn't know in advance."[64] Spencer and Roberts were leery. But Reagan knew, if they didn't, that the "new spontaneous approach" that he was suggesting had been market tested at 135 locations in 40 states before a quarter of a million people over a period of years. The managers decided to let Reagan give some trial performances. They were soon satisfied that the format worked. Thereafter, Roberts wrote a party activist in Santa Cruz,

> To get around the problem that Ron is just "speaking a part he memorized," we have asked for question-and-answer periods following most of his major engagements. These certainly are not prepared and people get an opportunity to test his intellectual capacity. He does not have all the answers; he is not a professional politician. . . . But, as time goes by, he learns more and more to add to the backlog of understanding which, we feel, he has.[65]

While candidate Reagan could change the public's perception of his supposed intellectual failings by demonstrating intelligence and grasp of the issues as he campaigned, there was nothing he could do about his lack of credentials as a public official. Accordingly, Spencer and Roberts decided to turn Reagan's inexperience in government to his advantage.[66] Public officials, particularly the governor, had made a botch of things. The electorate was ready for a citizen-politician untainted by the mess around him and owing no political debts. They had been primed in this conviction by movies such as *Meet John Doe* and *Mr. Smith Goes to Washington*. The stars of these films, Gary Cooper and Jimmy Stewart, were friends of Reagan's. He quoted lines from the movies in his speeches.[67]

"As the public grew more disillusioned with the rising crime rates, student protests, the war in Vietnam, and the ghetto riots," one observer commented, "they also became more suspicious of traditional, liberal politicians who had spent their careers expanding government entitlement, building state infrastructure, and reaching out to minorities. It was the beginning of the run-as-an-outsider trend that would soon sweep presidential politics."[68]

In June, the political outsider gained a lopsided primary victory, with 77 percent of the vote, over former San Francisco mayor George Christopher. The postelection analysis revealed that he had made significant gains in moderate Republican strongholds in the Los Angeles suburbs; he had, in effect, moved "M" to the right. And the "conservative belt" in Southern California was wider than ever. Pollster Lou Harris quantified that result: "Before this year, southern California was 40 percent conservative. The rest of the state was 18 percent conservative. Now southern California has increased to 50 percent and the rest to 30 percent conservative."[69]

The *New York Times* was alarmed: "California voters of both parties very nearly brought off a double disaster in Tuesday's primaries. The Republicans, against all counsels of common sense and political prudence, insisted upon nominating actor Ronald Reagan for Governor. . . . The Democrats, however, managed to pull back from the rim of the abyss and mustered a majority for Governor Brown."[70] The governor's primary opponent, Los Angeles mayor Sam Yorty, had espoused a conservative line and had received almost a million votes.

Edmund G. "Pat" Brown was a career politician. A lawyer, he had been running for office for almost forty years. His first attempt, for the state assembly in 1928 (as a Coolidge Republican!), was unsuccessful, as were some later runs as a Democrat. In 1950, after serving as San Francisco district attorney, he won his first statewide office, attorney general. In 1958, he was elected to his first term as governor, defeating

William Knowland, California's senior senator, who had decided to run for the state's highest executive office, in a highly visible campaign. In 1962, in a campaign that drew even more national attention, Brown defeated Richard Nixon, who had returned to California for a fresh political start after his narrow defeat by John Kennedy in the 1960 presidential election.[71]

After his two gubernatorial victories, Pat Brown was on a roll. Party registration in the state was Democratic by a two-to-one margin. One of the best-known governors in the United States, Brown called his program "responsible liberalism." But as his second term unfolded, a number of events occurred that weakened his political base. Race riots broke out in Watts, with widespread destruction and looting. Brown happened to be traveling abroad when the riots began. George Christopher said that Brown "fiddled while Los Angeles was burning."[72]

Students at the University of California at Berkeley mounted mass protests on the Vietnam war issue and proclaimed a "Free Speech Movement," often featuring obscene language. In the Democratic primary, Mayor Yorty of Los Angeles developed a "morality theme"—attacking the governor's stand on Vietnam protests, the Watts riots, and the student demonstrations at Berkeley—a "convenient catchall" to assault everything that happened during Brown's administration.

Ronald Reagan benefited from the primaries. His primary opponent, George Christopher, directed his campaign more against Pat Brown than against Reagan. Christopher's petulant defection in the fall was muted by the Republican State Committee's Eleventh Commandment: "Thou shall not speak ill of another Republican." The policy had been instituted to heal the sizable rift that had developed between the Goldwater Republicans and the less conservative members of the party. Democrats had no parallel policy. Brown won his primary, but Sam Yorty's strong showing and his half-hearted conciliation undoubtedly damaged Brown in the general election.

It has been suggested that Reagan picked up Yorty's morality theme.[73] In fact, that issue and others that played well in the fall—law and order and the danger of seeking solutions to community problems exclusively from government—had been staples of "The Speech" and its forerunners. The disillusioned electorate to whom Reagan now delivered it were probably even more ready to accept these positions than the GE audiences that had heard them for years. On November 8, Ronald Reagan defeated Governor Pat Brown by about a million votes, carrying fifty-five of the state's fifty-eight counties

Governor Reagan: the candidate could no longer be faulted for lack of credentials; he was the chief executive of the nation's largest state, with an economy greater than that of all but a few nations. Nor could "inexperience" be used to attack him in any future campaigns. Of course, the record would depend on his performance. Some of the hard conservative lines of campaign rhetoric now gave way to life in the real world. Reagan had entered office promising to lower taxes and reduce the size of government. After a short time in the state house, however, he found that he had inherited a deficit of almost $200 million and a virtually bankrupt state. He felt that he had to raise taxes—the largest increase in the state's history, in fact.[74] Other conservatives could now call into question whether he could run a government as he had said for many years that a government should be run.

Surrounded by close friends like Holmes Tuttle and Henry Salvatori (now part of what the press referred to as the "Kitchen Cabinet,"), Reagan began to govern. The Kitchen Cabinet recommended personnel to fill government jobs, as did old Hollywood friends such as Richard Zanuck of 20th Century Fox.[75] During the campaign, the press lauded the candidate for his role as an outsider. Now, when he departed from traditional sources for his appointees, he was characterized as a "novice."[76] A scandal involving his first chief of staff was handled well, with a competent replacement appointed before the situation got out of hand. At the end of Reagan's first term, Lou Cannon, then a reporter with the *San Jose Mercury-News*, described it as "responsible but undistinguished."[77]

1970

As Reagan ran for a second term, the electorate was changing in California as well as the rest of the country. The destructive and often violent student antiwar movement led to an increasing number of conservative-leaning Democrats. President Nixon referred to them as the "Silent Majority." In this atmosphere, Governor Reagan was featured on the cover of *Life* magazine and labeled "the hottest candidate in either party."[78] He was returned to office by a margin (not as large as his original plurality, but quite respectable) of half a million votes.

The increase in the state budget and the state's personal income and corporate taxes during Reagan's first term had taken some of the luster from his "cost-cutting" and "big government" campaign rhetoric. Accordingly, instead of relying on a global attack on government overkill as the theme of his second term, he focused on a single program. In his keynote address on his return to Sacramento, he said: "Welfare is the biggest single outlay of public funds at three different levels of government: federal, state, and county. And welfare is adrift without rudder or compass."[79]

Lemuel Boulware also felt strongly about welfare. "Millions of citizens now on welfare do not belong there," he wrote. "There is inevitable political corruption and other gigantic waste in handling the huge sums through political appointees."[80] He kept in touch with the governor. Their correspondence generally involved matters of economic or governmental policy.[81] As Boulware spoke around the country, he often forwarded copies of his speeches to Sacramento, including his remarks to the Monetary Conference sponsored by the prestigious Committee for Monetary Research and Education.[82] When one of Boulware's speeches was reprinted in *Human Events*, Reagan commented that "it has provided source material for some of my own speeches."[83]

Boulware focused on Reagan's power as a communicator. During Reagan's years in Sacramento, Boulware urged the governor to continue to use the banquet format to go directly to the people. Nor did he relent in his emphasis for enlisting businessmen in politics. "Also on the 'mashed potato' circuit," he wrote, "I hope you will exhort businessmen and others in the privileged top 10 percent to hurry in doing their obligated part to make good economics and good morals become 'good policies' with our sovereign public majority."[84]

Throughout the lean years of his first term, the governor had never given up on moving "M" to the right. His methods were not surprising. According to a *New York Times* correspondent, "his old skills as an after-dinner speaker proved highly potent in dealing with recalcitrant legislators by going over their heads to appeal his case to the public via television."[85] The results could be seen in the Welfare Reform Act of 1971 which was the centerpiece of Reagan's second term.

One legislator, Robert Moretti—a liberal Democrat who as speaker of the assembly was occasionally referred to as "the second most powerful man in Sacramento"—"was so inundated with letters that he begged

Reagan to stop the juggernaut."[86] Reagan's banquet speeches had done their job. The two men sat down face-to-face to work on welfare reform. Reagan was now "dealing with an equal"—following a key Boulware precept—and a genuine compromise was reached.

It took seventeen days of negotiations before the reform bill became law. Reagan prevailed on the issue of eligibility for benefits and Moretti gained higher benefits for those who were accepted into the program and an automatic cost-of-living increase for those who remained on welfare. California, which had been known as the "welfare capital of the nation," with a caseload growing at the rate of 40,000 per month, now became the model for reform. The monthly growth rate declined to 8,000, while the benefits to the "truly needy" increased by 40 percent. The net effect was to save taxpayers $2 billion and "bring the spiraling growth of state government under control."[87] Over the next two years, the state's welfare rolls were reduced by 300,000 people, a decline of 15 percent.

A robust economy contributed to the reduction. A surplus ensued, aided in part by a progressive withholding system for the state income tax. Here, Reagan reiterated one of his core positions: these monies belonged to the people who had paid the taxes. Billions were rebated to California taxpayers through statutes that Reagan pushed through the legislature.[88] Thus, the increase in taxes in a time of crisis, the surplus that developed when the crisis abated, and the ultimate rebate could be seen as part of long-range governmental policy. One of Ronald Reagan's key advisors saw a change in his chief after the welfare legislation. He observed, "It showed him that he could make some changes, that he could not only talk and move people to get things done, but he could actually move the mechanics of government to get things done. And I think that confidence that it gave Reagan was more important than most people realize."[89]

On other aspects of the governor's report card, New York Times reporter Robert Lindsey found that Reagan had "demonstrated great skill in selecting administrators to run state departments [and] left them alone to do their jobs."[90] The phrasing could easily have come from Ralph Cordiner.

Reagan's background in dealing with issues in a nonpartisan way also stood him in good stead. Wilson Riles had been elected as state superintendent of public instruction in a statewide vote, defeating Max Rafferty, the incumbent, who had become a darling of the conservatives. Riles was

California's highest-ranking black official. He viewed his office as "non-partisan." He did not want it to be "politicized." With that in mind, he called for a meeting with the governor, requesting direct and immediate access if he had a problem.

Riles later recalled that Reagan told him, "I fully understand what you mean; you'll have access." He delivered this verdict on his work with Reagan: "The bottom line on Ronald Reagan is that he is a conservative and articulates a very conservative position, but, at least in the field of education, which I know about, he did not try to manipulate it in a partisan way, he wasn't a racist, he did his homework, and he was well-organized. He was an administrator in the sense that he set the policies and directions and chose good people to carry them out."[91]

Ronald Reagan's record as governor of California made him a contender for the presidency. Legislator Bob Moretti focused on the particular skill that Reagan had perfected, much as FDR had made the new medium of radio his own: "Using his considerable talents to sell a point of view, he had repeatedly taken his case directly to the voters via television." Alan Post, a legislative analyst for the state during the Reagan years and often a critic, put this in the broader context of "going to the people." Post observed, "He's extraordinarily good at formulating a political issue to the public and getting them on his side."[92]

TWELVE

═══════

THE PRESIDENTIAL BUG

After the 1968 Republican National Convention, some of the press corps pursued Ronald Reagan for a postmortem. "Is the Presidential bug finally out of your system?" he was asked. "There never was a Presidential bug in my system," he replied.[1]

Nevertheless, just two years after he had won elective office for the first time, Reagan's age made him take a step that he probably would not have taken at this time if he had been younger. If Nixon gained the nomination in 1968, won the general election, and then served a second term, Reagan's next opportunity would be 1976. He would then be sixty-five years old. Only three men were older than that when elected to the presidency: Andrew Jackson, who was sixty-seven when he won in 1834; William Henry Harrison, who was sixty-seven when he won in 1840 (only to die soon thereafter from pneumonia contracted when he rode in the rain-drenched Inaugural Parade); and Dwight Eisenhower, who was sixty-six when he was reelected in 1956.

Richard Nixon seemed to have the nomination locked up. Lyndon Johnson had inadvertently helped Nixon by singling him out as a critic of Johnson's Vietnam policies at the time of Johnson's ill-conceived gambit to declare victory in his "Manila Communiqué." Moreover, Republicans anticipated a victory in November. The unpopularity of the Viet Nam war was their greatest asset, with Nixon's vaunted knowledge of foreign policy giving him the edge.

The Democrats were in disarray on the war issue, and their steadfast labor support also seemed to be falling apart. Walter Reuther led the UAW out of the AFL-CIO. He joined the Teamsters, who had been expelled from the AFL-CIO in the 1950s for corrupt practices, to form a short-lived "Alliance for Labor Action."[2] The broader traditional alliance was not politically aggressive enough for Reuther. His perception was confirmed four years later, when George Meany convinced the AFL-CIO to be neutral in the 1972 election.

Clif White thought Reagan had a chance to claim the nomination in 1968.[3] Although the "Arizona Mafia" had eased him out of the top spot in the 1964 general election campaign, White had masterminded the Draft Goldwater Committee's successful effort to wrest the party's nomination from Nelson Rockefeller. White remained the country's leading expert on delegate counting and convention management. He also knew the conservative power brokers throughout the country better than anyone else. Conservatives controlled many of the state delegations to the convention. Harry Dent in South Carolina, Clarke Reed and Wert Yerger in Mississippi, John Grenier in Alabama, and Charlton Lyons in Louisiana were all making complimentary noises about Reagan. None had committed to him, however, and neither had Strom Thurmond of South Carolina, the dean of the southern leaders.

White viewed Nixon's strength as wide but shallow. If Nixon didn't win on the first ballot, then, White believed, Reagan might run away with the vote. The key was the Florida delegation, given more than usual prominence because the convention was being held in Miami Beach. White felt he had a promise from Republican State Chairman Bill Murfin to the effect that Murfin would cast his vote in caucus for Reagan if White could gain the support of half the state's delegates. The delegation operated under the "unit rule," where all ballots would be cast for the candidate who had a majority. Florida came relatively early in the alphabetical roll call. It was possible that if Reagan captured Florida, the supposed Nixon majority could fall apart, especially if Reagan, who was present in Florida, could somehow gain the attention of the delegates.

Reagan played his part. The convention began with meetings of the plat-form committee. Before Reagan's testimony, the committee and the audi-ence sat in stony silence as the parade of witnesses presented their views. When the California governor covered a wide range of topics—including campus riots, the excesses of the welfare state, and the war in Vietnam—the audience and even the committee of jaded party regulars frequently broke into applause. Senator Everett Dirksen pounded his gavel to regain order. He was smiling as he did it. As a reporter from the *Times* of London ob-served, Reagan's appearance led to "the only spontaneous display of emo-tion for a witness throughout four days of public hearings."[4]

With various showings of public support and favorable soundings as he met with delegates, Reagan felt confident enough to move his candi-dacy out of the stealth mode. William Knowland—publisher of the *Oak-land Tribune*, former U.S. senator, and unsuccessful candidate for gover-nor of California in 1958—rose in his capacity as leader of the California delegation to make an announcement. The caucus had voted, he said, to "recognize [that] Governor Reagan [is] in fact a leading and bona fide candidate for President."[5]

Ronald Reagan was no longer just a "favorite son." Also present at the delegation's meeting at the Deauville Hotel, he was mobbed by reporters. He got a laugh when he said, "Gosh, I was surprised. It all came out of the blue." The word now spread through the other delegations. Harry Dent, who had attended many conventions, said, "The lightning struck. I have been in politics for I don't know how many years, and I have never seen anything like it."

At this point, Richard Nixon made what was widely viewed as a nearly fatal miscalculation. A rumor spread throughout the hall that Nixon was going to name Oregon's liberal Republican senator Mark Hatfield as his running mate. Senator Thurmond met with Nixon to express his objec-tion. Nixon turned a glaring error into a virtual assurance of victory by giving Thurmond a veto on the choice of vice president.

Thurmond and Reagan now sat down together. They met for over an hour. The senator expressed great admiration for the California gover-nor. But he had given Nixon his word that he would hold the Southern delegations in line. Reagan, for his part, declined the opportunity to run for vice president. Clif White learned that if Florida's Bill Murfin had ever given him an assurance on the delegation's support, it was now for-gotten. Murfin followed Thurmond's lead.[6]

Reagan might never have made his bid for the nomination had he not witnessed Boulware proceeding on the basis of focus groups and other sophisticated means of polling to pursue a course that flatly contradicted a head-to-head survey. Even though Jim Carey's poll showed that 87 percent of the IUE members favored a strike, Boulware refused to change GE's offer because he knew there was no depth to the union members' commitment to a strike. In Miami, every survey showed Nixon way ahead, but White and Reagan had contacted delegates directly and knew that Nixon's support was, as they had suspected, shallow. Boulware might have urged an earlier meeting with Thurmond—"meet with equals"—but Reagan probably felt that he first had to demonstrate his strength with the delegates by his convention performance, that is, going "over the heads" of the bosses to move the majority. In any event, the one-on-one with Thurmond came too late, and that was the ultimate turning point.

Ronald Reagan was game to the end. When the *Miami Herald* reported that Nixon would *still* name Hatfield as his running mate, Reagan joined Clif White in their communications trailer behind the convention hall to make calls to the delegates who would rebel at Nixon's continued apostasy. White purchased two thousand copies of the paper. In a move reminiscent of Boulware's direct transmission of materials to GE workers, White's operatives delivered them to every delegate and alternate they could find. Thurmond and Dent called the delegates to tell them the story was not true. The delegates stayed in line. The roll call for the nomination began at 1:19 A.M. When Nixon got a majority of the delegates, Ronald Reagan strode to the rostrum amidst a giant wave of applause to move that Nixon's nomination be declared unanimous.

1976

When he returned to California, Reagan announced that he would now "speak out for Republicanism and how we strayed from the visions of our founding fathers." He established an organization called "Citizens for the Republic" to "focus on these concerns."[7] Although he had done well as governor and had been elected chairman of the Republican Governors Conference,[8] he was still viewed as an outsider by much of the national Republican Party establishment. He saw this not as a disadvantage, but as an opportunity.

Although Speaker Moretti and others were correct in emphasizing Reagan's exceptional ability on television, the former governor turned to another medium when he resumed his life as a private citizen. He commenced a series of hundreds of radio addresses in the course of a weekly national program. Recently, a trove was discovered of some 670 of these talks written in his own hand.[9] In the midst of these talk, Citizen Reagan embarked on a bold, almost unprecedented course.

If Reagan had violated a basic rule of presidential politics in 1968 by attempting to gain the nomination before he had developed a record in public office, this paled in comparison to the conventional wisdom he rejected in his campaign for the nomination in 1976. An almost ironclad rule proclaimed that one never tried to wrest the party's nomination from an incumbent president of the same party. But much had happened since 1968. Richard Nixon had been elected in that year by the smallest percentage of the popular vote since Woodrow Wilson in 1912. Although he won a resounding reelection victory in 1972, Nixon resigned two years later in the aftermath of the Watergate scandal. His vice president, Spiro Agnew, had also resigned in disgrace. Nixon was succeeded as president by Gerald Ford, who called for a time of healing and was generally well received. On Sunday, September 8, 1974, however, President Ford announced that "pursuant to Article II, Section 2, of the Constitution . . . [I grant] . . . a full, free, and absolute pardon unto Richard Nixon."[10] The entire political landscape changed in an instant.

Reagan used his radio talks to strengthen his base as he moved to capture the party nomination. Two of the talks will be excerpted here because they dealt with issues that he had not stressed during his GE years. The first, abortion, was of increasing concern as a component of "social conservatism," with meaningful political impact in urban areas and throughout the South. The second, welfare reform, *had* been a subject of his earlier speeches but had gained new importance with his revolutionary treatment of the crisis in California and the failure of the federal government to accept a role in a national solution to the problem.

Ronald Reagan's radio address on abortion was aired in April of 1975.[11] He began by announcing the subject of the day's program: "An unborn child's property rights are protected by law—its right to life is not. I'll be right back." He promptly placed the issue into the framework of his governmental experience. "Eight years ago when I became Governor, I found myself involved almost immediately in a controversy over abortion. It was a subject I'd never given much thought to and one upon which I didn't really have an opinion. But now I was Governor and abortion was something I couldn't walk away from." Reagan referred to a bill filed in the legislature providing for abortion on demand. It had become an issue on which he had to have a position. He approached lawyers on his staff with questions about the rights of the unborn, for example, the right to inherit. He did not get a lot of helpful information, observing that "the only answer I got was that they were glad I wasn't asking the questions on the bar exam."

In time, he established a position, which he set out at the end of his radio address

> My answer as to what kind of abortion bill I could sign was *one* that recognized an abortion *is* the taking of a human life. In our Judeo-Christian religion, we *recognize* the right to take life in defense of our own. Therefore an abortion is justified when done in self-defense. My belief is that a woman has the right to protect her own life and health against even her own unborn child. I believe *also* that just as she has the right to defend herself against rape she *should* not *be made* to bear a child resulting from that violation of her person and therefore abortion is an act of self defense. I know there will be disagreement with this view but I can find no evidence whatsoever that a fetus is not a living human being with human rights.

Actually, the abortion issue *had* come up in Reagan's first campaign for governor. He was given a free pass at the time by a very powerful and politically sophisticated adviser. Francis McIntyre, the Roman Catholic cardinal from Los Angeles, suggested to the candidate that he wait until he knew what the legislature would do on this multifaceted issue. In the course of his campaign he cited the cardinal's view and was able to avoid the issue until, as stated in his radio address, the legislature forced him to inform himself and to take a stand.[12]

Reagan found little comfort and assistance in "The Speech" as he addressed the "social issues" that were becoming such a visible part of modern conservatism. In fact, this is the major difference between true Boulwarism and conservatism. An "inescapable moral requirement"[13] was always one of Boulware's major themes . But an examination of his teachings—his writings, the materials distributed while he was with General Electric, the various permutations of "The Speech" over the years, and Boulware's own speeches, beginning with "Salvation Is Not Free"—finds scant reference to "social issues" such as abortion, gun control, gay rights, and school prayer.

By and large, Reagan's radio addresses failed to concentrate on these subjects as well.[14] As his longtime secretary, Helene Von Damm, suggested in the 1970s, however, these social issues had become part of the fabric of the party's conservative wing, and Reagan supported, albeit without great fanfare, these views of the Republican right.[15] If he intended to make a fight for the Republican nomination, it was probably most important to carve out an acceptable position on the abortion issue, which is just what he did in his radio address of April 1975. (As president, on the tenth anniversary of the Supreme Court's *Roe v. Wade* decision, he took a more absolute position against abortion. He wrote an essay for *Human Life Review* entitled "Abortion and the Conscience of the Nation," which was later published as a small book.)[16]

Also in April 1975, the former California governor used another of his broadcasts to talk about welfare. In this instance, he portrayed himself as a reformer who had worked out a solution to an extremely difficult problem but who was getting a deaf ear from the Ford administration. After noting that sixty-two congressmen, Democrats and Republicans, were sponsoring a program of welfare reform at the national level, he reported that

> history does repeat itself. In 1969 the House Ways and Means Committee discovered the highest factor determining the size of the case load was the size of the grant. When the grant levels are too high there is no incentive to work. . . . Some time back a Rutgers University professor discovered what that English Royal commission learned 150 years ago. . . . When the old programs demonstrably fail, they are re-baptized and re-funded. . . . Sixty-two Congressmen are proposing a way to change this. They need our help. This is Ronald Reagan. Thanks for listening.[17]

At the end of his second gubernatorial term, Nancy had said, "As we left Sacramento that night, I honestly believed we were leaving politics forever."[18] While some of his close advisors were urging him to make a run for the 1976 nomination, others viewed the move as apostasy, or, at the

FIGURE 12 Lemuel Boulware's relationship with the fortieth president lasted until the end of Boulware's life. Pictured here in his later years, he maintained contact with Reagan for decades after they had both left GE. Reagan never wavered in the lessons learned during the GE years.
Source: Lemuel Boulware Papers, Rare Book and Manuscript Library, University of Pennsylvania.

least, impossible to achieve. Some early Reagan supporters were now Republican Party stalwarts. His possible candidacy was strongly opposed by Henry Salvatori and party officials, such as California Republican state chairman Paul Haerle. Spencer and Roberts had signed on with President Ford. Ford's chief delegate counter at the convention was none other than F. Clifton White.[19]

When asked whether he planned to contest the nomination with President Ford, Reagan replied, "A candidate doesn't make the decision whether to run for president, the people make it for him."[20] After testing the waters by contacting various Republican leaders and doing his best to determine the effectiveness of his campaign of going "over their heads" to the delegates and to the party members in state primaries, Reagan announced in November of 1975 that he would challenge Ford.

While Lemuel Boulware was lukewarm about a Reagan attempt to wrest the nomination from Ford, he felt that if Reagan *did* make such a move, the candidate must use his apparent weakness—lack of incumbency—as a strength. Reagan had done just that when he defeated Governor Pat Brown in his first bid for office. This time his opponent for the nomination, Gerald Ford, was a career professional politician, just as Brown had been. Reagan, the Washington "outsider," must complain about the mess in the nation's capital and fight to throw out the "Beltway" crowd. This must be not only the message of the Reagan campaign but the vehicle, as well—a citizens' campaign run by a citizens' committee.

Boulware's second book, *What You Can Do About . . . Inflation, Unemployment, Productivity, Profit, and Collective Bargaining,* was published in San Diego, California, in 1970, and was addressed to "the average citizen making up the public majority."[21] He cautioned that the average citizen "cannot afford to leave politics to the politicians." He recognized that "most political representatives" cannot risk losing votes by disagreeing with the current consensus." Now, as Citizen Reagan entered the political arena, Boulware drafted an advertisement. The ad, which he placed in the *Miami Herald* on March 8, 1976, described Reagan as a "take charge guy," a "budget balancer," a "sound insurance man" (i.e., Social Security), and a "moral mobilizer." The ad ended with a plea to "Cast Out Big Brother— Cast Your Vote for Ronald Reagan."[22] Of course, there was nothing in the ad that attacked the likeable Republican incumbent president by name.

His collected papers contain the printed ad and Boulware's original handwritten composition. One can only guess why he ran the ad and what he learned. His retirement home was now in Delray Beach, and the *Miami Herald* was a prominent local newspaper. Publication there would enable the old marketing expert to take an informal survey of fellow readers. One category of the sample would certainly be Ford partisans— perhaps even Ford convention delegates. The likely outcome was that they were not swayed. Why go against their party leader? In any event, the ad never appeared again. The headline that Boulware drafted—"Have You Had It?"—which for some reason was abandoned in the published version, would play well in 1980.

The premise of running on the Reagan record and using conservative themes was entirely consistent with the philosophy that had been set out in "The Speech." These ideas *had* been market-tested in the GE years and before the nation in the telecast of 1964. They had been reflected in the successes of the second term in Sacramento. The further concept of complementing the "outsider" appeal with a "citizens" organization as a base was new. It was also consistent. And, frankly, there was no other base available.

Reagan returned to the "mashed potato circuit," aided by Michael Deaver and Peter Hannaford from his Sacramento staff. He was soon "making eight to ten speeches a month for handsome sums." His syndicated column appeared in 174 newspapers, and his radio commentaries reached more than 200 stations. This was not an economic hardship for the candidate. Lou Cannon estimated that Reagan made $800,000 in 1975.[23]

Reagan made a fight of it, suffering a surprising loss to Ford in the New Hampshire primary at the beginning of the campaign but finishing well, with victories in a number of primaries in Southern states (the so-called "smaller states," on which Boulware had been concentrating for years). A month before the Kansas City convention, however, he took an unusual step that many observers thought cost him the nomination. He announced as his choice for vice president Senator Richard Schweiker of Pennsylvania, who was perceived by many Reaganites as a liberal.

Some of the adherents to the conservative themes expressed in Boulware's ad felt badly used. Clif White commented sarcastically that Reagan's campaign manager, John Sears, had "delivered his masterstroke— and handed the nomination to Gerald Ford."[24] Years later, Boulware was quoted as believing the Schweiker selection was "an abject sellout of principle."[25] The move appeared tricky. It unsettled many supporters who had always viewed Reagan as an upfront kind of guy.

Nevertheless, Reagan came remarkably close to gaining the nomination. At the convention on August 19, just after midnight, Ford prevailed by a tally of 1,187 to 1,070. Gerald Ford then gave his acceptance speech, regarded by most observers as the best address of his long career in politics. As the prolonged cheers subsided, the president waved to Ronald and Nancy Reagan, who were seated in the gallery, inviting them to join him at the podium. Now the Reagans came forward to join in a solid front for the Republican ticket. The crowd wouldn't quiet down until

Reagan said a few words. He spoke eloquently of the need for party unity. As a California delegate observed, "Ronald Reagan could get a standing ovation in a graveyard."[26]

Those journalists and pundits who wrote about Reagan on the day following the convention focused on one fact: If Ford won in the fall and served a full four-year term, Reagan would be sixty-nine years old in 1980. No man in history had run for the presidency at that age. If Democrat Jimmy Carter defeated Ford in the fall, the advantage of incumbency made a Reagan bid even more remote.

Still, Reagan had the last word. In some informal remarks to the campaign workers gathered at his hotel before he departed for California, he emphasized the cause in which they were all joined. He did *not*, however, indicate that he would pass the baton on to someone else. "We lost," he said , "but the cause, the cause goes on." He then quoted from an ancient Scottish ballad:

> I'll lay me down and bleed awhile;
> Though I am wounded, I am not slain.
> I shall rise and fight again.

"It's just one more battle in a long war and it's going to go on as long as we all live," he continued before the crowd of loyalists. "Nancy and I, we aren't going back and sit in a rocking chair and say, 'Well, that's all for us.' "[27]

1980

After Gerald Ford's defeat by Georgia governor Jimmy Carter, Ronald Reagan campaigned for the 1980 nomination for four years. He continued to go directly to the people. From 1975 through 1979, he taped more than 1,000 radio addresses.[28] He continued his weekly newspaper column. And he gave speeches. He rekindled Citizens for the Republic, organized funds, and garnered support using his political action committee, under the direction of Lyn Nofziger, a longtime aide.[29]

The radio talks, the mailings, and the Citizens for the Republic ads, as well as the former California governor's national speaking schedule, were all part of moving "M" further to the right. Of course, this was being done *"between"* elections."[30] Boulware contended that efforts to change the attitudes of the electorate had to be directed at "average citizens" and "there just isn't enough time to do so during a nominating or electing campaign."[31] Translating the formula from the labor wars to the national political scene, Reagan put the time to very good use.

The message set out in the ad that Lemuel Boulware had written before the 1976 convention—"Have You Had It?'—was similar to the theme of Reagan's four-year effort. He was appealing not only to the conservative wing of his own party but to the "cross-over" Democrats who would end up voting for him in 1980. The notion that he could win the general election was a persuasive factor in gaining support from potential delegates to the Republican convention in Detroit. In effect, this was a citizens' campaign, a refrain from the past and a taste of what was to come after the convention. Like all of Reagan's opponents, the opposition enhanced Reagan's position by underestimating him. Jimmy Carter and his strategists viewed Reagan as their "favorite opponent" among possible Republican nominees.[32]

George H.W. Bush of Texas was Reagan's principal opponent for the nomination. Bush won a surprise victory in the lead-off contest, the Iowa caucuses. (Campaign manager John Sears, who had advised Reagan not to campaign heavily in Iowa, was fired soon thereafter.) Reagan then won the nomination for two reasons—one pure Reagan, the other, pure Boulware.

At the televised debate in the key "first in the nation" primary in New Hampshire, Reagan wanted to include other Republican hopefuls, but Bush insisted that it be a two-man format. The moderator proceeded on Bush's plan; he turned off the microphone as Reagan attempted to introduce other Republican contenders who were present on stage. At that point, Reagan (whose committee was financing the telecast), in the words of campaign chronicler Theodore White, "jackknifes up from his chair, grabs the microphone in a single swoop, his temper flaring, and yells, 'I paid for this show. I'm paying for this microphone, Mr. Green [actually Breen].'" Reagan's firm, immediate action carried the day—and the debate and the primary. (Only later did it develop that Reagan's line came, almost verbatim, from presidential candidate Spencer Tracy in the 1948 movie, *The State of the Union*.)[33] Still, it was bold and effective. In the words of the pros, Regan had regained momentum.

There were a few impressive dying gasps from the Bush campaign. He won a majority of the voters in both Pennsylvania and Michigan, but

these were so-called popularity contests. The Reagan forces had so organized their efforts that they carried away the bulk of the delegates. After
winning New Hampshire, Reagan, took Vermont, Florida, and Illinois.
And then, as Theodore White observes, he won "the Southern states,
one after another."[34] These were the "smaller states" on which Boulware
had concentrated from the very outset of the campaign that began in
1958, a campaign that, for his "traveling ambassador," had never ended.

At the convention, the California governor asked George H. W. Bush
to accept the nomination for vice president. This act took place after negotiations with former president Gerald Ford, in which Ford declined the
opportunity to be the running mate. (Part of the problem was that Ford—
who, after all, had already served in the highest office—tended to view
Reagan as the running mate.)[35] Reagan's rationale with Bush, once Ford
was out of the picture, was simple: "George," he said, "it seems to me that
the fellow who came closest and got the next most votes for president
ought to be the logical choice for vice-president."[36] Bush agreed.

On Election Day, November 4, 1980—with only 5 percent of the vote
counted and with the polls still open in California and other Western
states—President Jimmy Carter called to concede. The Reagans joined
friends and supporters at the Los Angeles Century City Hotel, where
the grand ballroom rocked with enthusiasm. When the more complete
returns were in, they showed that Reagan had beaten Carter by ten
points, carrying forty-four states. (Carter, who had won virtually all of the
Southern states against Ford four years before, this time carried only his
home state of Georgia.) The developing trend in legislative elections
held that date was equally encouraging to the incoming administration.
Liberal Senators George McGovern, Frank Church, Birch Bayh, and
Warren Magnuson were defeated. Republicans took control of the Senate and added thirty new members in the House.[37]

Richard Wirthlin, Reagan's pollster and political strategist, described
a crucial element in the Reagan victory in these terms: "The only way
Ronald Reagan won in 1980 was reaching out and both by message and
by who he was to bring in the blue-collar, middle-class, Catholic ethnic
vote."[38] Looking back on the 1980 results, historians and political pundits saw something more than a personal victory. Arthur Schlesinger Jr.
commented that "no intellectual phenomenon has been more surprising
in recent years than the revival in the United States of conservatism as a
respectable social philosophy."[39]

Political columnist Max Lerner described Reagan's victory as an "earthquake." He believed that it represented "a long-range retreat from the liberalism of the New Deal welfare state." He continued, "Something like a class revolution has been taking place. Since the violent 1960s, the middle-middle and lower-middle classes have been seething with social resentments over the runaway changes in the culture. They, too, were part of the American dream—they had worked and scrimped, fashioned a trade or small business, built a house, raised a family. They felt threatened by the forces that seemed intent on taking this away from them." Lerner's list of "discontents" might have been taken from "Salvation Is Not Free" or "The Speech," with a nod to Reagan's Sacramento years: "foreign and defense policies, with taxes, welfare and social policies." Lerner found "pent-up social angers" in the Reagan constituency, and concluded that "this time the Populist revolt was led by conservatives."[40]

THIRTEEN

A PRESIDENT'S VISION

In the movie *The Candidate*, young Bill McKay (played by Robert Redford) wins a U.S. Senate seat from California. In the course of the campaign, which is handled by skilled professional managers, the candidate abandons or compromises almost everything he believes in. After he wins, in a rush of anxiety, he turns to one of his managers and asks, "What do we do now?"[1]

Regrettably, the candidate's position is not unusual. Most men and women who run for office have spent time—often years—in developing a strategy to win elections, with only a vague idea of what they want to do after they are elected. Ronald Reagan was different. He had spent years talking about and thinking about the course America should take. He had a vision.

"Vision" is the term used by many close observers to describe the outlook of the fortieth president, including aides such as George Shultz, White House Counselor Ed Meese, and leaders who sat across the conference table, such as Mikhail Gorbachev.[2] Nevertheless, it is a grand word. Certainly to those who characterized Reagan as "an amiable dunce"[3] or a sleeper through meetings or an actor hollowly repeating lines written by others, the notion of a man of vision would seem out of place. But to David Gergen, a seasoned national journalist who has worked with a number of presidents, including Reagan, "he was the best leader in the White House since Franklin Roosevelt."[4] And to a respected group of American historians who placed him eighth ("Near Great") among America's presidents in a recent poll, the word "vision" may be appropriate.[5]

George Shultz, who served as Reagan's secretary of state for six years, used "vision" to describe the president's core beliefs. This insight became his key to understanding Reagan. To him, the word explained the president's strengths and also his weaknesses. Shultz put it this way:

> Reagan had visionary ideas. In pursuing them, he displayed some of his strongest qualities: an ability to break through the entrenched thinking of the moment to support his vision of a better future, a spontaneous, natural ability to articulate the nation's most deeply rooted values and aspirations, and a readiness to stand by his vision regardless of pressure, scorn or setback. At the same time, he could fall prey to a serious weakness: a tendency to rely on his staff and friends to the point of accepting uncritically—even wishfully—advice that was sometimes amateurish and even irresponsible.[6]

To the Victor

Reagan embraced in their entirety the objectives announced by Lemuel Boulware in his "Salvation Is Not Free" speech at Harvard in 1949. Boulware had identified the opposition as "union officials" and the public officials who supported them. Reagan could turn his agenda into law because he had, by his campaigning and his election, defeated those who opposed it.

Labor historian Kevin Boyle describes the lengthy conflict in these terms: "For thirty-five years, from the end of World War II through the 1970s, the labor movement had occupied a preeminent place in national politics, providing one of the most important voices within the liberal New Deal order that dominated national discourse. Union leaders enjoyed easy access to the White House and Capitol Hill." But, Boyle goes on, "the Republican triumphs of the 1980s changed all that." In fact, the great labor adversaries whom Cordiner, Boulware, and Reagan had faced over the years were no longer on the scene. Walter Reuther and his wife had died in a plane crash in 1970. Jim Carey was felled by a heart attack in 1973. George Meany passed on at the beginning of 1980. Boyle concludes, "Now, after years of conservative attacks and liberal retreats, the American labor movement is little more than a hollow shell, unable to defend its members from corporate retrenchment, powerless to affect national policy, and devoid of political clout."[7]

THE VISION RESTATED: THE FIRST INAUGURAL

On January 20, 1981, Ronald Reagan delivered his first Inaugural Address. In a departure from past inaugurations, the ceremony was held on the west side of the Capitol. At the beginning the sky was overcast, but "Reagan luck" prevailed. As Reagan rose to speak, the sun burst through the clouds. His remarks on shrinking government, "lighten[ing] our punitive tax burden" and planning for the long term were familiar.[8]

"The Speech" had become the blueprint—the vision—for Reagan administration policy.[9] As political scientist John Sloan points out, "By repeating the same simple messages for so many years, Reagan became the embodiment of those messages." In his analysis of Reagan's leadership, Sloan quotes a Reagan White House speechwriter who explained that his function was to "plagiarize the president's old speeches." Columnist George Will commented that "it is hard for Reagan to avoid sounding like an echo of an echo."[10]

Hugh Sidey, the *Time/Life* journalist who interviewed every U.S. president from Eisenhower through George W. Bush, accompanied Reagan on trips to London and Moscow in Reagan's second term. He felt that the speeches the president gave in those cities were the finest ever given abroad by any American leader. When he asked a speechwriter who had penned these offerings, he was told: "Reagan. They were actually pretty much the speeches he had given when he worked for General Electric."[11]

THE VISION IS EXPEDITED

Two months after his inauguration—where he said "Progress may be slow"—an event occurred that accelerated the implementation of the

Reagan vision. The president was shot. The wound was serious, requiring surgery. As he was wheeled toward the operating room, he quipped to Nancy, "Honey, I forgot to duck," and commented to his surgeons, "I hope you're all Republicans." His "grace under pressure," to borrow Hemingway's phrase, earned him a special place in the hearts and minds of the American public.[12]

A week after he left the hospital, Reagan addressed a joint session of Congress. Ostensibly, the occasion was to present his plan to cut the federal budget and propose a controversial program of across-the-board tax cuts. It marked his return to good health and to the full pursuit of his office, however, and the federal legislators gave him (in his words) "an unbelievable ovation that went on for several minutes." As he delivered his address, some forty Democrats defied their leadership to stand up and applaud at a crucial point. He later joked, "That reception was almost worth getting shot for."[13] More important, Reagan's close encounter with death imbued the president with an even greater sense of mission. He wrote in his diary, "Whatever happens now I owe to God and will try to serve him in every way I can."[14]

An End to Burdensome Taxation

Reagan the negotiator now moved into action. On July 29, his diary entry read

> The whole day was given to phone calls to Congressmen except for a half dozen ambassadors. I went from fearing the worst to hope we'd squeak through. As the day went on though some how I got the feeling that something good was happening. Then late afternoon came word the Senate had passed its tax bill [ours] 89 to 11. Then from the House where all the chips were down, we won 238–195. We got 40 Democrat votes. On final passage almost 100 joined the parade making it 330 odd to 107 or thereabouts. This on top of the budget victory is the greatest political win in half a century.[15]

The insurgent Democrats were called the "boll weevils." They came largely from the South and a number later changed party affiliation. (Phil

Gramm of Texas, for example, was then a Democratic congressman and later sat in the Senate as a Republican.)[16] They provided the margin of victory. The president had gone over the heads of the party leaders to Democrat members who supported his program.

The tax plan was a victory for what was becoming known as "supply-side economics." Its premise was that a tax cut would actually bring *more* revenues to the government by unleashing the full vigor of the free economy. The writings of Jude Wininski, the use of the "Laffer Curve," and other contemporaneous happenings were properly given the lion's share of the credit for "Reaganomics."

THE DEFICITS: REMEMBERING HAZLITT AND HANEY

The most startling aspect of President Reagan's tax-restructuring legislative victory was that it was accomplished at a time when, as commander in chief, he refused to cut back on military spending. In time, administration critics would view the giant deficits incurred during the Reagan years as a failure of leadership. President Reagan disagreed.

"I did not come here to balance the budget," Reagan said at the time, "not at the expense of my tax-cutting program and my defense program."[17] The president's belief that he could spend large sums on the military while lowering taxes may have been based on his reading, as previously noted, of books by economists Hazlitt and Haney. Although the deficit was often cited in later years as proof of the failure of Reagan's economic policy, he did not seem overwrought by the criticism. As military costs diminished, he felt, with the Soviet collapse and the ultimate success of the Reagan doctrine, the economy would flourish. Congressional Budget Office predictions tended to confirm this view. Many Reagan supporters saw the reduction of Cold War expenses as a basic factor in the later bipartisan deficit reductions that occurred in the Clinton administration.[18]

Some observers saw another reason to justify the deficits. Richard Neustadt of Harvard, a revered historian of the presidency, put it this way: Reagan "tugged" his country "in a conservative direction" initially through his rhetoric and his tax cuts and "by tolerating substantial federal deficits, which had the effect of limiting congressional appetites for costly social welfare measures."[19]

The PATCO Incident: Pure Boulwarism

A few days after the passage of the tax program, air traffic controllers across the nation declared a strike. What became known as "the PATCO Incident," in the words of one Reagan watcher, "set the tone for [the Reagan] presidency."[20] Twelve thousand members of the Professional Air Traffic Controllers Organization announced they would not return to work until their demands for higher wages and reduced workloads were met. President Reagan, pointing out that the controllers were public employees who had taken an oath not to strike, gave them forty-eight hours to return to work. His position was doubly ironic because he himself had been a union leader and because PATCO was one of the few unions that had formally supported Reagan's candidacy. Nevertheless, when they did not return as ordered, he fired them.

Replacements were brought in. The president remained firm in his stand not to permit the striking air controllers to return. Fortunately for safety and politics, no plane crashed during the dispute. Even though replacements trained in the military and other areas were on hand, the risk had been enormous. Presentation of a full and fair offer and determination to stand by it was a practice that had become ingrained in the president. The PATCO incident had consequences outside of the narrow labor area. As a top White House aide commented in an oral history interview years later, "I think what is extraordinary about it is the impact it had way beyond domestic politics. Especially when you listen to George Shultz or Henry Kissinger talk about the impact it had on foreign policy, it was stunning. Basically the impact was that [foreign leaders] said, 'Oh my God, this President took on the unions and did it. He might do other things.' Which was true, of course."[21]

The NLRB Revisited

Kevin Boyle observes that in firing the air controllers, Reagan "signaled the end of an era [i.e. of union power] in American political life."[22] But what of the overall development of labor law? According to David Jacobs, an assistant professor of management at Kogod College of Business Administration at American University, "Reagan's National Labor Relations Board was . . . characterized by an unprecedented management tilt."[23] Jacobs observes that "Ronald Reagan had played his role in Boulware's strategy (receiving his salary from Boulware's public relations department), addressing employee groups as well as consumers. He perfected what he came to call 'The Speech,' a compact and persuasive appeal for conservative policies."[24] The implementation of some of these views could be seen at the NLRB.

Whereas the Reagan Board "took the employer's side in 60 percent of all cases . . . the Carter and Ford Boards . . . had favored employers about 28 percent of the time." Jacobs attributes this swing to the president's appointments of promanagement individuals to the board and its legal staff. Jacobs regards the Reagan administration's rejection of "bargaining" as "political Boulwarism." He preferred the policies of Massachusetts governor Michael Dukakis and his "appreciation of bargaining as a social tool." He had hope (in 1989, when his article was published) that President George H. W. Bush "would be a little more comfortable with Congressional compromise" than his immediate predecessor. Jacobs appeared to lament Reagan's policy as governor of California and later as president "to communicate with the voters directly" rather than deal with organizations that represented the citizens in articulating their independent concerns.[25]

FIRM BUT NOT INTRANSIGENT

Adherence to principle did not mean blind intransigence, however. In *The Truth About Boulwarism*, Lemuel Boulware states that 1948 "was the first and only time in my 14 years on the job that any union accepted such an initial all-inclusive offer. All subsequent ones were revised in major or minor ways." In *Boulwarism*, Northrup notes that GE had a "policy of making changes where 'new facts' so indicate."[26]

There are many instances of the principle in operation during the Reagan administration, the most prominent of which involved the Department of Education. In his 1980 campaign, Reagan spoke out for the elimination of the department. He believed that education was a matter for the states to handle, not the federal government.[27] Nevertheless, he made a stellar appointment to the cabinet post. Terrell Bell had experienced every level of education—public school teacher, administrator, college professor. What was not as widely known about the new secretary of education, was that Bell had served four years in the Pacific Theater in the Marines in World War II. He was not the kind of man who was prepared to give up strongly held beliefs easily.[28]

In 1983, the Department of Education published *A Nation at Risk: The Imperative of Education Reform*. The report, which Bell had commissioned , did not mince words. It said, "If an unfriendly foreign power had attempted to impose on America the mediocre performance that exists today . . . we might have viewed it as an act of war."[29] The idea of the Department of Education promulgating or endorsing standards to promote excellence in education appealed to President Reagan. The department, which was also proving to be more popular than candidate Reagan had anticipated three years before, remained intact. One historian of the American presidency went so far as to call Reagan America's "second education president," the first being Dwight Eisenhower, who had raised the federal officer in charge of education to cabinet rank.[30]

"A More Positive Press"

Looking back on the Reagan years, some members of the Washington press corps and pundits of the evening news felt that the fortieth president had received more favorable treatment than his recent predecessors. Tom Brokaw, then anchoring the *NBC Nightly News*, felt that Reagan got "a more positive press than he deserve[d]."[31] Ben Bradlee, the long-time executive editor of the *Washington Post*, commented, "We have been kinder to President Reagan than any President that I can remember since I've been at the *Post*."

In his book on the subject, Mark Hertsgaard attributes the favorable press to a skillful White House crew who understood how to "package the nation's top politician." Brokaw is somewhat more generous when he places the president himself in the formula. "Reagan's got that kind of broad-based philosophy about how he wants the government to run," he said, "and he's got all those killers who are willing and able to do that for him." Hertsgaard lists as the individuals primarily responsible for the White House's "extensive public relations apparatus" Michael Deaver and David Gergen.

Lou Cannon, Reagan's best-known biographer, attributes the fortieth president's favorable press to another source. He refers to the California years and points out that "Ronald Reagan was able to shift the debate when he didn't have Mike Deaver and he didn't have the White House. . . . The fact is that Reagan himself is the guy who does this." Lyn Nofziger, who handled Reagan's press in Sacramento, also notes that in Reagan "we had a candidate who comes across a hell of a lot better" than those who preceded him or opposed him.

Reagan's years on the road and in radio and television served him well. A president's State of the Union message has always been a significant media event. Radio coverage commenced in 1923 with Calvin Coolidge. Harry Truman's 1947 speech was the first to be telecast. In 1965, Lyndon Johnson moved it to prime time. But, as one commentator has observed, "it was one thing to televise the speech and another to turn it into a television show. The credit for that transformation goes to Mr. Reagan, who signaled the new order in 1982 when he pointed to the gallery to honor Lenny Skutnick, the man who had dived into the icy Potomac to save a woman after a plane crash."[32]

The carefully selected figures that pack today's galleries and help a president to "dramatize his message in human terms" are lineal descendants of Lenny Skutnick. They also reflect Reagan's experience on the plant tour and the mashed potato circuit, where he cited examples of the impact of government policy on "the average citizen" and "Joe Taxpayer" to bring his message home.

The Evil Empire

Reagan's undoubted talent for public relations and news management did not prevent him from occasionally making a statement that could curl the hair of some of the members of his administration. The March 1983 meeting of the National Association of Evangelists in Orlando, Florida, was one such occasion. It was no surprise that the president's speech to this audience would convey a high moral tone, but the occupants of the upper reaches of the State Department had not anticipated that the remarks would touch on foreign policy.

In fact, the end of the speech contained several references to the Soviet Union, including the following: "I urge you to beware the temptation of pride—the temptation of blithely declaring yourselves above it all and label both sides equally at fault, to ignore the facts of history and the aggressive impulses of an *evil empire,* to simply call the arms race a giant misunderstanding and thereby remove yourself from the struggle between right and wrong and good and evil" (Italics added).[33]

Actually, the diplomats of the Foreign Service and the public should not have been surprised by the president's confrontational language. The summer before, in a speech at Westminster, he had predicted the collapse of the Soviet Union, in equally tough terms: "The march of freedom and democracy . . . will leave Marxism/Leninism on the ash heap of history."[34] The phrase "ash heap of history" was one of Boulware's favorites, and he used it in "Salvation Is Not Free."[35]

In an era when official U.S. policy was based on containment and coexistence—even detente—Reagan's remarks marked a turning point. As Henry Kissinger later observed, "Reagan was the first postwar president to take the offensive."[36] Another Harvard professor, historian Harvey Mansfield, expanded on this point: "By taking the offensive Reagan brought final success to the largely defensive policy of containing communism that America had begun in 1945. He saw that America could 'stay the course' (a favorite phrase) by departing from the course, and looking back now [in 2004], one can see that this was his great achievement. . . . [H]e won the Cold War that America waged for forty-five years against one of the three worst regimes known to human history."[37]

The Strategic Defense Initiative

The media criticism of the "Evil Empire" speech was still in full swing, when, two weeks later, the president delivered his classic television address, "Defense and National Security." He introduced the subject of the Strategic Defense Initiative. There were traces of economists Hazlitt and Haney in his remarks; the defense budget, the president said, was not about "spending arithmetic." It *was* about America's need to maintain a "powerful military" to ensure that "any adversary concludes that the risk of attacking us outweighs any political gain." The question of whether military expenditures were justified in the Cold War was resolved according to the president's rationale when he described the Soviet Union as "an offensive military force."[38]

This time George Shultz *did* see the first draft of the speech. He wondered at first where the SDI idea had originated (Dr. Teller and Reagan's military advisors were often mentioned). But Shultz soon came to attribute the idea to Reagan directly.[39] In fact, in his book about his years at the helm of the State Department, Shultz first broaches his description of Reagan as a "visionary" in the course of discussing SDI. Shultz puts it this way: "But all along, the creation of what became the Strategic Defense Initiative was the vision of Ronald Reagan. . . . Once he was sold on this idea, he stuck with it and looked for ways to persuade others that his idea was right. It was a Reagan characteristic that I would observe again and again on important occasions."[40]

All in all, as George Shultz and others were to observe, the speech in which Reagan first referred to SDI was "an undeniable success with the public at large."[41] It is important to note that this was not simply the introduction of a popular new phrase or a passing piece of rhetoric. *Business Week* described SDI at the time as "the most radical change in strategic policy since the end of World War II."[42]

LET REAGAN BE REAGAN

It is one thing to have a vision and quite another to implement it. Throughout his career, Reagan was occasionally second-guessed by those who were supposed to be assisting him. They did not appreciate the full dimensions of his talent and, to use a phrase that came into vogue on these occasions, did not understand how to "Let Reagan be Reagan."[43] David Gergen concluded that Reagan was more than "comfortable in his own skin." He was "serene" and had a "clear sense of what he was trying to accomplish." He felt that the best thing the staff could do was to not treat the president as a "marionette" but to try to clear the obstacles from his path.[44]

Reagan's ideas—his good friend Margaret Thatcher once said they were few, "but all of them were big and all of them were good"[45]—were not random. In fact none of them were easily achieved. George Shultz put it this way: "[President Reagan] had a strong and constructive agenda, much of it labeled impossible and unattainable in the early years of his presidency."[46] Shultz said that he "found [Reagan] very good to work with. He asked lots of questions; he contributed ideas. But the main thing he contributed was a strong thread that guided him. And he knew what it was, and he knew when we were getting off that beat, and he would get us back on it again."[47]

One of the reasons why Reagan was able to promote and implement his vision of America was that many of those who "Let Reagan be Reagan" had a sense of history. They had come to his administration from the academic community. Shultz, of course, had been dean of the business school at the University of Chicago before he entered government during the Nixon administration. Jeane Kirkpatrick, whom Reagan appointed U.S. permanent representative to the U.N. after he had read her article "Dictatorships and Double Standards"—written when she was Leavey Professor of Political Science at Georgetown University— has commented on the abundance of former professors who served under Reagan. She wrote that although it "has generally escaped notice," she was impressed with "how relatively many academics [were] present in [the Reagan administration] at relatively high policy-making levels."[48]

Moving "M"

On Election Day, November 6, 1984, Ronald Reagan defeated his opponent Walter Mondale by garnering 59 percent of the popular vote and carrying forty-nine states. He gained more electoral votes than any of his predecessors. His hortatory skills played a significant part in his win, but his message hit home, as well. As Lou Cannon has observed: "Reagan was not believable because he was the Great Communicator; he was the Great Communicator because he was believable."[49] After the election, House Speaker Tip O'Neill told Reagan: "In my fifty years in public life, I've never seen a man more popular than you with the American people."[50] With this giant mandate, he turned more to foreign policy in his second term, which saw the greatest achievement and the greatest crisis of his presidency. The lessons he learned during the GE years were much in evidence.

The Reagan Doctrine

In February 1985, Secretary of State Shultz gave a speech to the Commonwealth Club in San Francisco. He said, "A revolution is sweeping the world today—a democratic revolution. This should not be a surprise. Yet it is noteworthy because many people in the West lost faith, for a time, in the relevance of the idea of democracy." Shultz took issue with the message sent out from Moscow to the nations of the world: "What's mine is mine. What's yours is up for grabs." The United States cannot not shrink from leadership, Shultz maintained, and permit a vacuum into which its adversaries could move. He later commented that he had gone over the speech in advance with the president, who "approved wholeheartedly." The policy became known as the Reagan Doctrine.[51]

In fact, Larry Beilenson had also set out the doctrine five years earlier in *Survival and Peace in the Nuclear Age*. Beilenson expressed some ground rules for the policy, the most relevant of which was: "All revolution must come from within; the United States can merely help." The doctrine did not necessarily involve sending U.S. troops. As Beilenson had written years before in *Power Through Subversion*, "The United States should give to the dissidents against all Communist governments protracted sustained aid—initially money for propaganda—agitation with supplies and arms where feasible and warranted by the developing situation."[52]

The president himself had rejected "containment" as way to stop "Russian aggression on the world front" in January 1962, in the version of "The Speech" he was then giving on the banquet circuit, when he addressed Chamber of Commerce in Fargo, North Dakota at its annual meeting.[53] An article that appeared at about that time in GE's *Defense Quarterly*—which is cited above for its early reference to a nuclear shield defense—had called for "a *doctrine* for dealing with Communist engendered 'wars of national liberation' which creates the full range of political, military, and economic means for implementation" [italics added].[54] As noted earlier, a coauthor of the article, Dr. Robert Strausz-Hupe, was appointed ambassador to Turkey by Ronald Reagan.

The foreign policy goals that Ronald Reagan sought to attain were massive—the defeat of the Soviet Union, the Reagan Doctrine, initiation of the Strategic Defense Initiative, and the zero option in nuclear disarmament. Any one of these would have been a major accomplishment. To pursue them simultaneously invited expanded opposition, popular protests, vicious counterattacks, and streams of ridicule. The president's offensive featured two familiar weapons: skill in negotiation and going over the heads of the opposition directly to the people.

The Great Negotiator

Four U.S.-Soviet summits were held during the Reagan administration, all in his second term. The first occurred in Geneva, Switzerland, on November 21, 1985. During his meeting with Soviet leader Mikhail Gorbachev, Reagan's "personal" approach to summitry seemed to pass muster with press and colleagues.[55] His primary objective was get to know Gorbachev well and let Gorbachev get to know him. As George Shultz reported after the meeting: "The first Reagan-Gorbachev summit had come to an end. The fresh start that the president wanted had become a reality in Geneva, not the least because the two leaders had come to like and respect each other. They had agreed; they had disagreed. We had heated moments; we had light moments. We had come in order to get to know each other as people by working hard on the issues, and we did, as did the two leaders, who spent almost five of the fifteen hours of official meetings talking privately." Shultz concluded: "Ronald Reagan's one-on-one meetings with Mikhail Gorbachev were clearly productive."[56]

Media commentary on President Reagan's head-to-head approach turned harsh a year later after the second Reagan-Gorbachev meeting, in Reykjavik, Iceland, in October 1986.[57] The event was widely regarded as a failure, with attacks from critics on all sides. No agreement was reached because Reagan had not been willing to give up the Strategic Defense Initiative. SDI, now popularly dubbed and derided as "Star Wars," was the Soviet price for the bargain.

Shultz describes the SDI situation in the following words:

> Ronald Reagan said that the Strategic Defense Initiative would never be a bargaining chip. In our subsequent negotiations with the Soviets, the integrity of the basic research and development program was never compromised. But SDI proved to be of deep concern to the Soviets. . . . [They] were genuinely alarmed by the prospect of American science 'turned on' and venturing into the realm of space defenses. The Strategic Defense Initiative in fact proved to be the ultimate bargaining chip. And we played it for all it was worth.[58]

The financial impact of SDI research on the Soviet economy had been in Reagan's thinking for some time. The GE *Public and Employee News* of December 1957, an issue devoted to "Better Defense or Better Living or

Both," stressed the greater impact of defense spending would have on the Soviet economy than on that of the United States.[59] The Strausz-Hupe article, discussed in detail earlier, mentioned not only the military importance of "achieving an effective anti-missile defense," but also the fact that the Soviet Union was "devoting a far greater percentage of its total R & D effort" toward developing the system than the United States.[60]

With the notable exception of Senator Daniel Patrick Moynihan, there were few in Washington at the time of the Reagan-Gorbachev summits who acknowledged the frailty of the Soviet economy. The financial pinch created by SDI generated the greatest pressure at the bargaining table—and made it so significant a bargaining chip.

THE PRESIDENT AS ADMINISTRATOR: IRAN-CONTRA AND THE CORDINER MODEL

Events that occurred between the second and third summits almost derailed the negotiations with the Soviets and destroyed the Reagan presidency.[61] The Iran-Contra scandal involved a scheme for the sale of arms to Iran and the use of the profits to fund Nicaraguan guerillas known as "Contras." These activities were in direct contravention of U.S. policy set forth by the Senate in the Boland Amendment. In a speech on November 13, 1986, the president said that reports of arms being traded for hostages were wrong and, in effect, he denied any knowledge of the situation. A poll taken immediately after the speech showed that only 14 percent of the public believed him.[62]

The U.S. sale of arms to Iran was first brought to world attention in *Al-Shira*, a Lebanese publication, on November 3. As the matter continued to unravel, it seemed likely that the administration was violating not only the Boland Amendment but the U.S. Constitution and long-standing legislation prohibiting expenditure of funds without appropriation. NATO ambassador David Abshire, whom the president put in charge of investigating Iran-Contra, said in his later account that if the president were guilty of the charges being leveled, "the acts would be grounds for impeachment."[63]

The president's approval rating plummeted to 41 percent. Three other presidents in the second half of the century suffered similar declines in public confidence after unpopular policies or scandals. Lyndon Johnson decided not to run for reelection. Richard Nixon resigned, and Bill Clinton was impeached. Ronald Reagan was in serious trouble. It will be recalled that at the same time that George Shultz praised Reagan as a visionary, he found a "serious weakness" in the fortieth president. Reagan had "a tendency," Shultz observed, "to rely on his staff and friends to the point of accepting uncritically—even wistfully—advice that was sometimes amateurish and even irresponsible."[64] Nowhere was this weakness more apparent than in the Iran-Contra situation.

The likely administrative model for Reagan was the system of governance in place at General Electric during Reagan's years with the company. The brief summaries the two chief executives used in describing their approaches are illuminating. Cordiner, in his Columbia lectures, said, "The President [of the corporation] is of course unable to do all the work himself, and he delegates the responsibility for portions of the total work through organization channels to individuals who have the talents and knowledge required to do it." Reagan, in responding to a question by Andrea Mitchell in a press conference at the time of Iran-Contra, said: "I've been reading a great deal about my management style. I think that most people in business will agree that it is a proper management style. You get the best people you can to do the job; then you don't hang over their shoulder criticizing everything they do or picking at them on how their doing it."[65]

Under Cordiner's leadership, GE constantly met and exceeded its objectives. By and large, his system worked well. With the exception of the World War II years, GE had a higher average annual pretax return on equity under Cordiner than any of its CEOs from 1915 to 1990.[66] But when the system failed, it did so in spectacular fashion. It cost the company hundreds of millions of dollars in civil damage claims, and shares plummeted. GE's antitrust violations led to one of the greatest debacles in the history of American corporations.[67] Cordiner's administrative program encouraged the rogue. At GE, delegation without adequate supervision led to a sprawling antitrust conspiracy. Certain division leaders who met and exceeded their goals at GE were among the first U.S. corporate executives to go to prison under the antitrust laws. Ralph Cordiner had his Bill Ginn; Ronald Reagan, his Oliver North.

Ronald Reagan's reliance on staff had worked well in his years as governor. Actually, the most talked about "scandal" in his first term involved the replacement of his powerful chief of staff, Phil Battaglia. But the situation was resolved, and the governor's office continued to function well. Lou Cannon credits the appointment of William P. Clark Jr. as Battaglia's successor. "Under Clark," Cannon wrote, "Reagan adopted a 'chairman of the board' style that became his preferred method of governance in Sacramento and during the first term of his presidency."[68] This approach was similar to that of a U.S. president whose leadership qualities were held in high esteem by Ronald Reagan: Franklin Delano Roosevelt.

THE VISIONARY AS AN ADMINISTRATOR: FDR AND REAGAN

Reagan voted for Roosevelt four times and had "followed FDR blindly."[69] Even after he and Boulware came to disagree with Roosevelt, almost categorically, on points of policy, they still respected his leadership skills. Undoubtedly, part of Reagan's devotion came from his admiration of FDR's style. As presidential speechwriter James Humes observed, "Roosevelt . . . was a born actor."[70]

Soon after his inauguration in 1933, Franklin Roosevelt started a whirlwind of domestic-policy legislation. The surge of statutory proposals from the White House redefined presidential history. Thereafter, the standard against which administrations were measured was the accomplishments during their "First Hundred Days." Ironically, Reagan's devotion to his idol's methods came to be regarded as his "Achilles heel."[71]

The impetus for the New Deal legislation was the Great Depression that had strangled the American economy. During the transition before his inaugural, FDR's "Brain Trust"—Professors Moley, Berle, Tugwell and others coming largely from the Columbia University faculty—fashioned a panoply of statutes running the gamut from alphabetical agencies to stimulate the economy to tightening of securities laws to prevent unfettered abuse by banking institutions. The president supplemented his pressure for legislation by going directly to the voters in his "Fireside Chats" on a new medium, radio. When he ran for reelection at the end of his first term, he won all but two states in the greatest election victory, to that time, in American history.

During the transition after the 1980 election before his own presidency, Reagan established a number of policy-defining task forces under the direction of Martin Anderson, once of Columbia University and more recently of Stanford. In addition, starting in 1979, the Heritage Foundation had prepared *A Mandate for Leadership*, developed by a panel of several hundred experts under the direction of the foundation's chief executive, Edwin J. Feulner Jr. This was a conservative blueprint, directed especially at the first hundred days. Even before its publication in early 1981, a draft was made available to Reagan's transition task forces. The president also gave a copy to each member of his cabinet and directed them to read it.[72]

Historians have raised questions about the administrative competence of both presidents. They each used a "troika" effectively during a crucial time of their presidencies. In his first term, Reagan used a three-man team at the White House to move his program forward. It was composed of a pragmatist (Chief of Staff James Baker), a publicist (counselor Michael Deaver) and an ideologue (counselor Ed Meese). In the final two years of the war, Roosevelt was well-served by a three-man team at the White House: "Harry Hopkins as emissary to the Allied leaders, Admiral William Leahy as his link with the military, and James F. Byrnes as the overall director of the domestic war effort."[73]

According to political scientist Fred Greenstein, Roosevelt's reliance on his three strong staff subordinates, "tempered his organizational idiosyncrasies."[74] Absent their influence, FDR's administrative techniques were often viewed as "Byzantine" and "competitive," frequently pitting one of his team against another.[75] The president was often accused of lack of candor; witness the surprising number of prominent members of his administration who thought they had been promised the vice presidency by FDR.

Similarly, the exodus of *his* troika preceded the lowest point of the Reagan administration, the Iran-Contra crisis. Secretary of the Treasury Donald Regan had exchanged jobs with Chief of Staff Jim Baker. Deaver and Meese also left the White House, Meese to become Attorney general. In the now familiar phrase, Don Regan would not "Let Reagan be Reagan."[76] The first lady was infuriated by what she viewed as a failure to serve the president properly. "He liked the word 'chief' in his title," she said about Regan, "but he never really understood that his title also included the word 'staff.'"[77]

In fact, Don Regan was obsessed with micromanaging the president. "In focusing on the top of the White House pyramid," observes Greenstein, "Regan was inattentive to its base." Greenstein notes that the pyramid's base included the National Security Council. An "obscure functionary" of the NSC was Colonel Oliver North, a prime mover in the Iran-Contra scheme.[78] Nancy Reagan, who had supplied steel resolve when John Sears was fired as campaign manager during the 1980 primaries, now filled that role once again. Donald Regan was summarily fired.

If Roosevelt was too Machiavellian in his work with subordinates, Reagan was too trusting. Both men were poor in dealing with details. In the final years of their presidencies, neither man was at his best. Roosevelt was sixty-three years old when he died in 1945 and had been seriously ill for some time.[79] Reagan was seventy-seven when he left the presidency in 1989.

There have been questions as to whether the Alzheimer's disease that claimed President Reagan in 1994 may have affected the president during his White House years. Certainly, Ronald Reagan had slowed down some from his first term, when he took homework to the residence in the evenings and returned it with his comments written in the margins in the following mornings. But former senator Howard Baker (the new chief of staff) and the team he had assembled to replace Donald Regan made it a point to observe President Reagan before they finally committed to serve him. They wanted to make sure that he still had the capacity to carry out the constitutional duties of the most demanding job in the world. They found that he did.[80] Biographer Edmund Morris's review of Reagan's diaries comes to the same conclusion: there was no "hint of mental deterioration" toward the end of Reagan's second term.[81] Still, the president was then in his late seventies.

There is one other parallel between Presidents Roosevelt and Reagan. Both believed in personal diplomacy. The close bond between FDR and British prime minister Winston Churchill was a pillar in the U.K.-U.S. alliance. Churchill actually stayed in the family quarters at the White House when he was in Washington, sometimes for an extended period. While Reagan had a good relationship with Margaret Thatcher, it did not approach the closeness of the Churchill-Roosevelt friendship.

Roosevelt fared less well than Reagan in his relationship with the leader of the Soviet Union. Joseph Stalin was barely approachable and was determined to come out of the Second World War in control of Eastern Europe. FDR was ill when the two met at the summit in Yalta. The U.S. president has been criticized in retrospect for relying too much on his confidence in his ability to personally sway Stalin to his own goal of the end of imperialism and the enhancement of democracies. Reagan's opposite number, Mikhail Gorbachev, on the other hand, was receptive to Reagan's personal approach and realistic about the true economic and military strength of his country.

GOING OVER THEIR HEADS

Ronald Reagan, with his popularity at its lowest ebb after the Iran-Contra revelations, knew that he could not resolve his problems by try-ing to deal with the country's legislative leaders. Many of them differed with his approach to the "Evil Empire," disagreed with his tax policy, and were opposed to SDI. They had no incentive to let him off the hook of Iran-Contra. Opposition leaders saw that the scandal had, to some extent, restored the balance between the legislative and executive branches. Accordingly, Reagan moved into dramatic action. He put former NATO ambassador David Abshire in charge of the Iran-Contra matter, with cabinet rank. This was in response to a memo by aide Patrick Buchanan, counseling the president to provide for two administrative tracks, one engaged entirely with Iran-Contra, to "allow peak-period White House business to go forward in January uninterrupted by Iran issues."[82]

Although Attorney General Ed Meese and the Tower Commission investigated the matter, it was Abshire, carrying out his role in exemplary fashion, who enabled the executive branch to continue to function. The procedure was the opposite of the all-consuming Watergate cover-up that had destroyed the Nixon presidency. Reagan then did what few presidents have been able to do effectively in times of crisis. He spoke directly to the people.

Using the medium that he had mastered as had no president before him—television—Ronald Reagan spoke to the nation from the Oval Office: "A few months ago, I told the American people I did not trade arms for hostages. My heart and my best intentions still tell me that's true, but the facts and the evidence tell me it is not. As the Tower Board reported, what began as a strategic opening to Iran deteriorated, in its implementation, into trading arms for hostages. This runs counter to my own beliefs. There are reasons why it happened, but no excuses. It was a mistake."[83] The president took full responsibility. Overnight, his approval rating rose from 42 to 51 percent

A number of prominent voices maintained an ominous public clamor on disarmament policy. Soviet intransigence began to melt, however, and with it, much of Reagan's domestic opposition (e.g., Caspar Weinberger of his own cabinet and Nixon and Kissinger). A letter from Gorbachev now appeared to agree to a zero option for intermediate-range missiles. There was no doubt in George Shultz's mind about the reason for the change: "The creation of SDI," he noted, "has produced this [Soviet] proposal to reduce nuclear weapons to zero."[84]

Reagan did not soften his public stance. On June 12, 1987, he stood before the Brandenburg Gate. In one of the most memorable speeches in the history of the American presidency, he used this internationally televised event to address Mikhail Gorbachev directly: "General Secretary Gorbachev, if you seek peace, if you seek prosperity for the Soviet Union and Eastern Europe, if you seek liberalization: Come here to this gate! Mr. Gorbachev, open this gate! Mr. Gorbachev, tear down this wall!"[85]

Six months later, the American president met the Soviet premier in Washington, D.C., for their third summit. On December 8, 1987, the two leaders signed the INF Treaty, eliminating "an entire class of U.S. and Soviet nuclear missiles."[86] The Soviets gave way on positions they had held for years. American protestors had demanded a "nuclear freeze." Reagan had done them one better. Following the zero-option position he had advanced in 1981, the INF Treaty marked the first time in history that nations had agreed to destroy nuclear weapons rather than just slow down the arms race. Gorbachev called it a step toward the "demilitarization of human life."[87]

The American president's work was not over, however. The disarmament treaty was opposed by a significant number of senators, perhaps enough to defeat ratification. All congressmen and senators knew when they dealt with the president that he had carried their states in his reelection campaign. (The only exception was Minnesota, the home state of his 1984 opponent, Walter Mondale.) The White House contacted key congressional leaders and mounted an intensive media campaign. Reagan won the battle in May 1988 and signed the treaty.[88]

The fourth summit between the U.S. and Soviet leaders took place in Moscow that May. There were no major substantive accomplishments, but the momentum toward the START disarmament talks continued, as did the unwinding of the Soviet Union. Reagan delivered an address at Moscow State University in which he discussed freedom as "the continuing revolution of the marketplace. . . . It is the right to put forth an idea, scoffed at by the experts, and watch it catch fire among the people." The president was "extremely well-received in the Soviet capital."[89]

When Mikhail Gorbachev was invited to address the United Nations in New York City in December 1988, he asked President Reagan, then nearing the end of his administration, to join him there. Only two weeks before, that "most realistic of the cold warriors," Margaret Thatcher, had declared that the cold war was over.[90] While she had been among the first to advance the notion that Gorbachev was a "man with whom we can do business,"[91] she had no doubt about Reagan's role in the outcome. "He won the Cold War," she said, "without firing a shot."[92]

Not everyone gives Reagan credit for the collapse of the Soviet Union. Certainly, Pope John Paul II and others played major roles. Some observers single out Mikhail Gorbachev. Liberal activist Frances Fitzgerald, for example, writes that the "revolution [which led to the demise of the Soviet Union] was in essence a series of decisions made by one man," Gorbachev. Even so, Fitzgerald admits that while "it was Gorbachev who changed the Soviet Union . . . Reagan's 'embrace' of him as an individual was surely the most important contribution the United States made to the Soviet revolution until after the disintegration of the Warsaw Pact." Fitzgerald comments that "Reagan did not see exactly what he had done," ignoring Reagan's record of well-defined policy initiatives about the USSR.[93] She does not see any vision in Reagan's approach. In this view, she differs not only with George Shultz and Margaret Thatcher but with Mikhail Gorbachev.

In the course of their summits, the Soviet leader had come to recognize that there were some core positions that the American president would never abandon. This he viewed as Reagan's strength, and it was never more apparent than in their personal, head-to-head confrontations. Gorbachev confided to Anatoly Dobrynin, the perennial Soviet ambassador to the United States, that "Reagan was a visionary making 'great decisions.'"[94]

We have a tendency in discussing national policy to divide domestic and foreign matters into separate, watertight compartments. In her *Statecraft*, Margaret Thatcher assesses Reagan's vision as an integrated whole. "The conservative revolution spearheaded by Ronald Reagan," she writes, "and pushed by me in Britain and like-minded political leaders elsewhere, ensured that national economies were opened up to international competition."[95]

In 1989, Ronald Reagan left office with a 68 percent approval rating, the highest of any postwar president at the end of his term.[96]

A CELEBRATION

On June 3, 1985, a luncheon was held at the General Electric headquarters, now located in Fairfield County, Connecticut.[97] The guest of honor was Lemuel Boulware, then ninety years old. At the time, the Boulwares were still renting a home each summer in Greenwich. The party was the brainchild of Art Puccini, a former GE vice president who was one of those who had followed Boulware in the job of VP for public and labor relations. Puccini found that all of Boulware's successors were still alive and invited them to the luncheon.

Jack S. Parker, who had risen to the position of vice chairman of the board, was there. Virgil Day, who had held the job but left for a tour of public service in Washington and then gone on to a highly successful career as a labor lawyer, was present, as were John Burlingham and Frank Doyle, the latter having been given the job of "dismantling Boulwarism" after Boulware's departure. Doyle had found much to preserve, however, and had used Boulware's communication and education programs effectively.

At the end of the luncheon, amidst nostalgia and toasts, Art Puccini rose and read a "Dear Lem" letter from the president, who commented that "Nancy and I will be thinking of you on June 3, as we always do, with affection."[98] A surprise guest—who was not one of Boulware's successors in the vice presidency for employee relations—was GE's dynamic CEO Jack Welch. Typically, he didn't mince any words when it came his time to speak. He observed that he had not known Boulware during his years of service with GE but since then had "met and loved Lem." He raised his glass toward the guest of honor. His words formed the ultimate rehabilitation of the old prophet in his own company.[99]

On November 7, 1990, Lemuel Boulware died at his home in Delray Beach, Florida. At the time of his death, he was virtually unknown to the general public. The *New York Times* published a three-column lead obituary, but to most readers it must have seemed ancient history.[100] After all, Boulware had lived for almost a century. The term "Boulwarism" gave him an immortality of sorts. Still, the word is known today largely among labor lawyers and readers of law reviews.

Ronald Reagan was keenly aware of the role that the GE years and his mentor Lemuel Boulware had played in the development of his agenda and political skills and in his ultimate achievement of the highest office. Among Boulware's collected papers, there is a photograph of Reagan's first inauguration. It is inscribed in the president's own hand.[101] One can imagine Boulware, in his final year, when a stroke and a debilitating illness had finally slowed him down, taking the photo from his desk drawer occasionally and scanning the inscription, which reads: "Thanks to your help this moment was possible."

APPENDIX

═══════════

SPEECHES OF REUTHER, BOULWARE, AND REAGAN

The appended speeches have been referred to in the course of the book. They are given in full here because they spell out in detail what the speakers believed and what they hoped to accomplish. Their style may seem strange in this era of sound bites and misinformation. But in their time, these words defined a great contest, and the men who uttered them moved a nation.

APPENDIX

==========

LABOR AND THE COMMUNITY

WALTER P. REUTHER

HOWARD UNIVERSITY
MAY 13, 1947

It is a sign of American labor's increasing maturity that greater and greater sections of it are realizing that unions can no longer operate as narrow pressure groups, concerned only with their own selfish interests. The test of democratic trade unionism in a democratic society is its willingness to lead the fight for the welfare of the whole community. To a continuously increasing degree, American labor is meeting that test today.

This approach to labor's relation to the rest of the community has always been inherent in basic trade union philosophy but much of the time in the past it has been submerged in and subordinated to the struggle of workers to organize, to make their organizations secure and to meet, often from short-sighted point of view, the problems that an even more short-sighted industrial and business management threw in their path.

These "notes" for the address have been obtained from and printed here with permission of the Archives of Labor and Urban Affairs, University Archives, Wayne State University, Detroit, Michigan.

In the last decade or more, labor's awareness of its relation to the rest of the community has been brought to the surface and given concrete expression by a complex interplay of a large number of social and economic forces.

One of these was the development of industrial organization which brought into the labor movement millions of semi-skilled and unskilled workers and established effective collective bargaining for the first time in America's vast mass production industries.

It had been possible for highly skilled workers in some crafts to gain limited advantages and some security, although a temporary and uncertain security, through a narrow, selfish approach to their own particular problems. Hence we had, and still have in some instances, craft unions which restrict competition for jobs in their trades through high initiation fees and dues, through discrimination because of race or color or creed or through other anti-social methods.

By its very nature, industrial unionism cannot tolerate such practices. Complete and effective organization of mass production industries demands low initiation fees and dues; it rules out racial discrimination; it rules out any practice that would make any worker ineligible for membership or which would restrict his participation in union activities.

By the same token, industrial unionism cannot accept and try to adapt itself to an economy of scarcity with its periodic depressions and mass unemployment. That would be suicide for unionism, if not for the economy. Industrial unionism must necessarily fight for an economy of abundance, of full production, full employment and full consumption.

A union, or even the whole o[f] organized labor, cannot fight for that kind of economy for its members alone. A permanent, healthy prosperity, like peace, is indivisible. Its beneficiaries must be all sections of the community, all sections of the Nation—farmers, small business men, professional people, white collar workers and industrial workers; they must be of all races, colors and creeds.

At the same time that labor's interest has turned to the welfare of the whole economy, its concern has broadened to more than just the shop problems of the wages, hours and working conditions of its members. A happy and prosperous people and nation call for adequate housing, medical aid that is available to all, better educational facilities and opportunities for our children.

Labor cannot fight for better housing in the nation or in the community just for union members. It has to fight for better housing for all who need it and it has to fight for it with the rest of the community.

Labor cannot fight for more adequate medical aid just for the children of its members.

Those are projects in which the whole community has a vital concern and for which the whole community must fight, with labor working as an important and integral section of the community.

2.

The most dramatic and concrete example of labor's concern for the welfare of the whole community has been its fight against inflation and for an economy of lasting prosperity.

Beginning with the struggle of the General Motors workers immediately after V-J Day, labor has fought a two-front battle to keep the nation's purchasing power at a high enough level to insure full employment, full production and full employment. It is a battle not only for higher wages but for lower prices so that the whole community and the whole nation can benefit.

The General Motors workers completely abandoned the traditional attitude of pressure groups who say, "Let's get ours and to hell with everybody else." They demanded that the General Motors Corporation pay wage increases without increasing the prices of its products to consumers generally. And they declared that if General Motors could show that it was unable to pay the full amount of the wage increase demanded without increasing prices, they would scale their demand down to what the corporation could pay without price increase. General Motors never accepted that challenge but the case of the GM workers was upheld by a special Presidential Fact Finding Committee which said that not only General Motors but the whole automobile industry could pay a $19^1/_2$ cents an hour wage increase without increasing prices.

In the past year practically all of labor has waged a vigorous fight for greater purchasing power for all consumers through its fight not only to prevent price increases but to bring about general price reductions.

Labor has recognized that what is important is not the amount of dollars in the pay envelope each week but how much food, clothing and services those dollars will buy. It has recognized that other consumers must be able to buy the products of industry if industrial workers are to be employed.

Labor's fight for greater purchasing power for all instead of higher wages for the few will continue. It is a concrete expression of labor's realization that its welfare is tied in directly with that of the rest of the community. It knows that no one section of the community can make progress permanently at the expense of other sections. We must all progress together if we are to progress at all.

3·

Labor's approach to race relations is dictated by the same forces which have determined its relation to the rest of the community.

The artificial barriers of race, color and religion have been obstacles in the way of achieving an economy of abundance and a sound, healthy prosperity. They must be removed.

Industrial workers have already learned the elementary lesson that a wage differential between Negro and white workers on the same job is a threat to the wage standards of all, and in the automobile industry those differentials have been eliminated.

They are learning by the same reasoning that the segregation of Negro workers into the unskilled, lowest paid, most disagreeable jobs or the complete denial of job opportunities to Negroes because of their race are equally as serious threats to the living standards of all workers.

In its fight along with the rest of the community for better housing, medical aid, more adequate educational facilities and opportunities, labor has learned that it must fight for the same standards for Negroes or else the standards of all will suffer. And it has learned that the same standards cannot be maintained if segregation is permitted to exist.

It has learned that Jim Crow's roots are economic and the Jim Crow is a drag on the progress of white workers as well as Negro workers.

But while we fight for these long range goals, we cannot and do not neglect the immediate problems. While we fight for full employment, we must also fight for legislation to enforce fair employment practices. While we fight for better housing, better schools and medical aid for all, we must fight for abolition of the poll tax so that the disfranchised Negro and white workers of the Southern states can have full political expression and add their political strength to the achievement of those goals.

With this approach in mind, we have in the UAW-CIO a Fair Practices and Anti-Discrimination department which not only conducts a long range educational program for tolerance, but does the day-to-day job of correcting and eliminating instances of discrimination wherever they may arise in the industry or within the union itself.

4·

There is a part missing to this picture of an interrelated, interdependent democratic community.

That is the development of a sense of social responsibility on the part of big business to match the growing sense of social responsibility on the part of labor and other sections of the community.

No better illustration of this lack of responsibility by industry can be found today than industry's resistance to appeals from practically all other quarters that it reduce prices before it is too late in order to avoid a depression.

Industry's determination to milk all it can from a seller's market, regardless of the consequences to the economy and to the rest of the nation, is a frightening display of the most reckless kind of irresponsibility. It is willing to gamble the welfare of the whole nation in order to collect exorbitant and outrageous profits in a brief period of boom when the wiser course for both business and the nation would be to maintain continuous and stead prosperity even though current profits would be lower.

A comparatively few large, monopolistic corporations dominate [the] American economy. The welfare of 130,000,000 people depends upon policies and actions decided upon by the handful of people who control those corporations. Yet this handful has no responsibility to the public and only a limited responsibility to the government. In theory they are responsible to the stockholders. In actual practice, they are responsible only to themselves.

The continuation of a free society in America and in the world depends upon the development of a sense of social responsibility by industry. America offers the greatest opportunity for the development of a truly free democracy, both an economic and political democracy. We cannot have such a democracy unless industry acquires a social consciousness. If it is imposed upon industry by legislation or governmental fiat, then we have abandoned our free society. Our only weapon is the force of public opinion. The use of that weapon to compel industry to accept and meet its responsibilities to the rest of the Nation is the principal problem of labor and the community today.

====

SALVATION IS NOT FREE

LEMUEL BOULWARE

HARVARD UNIVERSITY
JUNE 11, 1949

Every one of you must already be a pronounced success in your business or profession—successful in what has long been thought was the principal, and maybe only, field [or] activity for which society held you individually responsible.

But I assume you share my embarrassed realization that we here—and others like us everywhere—must not have been doing our whole duty.

What's the evidence [that] we—and too many other[s] like us—have not been doing this whole duty?

The evidence is clear. It's the too-common economic illiteracy among us businessmen, among our employees and their families and neighbors, and among the representatives of all of us in government, in unions, in education, in the clergy, and elsewhere.

In *The Truth About Boulwarism*, 159–67, Lemuel Boulware appends these remarks and describes them as excerpts from his 1949 Harvard speech "which may still be significant."

Too many of us just do not understand how we got this standard of living that's the envy of the rest of the world.

Too many of us working, and buying, and voting adults just don't understand the parts played by the customer, the worker, the manager, as well as the saver . . . that each of these has a necessary part to play, but not one of them can play it, or will even try, unless the incentive is there, unless he thinks he is going to get what's right from the others for what he does.

The penalty for such economic ignorance can be—is already—very great in both the economic and political fields. Our free markets and our free persons are at stake.

We don't like the proposals for further greatly enlarged government expenditures now being urged on the public by a combination of government and union officials.

The size of taxes—now and proposed—is bad enough.

But the manner of their collection is disgracefully worse—is infinitely more ominous for our whole future as well as for the future of any free market and any free person—for our taxes are now being based on political rather than economic considerations.

We see all this unsound program being misrepresented, "sold" to the public, if you will—by the public's own representatives in government and in unions—as though it were a free service by a great and wealthy and indulgent government. And we see our government keep trying to give the impression to the vast majority of citizens that it can get the money from somebody else—right while the costs of the current so-called "free" benefits are at the very moment being taken directly and indirectly out of the pockets of the whole public—from you and me—from all our employees—from everybody.

The costs are being collected from everybody in the taxes the government hides in consumer prices . . . in the inflation, from deficit spending and unsound monetary practices, which also turn right up in consumer prices . . . in the prices that are higher than they would be, even under these circumstances, if it had not become "the thing to do" to tax unfairly, and otherwise be hostile to, the income and savings of the very people who would finance more arm-lengthening equipment and methods to make bigger real values available in every store.

Despite these real causes, we see the profits and other supposed inhumanities of businessmen or their corporations all the while being blamed for high prices—for supposedly keeping the worker from getting back more of what he produces.

There are other things we don't like—other things that are frightening—in the public's misinformation and consequent vulnerability to current economic and political demagoguery.

We all believe, of course, that good unions are possible and have a useful function they can perform in the employee and public interest. We have had ample evidence of how wise government representatives can promote that free play of incentives and rewards which brings a higher standard of living.

But we are horrified at the way representatives, both in government and in unions, so frequently say and do things they—as well as we—know to be economically unsound.

We can hardly believe our eyes when we see the platforms of our two major parties incorporating just about the same unsound economics—just about the same something-for-nothing promises.

There seems never, never any honest explanation that all of us pay the bill, and pay it soon, if not immediately. We've got to learn that—in government programs as elsewhere—there isn't any such thing as "a free lunch." I think we have maybe got to get something like the Better Business Bureau after our office holders and politicians—low and high—in all parties.

If it were not for what we see along this line over here in America, we would be hard-put to explain why the British Conservative Party platform for next year is so shockingly close to being economically the same as the British Socialist Labor Party platform.

The plain fact is that most all politicians in all parties and all lands—no matter what their private convictions on economic matters—think that the majority of adults everywhere are so misinformed that they not only believe "something-for-nothing" is really possible, but demand it. They think the public just would not understand or support them if they spoke and acted soundly.

Hence so many public leaders openly espouse and support unsound schemes. For years, from within our own government has come a persistent endorsement and following of such unsound and demagogic ideas—so much so as to be an actual attack from within on the very free economic and political system our officials are sworn to defend and protect. You all may know—as I do—government and union officials who are appalled, even frightened, at what they find themselves saying and doing in order to fit in with public ignorance of economic facts.

But I suspect our greatest consternation—our deepest distress of all—is over the low estate in which we businessmen find ourselves before our employees and the public.

Here we are—with incredible achievements to show for our management of the business side of our wonderful system of freedoms, incentives, and competition.

We are great physicists, chemists, engineers. We are phenomenal manufacturers. We have been fabulous financiers. We are superb in individual selling and mass marketing.

People like—and respect—the results of our separate professional skills.

But taken as the whole man of business, each of us is too likely to be condemned by a majority of the public as anti-social. We always seem to be coldly against everything—never seem to know clearly what are the good objectives we *claim* to be seeking—never seem to be willing or able to speak up warmly and convincingly to prove that what we are doing is for the common good.

As a result, too many of our employees and too many of their friends and representatives—in unions, in government, among educators and clergy, in the whole public—in other words too many of our real bosses—not only do not respect us but also do not like us. They do not understand or appreciate what we are trying to do. And let's be frank about it—there are times when it looks like *we* don't, either.

Too many people just don't think that the jobs we provide are what they ought to be. They don't think that the economic and social consequences of our activities, and the system back of our activities, are what they ought to be for the good of each community and of the nation.

They do not even credit us with good intentions toward them—with being on their side—whereas we thoroughly believe that being on their side is being on the side of what's good for all.

They even doubt our honesty and competence in this broader economic and social field—where they have been led to believe some magic, some escape from the rules of arithmetic, is possible.

Hence, our participation is not sought—or even tolerated—in important public affairs.

It has become popular, and therefore politically expedient, to heap injustices upon us, and even to put limitations on our carrying out what people want us to do for them.

Yet we are the same people who give those very folks, who distrust us, the products and prices and responsible guarantees which they have proved they trust and like—proved in the hundreds of millions of individual instances of daily customer preferences in millions of separate free markets.

We have got to admit that our business system and our businessmen have produced a fantastic fairyland of well-being . . . especially when we think of the new burdens we are carrying and when we think of what is now, or has ever been, possible anywhere else in the world. But people are being taught to look right at this and not see it—to see something different and *bad*.

How do people all over the world get this way? Why do they reject businessmen, who have a fine record of raising the standard of living through voluntary action inspired by the incentive to save and to compete? Why do so many choose, instead, the government planners—skimming off for state purposes everything above a bare subsistence standard of living—and with their inevitable necessity in the end, directly or indirectly, of having to shut off free choice and free speech in order that their planning failure will be masked?

This can only be the fault of us businessmen ourselves. We have been looking right at this new kind of robber barons who have gotten more and more successful elsewhere out around the world during the last thirty years. They always get themselves cloaked in the mantle of the common man. But their objective is power—and power direct rather than through money. Their methods are therefore political and not commercial.

Businessmen, unthinkingly continuing to devote themselves purely to the customary commercial pursuits, where their only skill has been, have meanwhile in country after country been gradually weakened and then displaced. Along with their displacement went freedom—for all the people—freedom and any hope of human dignity, plenty, and the good life.

This can only prove that just too pitifully few businessmen had the alertness to know when they were pushed beyond the commercial field into the political arena. And when they did awaken to their state, too few businessmen seemingly had the courage, or intelligence, or energy to go about correcting misinformation and teaching sound economics.

Yet when most businessmen face essentially this exact type of spurious emotional attacks and something-for-nothing appeals in the commercial field, they have no trouble or the slightest hesitancy in dealing with them devastatingly.

We businessmen are bold and imaginative before commercial competitors.

We are cowardly and silent in public when confronted with union and other economic and political doctrines contrary to our beliefs.

Incidentally, a distinguished professor recently told me that he was beginning to believe that the missing ingredient in the businessman's employee relations, community relations, and public relations is summed up in the one word "politics"—not *party* politics, of course, but private and public political action by managers, farmers, stockholders, bond holders, insurance policy holders, savings bank depositors, pensioners, and any other upstanding citizens with an interest in keeping the value of money honest, the standard of living rising, and the freedom of choice, speech, worship, and movement really free—in other words, the insistence by citizens on the mastery of sound economics by themselves and then on sound economic teaching and practices by their representative in government, in unions, even in education and the clergy, as well as in business.

We have got to get just as aroused and just as active about all kinds of socialists as we are about the communist brand of socialist. Our real danger is that, while we are scared to death of communism, too many of us seemingly haven't even come to fear socialism at all. The intentions of communists are, of course, the ultimate in the wrong direction. But the potentialities for evil of the socialists—who are careful not to be known as such—are just out of this world, and simply because we are not alerted at all.

Fortune sagely points out that "a democratic government can corrupt an unvigilant people" because of the failure of "so many of its citizens to act on or even fully understand two basic, timeless facts:

1. In the long run the government can give them only what it takes out of their pockets, and
2. Sometimes the government may seem to be doing many of them good when it is only debauching and corrupting them all."

... A vivid but hard lesson that's right at the core of what we have got to learn about representation in government and unions and other organizations—is that leaders are just not often leaders any more. They are followers. They do, and are supposed to do, what the folks back home—or the people represented—want done, regardless of the ignorance that prompts those wants.

If we want bad—or even good—leaders to do what is right economically and politically, we must see that a majority of us, *as citizens at the grass roots*—know what is right economically, do what is accordingly right within the area of our own economic and political activities, and then get and stay forcefully articulate—in private and public—in getting our representatives in government, unions, and elsewhere to act with economic and political horse-sense.

Let's keep in mind that communism and socialism have only recently—and erroneously—come to be thought of by the public as two different things. Communism is just a slight variant of socialism, as were facism and nazism, and is now the British type which is just communism a little less brutal, a little more gentlemanly yet, and in not so much of a hurry.

Our great problem in this country—and the world—is to learn the economic fallacies of the whole socialist theory—and then to act accordingly to keep people from being fooled and pauperized and silenced and enslaved, and to keep our great nation—as we know and love it—from going on the ash-heap of history.

A really free people can live well materially and spiritually where there is the incentive to work, create, compete, save, invest, and profit.

But there must be either force to *drive* men to work. Or there must be incentive to make men *want* to work.

It's "the carrot or the stick"—now, as in all history of man or other animal. And that applies to each of us right here in this room.

People that start out free—with no force over them, but also with no incentive—will starve in any organized society having a subdivision of effort—any society except in that modern-times impossible one where each person serves all his own wants.

Let's watch our British friends to see what happens in their experiment. Probably the only thing that can save British socialism is for us in America to stay strong enough to keep helping them—for us not to debilitate ourselves by continuing our drift into that same socialism. In other words, the recipients of free drinks in this international barroom of socialism have got to see that the American bartender doesn't become a drunk, too.

Meanwhile, what do we have to do to be saved here? What can management do to promote sound economic understanding and resulting sound public action?

We have simply got to learn, and preach, and practice what's the good alternative to socialism. And we have to to [sic] interpret this to a majority of adults in a way that is understandable and credible and attractive.

What we have to do is show the worker and farmer and other citizen that profitable, competitive business does more for him now, and offers the promise of more of the things he wants in the future, than do any of the unsound substitutes being put forward.

So what we really have to do is only just exactly, and faithfully, and every bit as we do when we encounter any other unfair or dishonest salesman out with an unsound product trying to compete for our good customer's favor.

In fact, I'll bet all you honorable and experienced businessmen here hope for no greater blessing than that your competitors will show up as liars and with bad products.

You know that a few—or many—customers may be fooled for a while. But you also know that if you keep your product honest, and if you keep warmly plugging the truth to those customers, you will keep most of them and soon get the rest back.

We have become sophisticated in the product field—we don't expect to get something for nothing or, as businessmen, to have to offer it. Millions of man-days of hard and honest selling have done that for us.

We have become just as sensible and sophisticated in the field of morals. A few husbands will fall for the harlots, but about 99.44 percent of the time the wife today triumphs over the mistress. That's the triumph of millions upon millions of character lessons taught at the mother's knee, or at church, or in the hard knocks of life.

With triumphs like these—in the very difficult fields of products and morals—to show what we can do when we really try, there is just no sense in our having the slightest hesitancy in taking on the selling of whatever our study together teaches us to be the sound, and honest, and good, and richly rewarding economic program that's really the one for us all here in America.

Just as in the case of any parents facing up finally to telling the truth about Santa Claus, we are quite likely to be worse off in some quarters before beginning to be better off.

Even if the employee—and his family and neighbors—feel he has got the best pay, best working conditions, and best boss in town—if he feels his boss and company have been literally "born again," are on his side, and are really putting human considerations first—it still isn't enough.

He goes into the grocery or other store, finds prices that seem outlandishly high. In a flash, this seems to confirm a lot he has been told—told by the agents of those very ones who have been doing the diluting of the money and causing the high prices while blaming businessmen.

He concludes that the grocer—and his own boss back at the shop—are the representatives of a system that is not being operated by people on his side, but by people who are against him—who are maybe even exploiting him, as claimed.

His family and neighbors are too likely to conclude the same.

Unfortunately, the facts will not speak for themselves in this area any more than they will in the commercial area. The facts have got first to be good—but then they have got to be constantly pointed out and explained and repeated to him—just as the commercial customer has to be both initially sold and then kept constantly reminded.

For us to accomplish this—and have a favorable climate for our further operations—the public has got to be helped to understand the rudiments of sound economics, and then the public has got to have itself and its representatives be guided by the sound principles of economics so learned.

This is a big and hard job. But we think it can be done, and that it's got to be done if business management—in fact, [i]f our free system of incentives and competition, is to survive.

But this is no job for *one* company or for the employers and other good citizens in a *few* communities. It's the job for every businessman—every citizen—to go back to school on economics individually, in small groups, in big groups . . . to learn from simple text books, from organized courses, from individual discussions with business associates, in neighborhood groups, at the club or bar, on the train or bus.

Let's learn again that socialism is just communism in not so *much* of a hurry—but in *quite* a hurry.

Let's appreciate again how silence and lack of sophistication by us businessmen and other free enterprisers in the last thirty years have guaranteed the coming of the things that now terrify us.

Let's consider the tragedy—and the peril—in how pitifully few of us in management at the moment are really competent to do anything about it—have the energy and courage to be even trying!

The current rapid trend has got to be changed, or we are through with every good thing we cherish.

And we businessmen have got to do the job. It will not be done by others—we are the only ones left to do it.

So—let's do it.

Let's here at this moment covenant together that we ourselves—without waiting for any others—are now individually going to make the start . . . that we are each going to study until we understand this wonderful system of ours . . . that we are going to find out how to preserve and improve it rather than let it be damaged or even perish along with our free market and our free persons . . . that we are going to do our part in seeing that a majority of citizens understand the economic facts of life, the proper working of our system toward its good ends, and the fallacy of all these contrary something-for-nothing fairy tales . . . that we ourselves are then going to act with economic and political horse-sense in our daily business and personal lives, and that we are publicly going to encourage an increasing majority of citizens to insist very vocally on their representatives acting with the same economic and political horse-sense toward the greatest and surest further attainment of our material and spiritual needs and desires.

And let us businessmen stop being Nervous Nellies about this! There is no such thing as a humiliating defeat in a just cause. And, anyhow, let's go at this job fearlessly—recognizing that mightier than armies is the power of a righteous idea whose time has come.

So let's boldly take—and continue from there on—the leadership that's expected of people like us in this patriot's job of standing up, speaking out, and being counted—no matter who has to be contradicted!

A TIME FOR CHOOSING ("THE SPEECH")

RONALD REAGAN

LOS ANGELES, CALIFORNIA
OCTOBER 27, 1964

I am going to talk of controversial things. I make no apology for this. I have been talking on this subject for ten years, obviously under the administration of both parties. I mention this only because it seems impossible to legitimately debate the issues of the day without being subjected to name-calling and the application of labels. Those who deplore use of the terms "pink" and "leftist" are themselves guilty of branding all who oppose their liberalism as right wing extremists. How long can we afford the luxury of this family fight when we are at war with the most dangerous enemy ever known to man?

If we lose that war, and in so doing lose our freedom, it has been said history will record with the greatest astonishment that those who had the

Ronald Reagan delivered this speech during his years with GE and thereafter and on behalf of Republican presidential candidate Barry Goldwater in 1964. He continued to give variations of The Speech after 1964. This version, which is appended to his 1965 autobiography, *Where's the Rest of Me?*, does not mention candidate Goldwater.

most to lose did the least to prevent its happening. The guns are silent in this war but frontiers fall while those who should be warriors prefer neutrality. Not too long ago two friends of mine were talking to a Cuban refugee. He was a business man who had escaped from Castro. In the midst of his tale of horrible experiences, one of my friends turned to the other and said, "We don't know how lucky we are." The Cuban stopped and said, "How lucky you are! I had some place to escape to." And in that sentence he told the entire story. If freedom is lost here there is no place to escape to.

It's time we asked ourselves if we still know the freedoms intended for us by the Founding Fathers. James Madison said, "We base all our experiments on the capacity of mankind for self-government." This idea that government was beholden to the people, that it had no other source of power except the sovereign people, is still the newest most unique idea in all the long history of man's relation to man. For almost two centuries we have proved man's capacity for self-government, but today we are told we must choose between a left and right or, as others suggest, a third alternative, a kind of safe middle ground. I suggest to you there is no left or right, only an up or down. Up to the maximum of individual freedom consistent with law and order, or down to the ant heap of totalitarianism; and regardless of their humanitarian purpose those who would sacrifice freedom for security have, whether they know it or not, chosen this downward path. Plutarch warned, "The real destroyer of the liberties of the people is he who spreads among them bounties, donations and benefits."

Today there is an increasing number who can't see a fat man standing beside a thin one without automatically coming to the conclusion the fat man got that way by taking advantage of the thin one. So they would seek the answer to all the problems of human need through government. Howard K. Smith of television fame has written, "The profit motive is outmoded. It must be replaced by the incentives of the welfare state." He says, "The distribution of goods must be effected by a planned economy."

Another articulate spokesman for the welfare state defines liberalism as meeting the material needs of the masses through the full power of centralized government. I for one find it disturbing when a representative refers to the free men and women of this country as the masses, but beyond this the full power of centralized government was the very thing the Founding Fathers sought to minimize. They knew you don't control things; you can't control the economy without controlling people. So we have come to a time for choosing. Either we accept the responsibility for our own destiny, or we abandon the American Revolution and confess that an intellectual belief in a far-distant capitol can plan our lives for us better than we can plan them ourselves.

Already the hour is late. Government has laid its hand on health, housing, farming, industry, commerce, education, and, to an ever increasing degree, interferes with the people's right to know. Government tends to grow; government programs take on weight and momentum, as public servants say, always with the best of intentions, "What greater service we could render if only we had a little more money and a little more power." But the truth is that outside of its legitimate function, a government does nothing as well or as economically as the private sector of the economy. What better example do we have of this than government's involvement in the farm economy over the last thirty years. One-fourth of farming has seen a steady decline in the per capita consumption of everything it produces. That one-fourth is regulated and subsidized by government.

In contrast, the three-fourths of farming unregulated and unsubsidized has seen a 21 per cent increase in the per capita consumption of all its produce. Since 1955 the cost of the farm program has nearly doubled. Direct payment to farmers is eight times as great as it was nine years ago, but farm income remains unchanged while farm surplus is bigger. In that same period we have seen a decline of five million in the farm population, but an increase in the number of Department of Agriculture employees.

There is now one such employee for every 30 farms in the United States, and still they can't figure how 66 shiploads of grain headed for Austria could disappear without a trace, and Billy Sol Estes never left shore. Three years ago the government put into effect a program to curb the over-production of feed grain. Now, $2.5 billion later, the corn crop is 100 million bushels bigger than before the program started. And the cost of the program prorates out to $43 for every dollar bushel of corn we don't grow. Nor is this the only example of the price we pay for government meddling. Some government programs with the passage of time take on a sacrosanct quality.

One such considered above criticism, sacred as motherhood, is TVA. This program started as a flood control project; the Tennessee Valley was periodically ravaged by destructive floods. The Army Engineers set out to solve this problem. They said that it was possible that once in 500 years there could be a total capacity flood that would inundate some 600,000 acres. Well, the engineers fixed that. They made a permanent lake which inundated a million acres. This solved the problem of the floods, but the annual interest on the TVA debt is five times as great as the annual flood damage they sought to correct.

Of course, you will point out that TVA gets electric power from the impounded waters, and this is true, but today 85 per cent of TVA's electricity is generated in coal burning steam plants. Now perhaps you'll charge that I'm overlooking the navigable waterway that was created, providing cheap barge traffic, but the bulk of the freight barged on that waterway is coal being shipped to the TVA steam plants, and the cost of maintaining that channel each year would pay for shipping all of the coal by rail, and there would be money left over.

One last argument remains: The prosperity produced by such large programs of government spending. Certainly there are few areas where more spending has taken place. The Labor Department lists 50 per cent of the 169 counties in the Tennessee Valley as permanent areas of poverty, distress, and unemployment.

Meanwhile, back in the city, under Urban Renewal, the assault on freedom carries on. Private property rights have become so diluted that public interest is anything a few planners decide it should be. In Cleveland, Ohio, to get a project under way, city officials reclassified eighty-four buildings as substandard in spite of the fact their own inspectors had previously pronounced these buildings sound. The owners stood by and watched 26 million dollars worth of property as it was destroyed by the headache ball. Senate Bill 628 says: "Any property, be it home or commercial structure, can be declared slum or blighted and the owner has no recourse at law. The Law Division of the Library of Congress and the General Accounting Office have said that the Courts will have to rule against the owner."

Housing. In one key Eastern city a man owning a blighted area sold his property to Urban Renewal for several million dollars. At the same time, he submitted his own plan for the rebuilding of this area and the government sold him back his own property for 22 per cent of what they paid. Now the government announces, "We are going to build subsidized housing in the thousands where we have been building in the hundreds." At the same time FHA and the Veterans Administration reveal they are holding 120 thousand housing units reclaimed from mortgage foreclosure, mostly because the low down payment and the easy terms brought the owners to a point where they realized the unpaid balance on the homes amounted to a sum greater than the homes were worth, so they just walked out the front door, possibly to take up residence in newer subsidized housing, again with little or no down payment and easy terms.

Some of the foreclosed homes have already been bulldozed into the earth, others it has been announced, will be refurbished and put on sale for down payments as low as $100 and thirty-five years to pay. This will give the bulldozers a second crack. It is in the area of social welfare that government has found its most fertile growing bed. So many of us accept our responsibility for those less fortunate. We are susceptible to humanitarian appeals.

Federal welfare spending is today ten times greater than it was in the dark depths of the Depression. Federal, state, and local welfare combined spend 45 billion dollars a year. Now the government has announced that 20 per cent, some 9.3 million families are poverty-stricken on the basis that they have less than a $3,000 a year income.

If this present welfare spending was prorated equally among these poverty stricken families, we could give each family more than $4,500 a year. Actually, direct aid to the poor averages less than $600 per family. There must be some administrative overhead somewhere. Now, are we to believe that another billion dollar program added to the half a hundred programs and the 45 billion dollars, will, through some magic, end poverty? For three decades we have tried to solve unemployment by government planning, without success. The more the plans fail, the more planners plan.

The latest is the Area Redevelopment Agency, and in two years less than one-half of one per cent of the unemployed could attribute new jobs to this agency, and the cost to the taxpayer for each job found was $5,000. But beyond the great bureaucratic waste, what are we doing to the people we seek to help?

Recently a judge told me of an incident in his court. A fairly young woman, with six children, pregnant with her seventh, came to him for a divorce. Under his questioning it became apparent her husband did not share this desire. Then the whole story came out. Her husband was a laborer earning $350 a month. By divorcing him she could get an $80 raise. She was eligible for $350 a month from the Aid to Dependent Children Program. She had been talked into the divorce by two friends who had already done this very thing. But any time we question the schemes of the do-gooders, we are denounced as being opposed to their humanitarian goal. It seems impossible to legitimately debate their solutions with the assumption that all of us share the desire to help those less fortunate. They tell us we are always against, never for anything. Well, it isn't so much that liberals are ignorant. It's just that they know so much that isn't so.

We are for a provision that destitution should not follow unemployment by reason of old age. For that reason we have accepted Social Security as a step toward meeting that problem. However, we are against the irresponsibility of those who charge that any criticism or suggested improvement of the program means we want to end payment to those who depend on Social Security for a livelihood.

Fiscal Irresponsibility. We have been told in millions of pieces of litera-ture and press releases that Social Security is an insurance program, but the executives of Social Security appeared before the Supreme Court in the case of *Nestor v. Fleming* and proved to the Court's satisfaction that it is not in-surance but is a welfare program, and Social Security dues are a tax for the general use of the government. Well it can't be both: insurance and welfare. Later, appearing before a Congressional Committee, they admitted that So-cial Security is today 298 billion dollars in the red. This fiscal irresponsibil-ity has already caught up with us.

Faced with a bankruptcy we find that today a young man in his early twenties, going to work at less than an average salary, will with his em-ployer, pay into Social Security an amount which could provide the young man with a retirement insurance policy guaranteeing $220 a month at age 65, and the government promises him $127.

Now are we so lacking in business sense that we cannot put this program on a sound actuarial basis, so that those who do depend on it won't come to the cupboard and find it bare, and at the same time can't we introduce vol-untary features so that those who can make better provision for themselves are allowed to do so? Incidentally, we might also allow participants in Social Security to name their own beneficiaries, which they cannot do in the pres-ent program. These are not insurmountable problems.

Youth Aid Plans. We have today 30 million workers protected by indus-trial and union pension funds that are soundly financed by some 70 billion dollars invested in corporate securities and income-earning real estate. I think we are for telling our senior citizens that no one in this country should be denied medical care for lack of funds, but we are against forcing all citi-zens into a compulsory government program regardless of need. Now the government has turned its attention to our young people, and suggests that it can solve the problem of school dropouts and juvenile delinquency through some kind of revival of the old C.C.C. camps. The suggested plan prorates out to a cost of $4,700 a year for each young person we want to help. We can send them to Harvard for $2,700 a year. Of course, don't get me wrong—I'm not suggesting Harvard as the answer to juvenile delinquency.

We are for an international organization where the nations of the world can legitimately seek peace. We are against subordinating American inter-ests to an organization so structurally unsound that a two-thirds majority can be mastered in the U.N. General Assembly among nations representing less than 10 per cent of the world population.

Is there not something of hypocrisy in assailing our allies for so-called vestiges of colonialism while we engage in a conspiracy of silence about the peoples enslaved by the Soviet in the satellite nations? We are for aiding our allies by sharing our material blessings with those nations which share our fundamental beliefs. We are against doling out money, government to government, which ends up financing socialism all over the world.

We set out to help nineteen war-ravaged countries at the end of World War II. We are now helping 107. We have spent 146 billion dollars. Some of that money bought a $2 million yacht for Haile Selassie. We bought dress suits for Greek undertakers. We bought one thousand TV sets, with 23-inch screens, for a country where there is no electricity, and some of our foreign aid funds provided extra wives for Kenya government officials. When Congress moved to cut foreign aid they were told that if they cut it one dollar they endangered national security, and then Senator Harry Byrd revealed that since its inception foreign aid has rarely spent its allotted budget. It has today $21 billion in unexpended funds.

Some time ago Dr. Howard Kershner was speaking to the Prime Minister of Lebanon. The Prime Minister told him proudly that his little country balanced its budget each year. It had no public debt, no inflation, a modest tax rate and had increased its gold holdings from $70 to $120 million. When he finished, Dr. Kershner said, "Mr. Prime Minister, my country hasn't balanced its budget 28 out of the last 40 years. My country's debt is greater than the combined debt of all the nations of the world. We have inflation, and we have a tax rate that takes from the private sector a percentage of income greater than any civilized nation has ever taken and survived. We have lost gold at such a rate that the solvency of our currency is in danger. Do you think that my country should continue to give your country millions of dollars each year?" The Prime Minister smiled and said, "No, but if you are foolish enough to do it, we are going to keep on taking the money."

9 Stalls for 1 Bull. And so we built a model stock farm in Lebanon, and we built nine stalls for each bull. I find something peculiarly appropriate in that. We have in our vaults $15 billion in gold. We don't own an ounce. Foreign dollar claims against that gold total $27 billion. In the last six years, fifty-two nations have bought $7 billion worth of our gold and all fifty-two are receiving foreign aid.

Because no government ever voluntarily reduces itself in size, government programs once launched never go out of existence. A government agency is the nearest thing to eternal life we'll ever see on this earth. The United States Manual takes twenty-five pages to list by name every Congressman and Senator, and all the agencies controlled by Congress. It then lists the agencies coming under the Executive Branch, and this requires 520 pages.

Since the beginning of the century our gross national product has increased by thirty-three times. In the same period the cost of Federal government has increased 234 times, and while the work force is only $1^1/_2$ times greater, Federal employees number nine times as many. There are now $2^1/_2$ million Federal employees. No one knows what they all do. One Congressman found out what one of them does. This man sits at a desk in Washington. Documents come to him each morning. He reads them, initials them, and passes them on to the proper agency. One day a document arrived he wasn't supposed to read, but he read it, initialed it and passed it on. Twenty-four hours later it arrived back at his desk with a memo attached that said, "You weren't supposed to read this. Erase your initials, and initial the erasure."

While the Federal government is the great offender, the idea filters down. During a period in California when our population has increased 90 per cent, the cost of state government has gone up 862 per cent and the number of employees 500 per cent. Governments, state and local, now employ one out of six of the nation's work force. If the rate of increase of the last three years continues, by 1970 one-fourth of the total work force will be employed by government. Already we have a permanent structure so big and complex it is virtually beyond the control of Congress and the comprehension of the people, and tyranny inevitably follows when this permanent structure usurps the policy-making function that belongs to elected officials.

One example of this occurred when Congress was debating whether to lend the United Nations $100 million. While they debated the State Department gave the United Nations $217 million and the United Nations used part of that money to pay the delinquent dues of Castro's Cuba.

Under bureaucratic regulations adopted with no regard to the wish of the people, we have lost much of our Constitutional freedom. For example, federal agents can invade a man's property without a warrant, can impose a fine without a formal hearing, let alone a trial by jury, and can seize and sell his property at auction to enforce payment of that fine.

Rights by Dispensation. An Ohio deputy fire marshal sentenced a man to prison after a secret proceeding in which the accused was not allowed to have a lawyer present. The Supreme Court upheld that sentence, ruling that it was an administrative investigation of incidents damaging to the economy. Someplace a perversion has taken place. Our natural inalienable rights are now presumed to be a dispensation of government, divisible by a vote of the majority. The greatest good for the greatest number is a high-sounding phrase but contrary to the very basis of our nation, unless it is accompanied by recognition that we have certain rights which cannot be infringed upon, even if the individual stands outvoted by all of his fellow citizens. Without this recognition, majority rule is nothing more than mob rule.

It is time we realized that socialism can come without overt seizure of property or nationalization of private business. It matters little that you hold the title to your property or business if government can dictate policy and procedure and holds life and death power over your business. The machinery of this power already exists. Lowell Mason, former antitrust law enforcer for the Federal Trade Commission, has written "American business is being harassed, bled and even black-jacked under a preposterous crazy quilt system of laws." There are so many that the government literally can find some charge to bring against any concern it chooses to prosecute. Are we safe in our books and records?

The natural gas producers have just been handed a 428 page questionnaire by the Federal Power Commission. It weighs ten pounds. One firm has estimated it will take 70,000 accountant man hours to fill out this questionnaire, and it must be done in quadruplicate. The Power Commission says it must have it to determine whether a proper price is being charged for gas. The National Labor Relations Board ruled that a business firm could not discontinue its shipping department even though it was more efficient and economical to subcontract this work out.

The Supreme Court has ruled the government has the right to tell a citizen what he can grow on his own land for his own use. The Secretary of Agriculture has asked for the right to imprison farmers who violate their planting quotas. One business firm has been informed by the Internal Revenue Service that it cannot take a tax deduction for its institutional advertising because this advertising espoused views not in the public interest.

A child's prayer in a school cafeteria endangers religious freedom, but the people of the Amish religion in the State of Ohio, who cannot participate in Social Security because of their religious beliefs, have had their livestock seized and sold at auction to enforce payment of Social Security dues.

We approach a point of no return when government becomes so huge and entrenched that we fear the consequences of upheaval and just go along with it. The Federal Government accounts for one-fifth of the industrial capacity of the nation, one-fourth of all construction, holds or guarantees one-third of all mortgages, owns one-third of the land, and engages in some nineteen thousand businesses covering half a hundred different lines. The Defense Department runs 269 supermarkets. They do a gross business of $730 million a year, and lose $150 million. The government spends $11 million an hour every hour of the twenty-four and pretends we had a tax cut while it pursues a policy of planned inflation that will more than wipe out any benefit with depreciation of our purchasing power.

We need true tax reform that will at least make a start toward restoring for our children the American dream that wealth is denied to no one, that each individual has the right to fly as high as his strength and ability will take him. The economist Sumner Schlicter has said, "If a visitor from Mars looked at our tax policy, he would conclude it had been designed by a Communist spy to make free enterprise unworkable." But we cannot have such reform while our tax policy is engineered by people who view the tax as a means of achieving changes in our social structure. Senator [Joseph S.] Clark (D.-Pa.) says the tax issue is a class issue, and the government must use the tax to redistribute the wealth and earnings downward.

Karl Marx. On January 15th in the White House, the President [Lyndon Johnson] told a group of citizens they were going to take all the money they thought was being unnecessarily spent, "take it from the haves and give it to the have-nots who need it so much." When Karl Marx said this he put it: . . . "from each according to his ability, to each according to his need."

Have we the courage and the will to face up to the immorality and discrimination of the progressive surtax, and demand a return to traditional proportionate taxation? Many decades ago the Scottish economist, John Ramsey McCulloch, said, "The moment you abandon the cardinal principle of exacting from all individuals the same proportion of their income or their property, you are at sea without rudder or compass and there is no amount of injustice or folly you may not commit."

No nation has survived the tax burden that reached one-third of its national income. Today in our country the tax collector's share is thirty-seven cents of every dollar earned. Freedom has never been so fragile, so close to slipping from our grasp. I wish I could give you some magic formula, but each of us must find his own role. One man in Virginia found what he could do, and dozens of business firms have followed his lead. Concerned because his 200 employees seemed unworried about government extravagance he conceived the idea of taking all of their withholding out of only the fourth paycheck each month. For three paydays his employees received their full salary. On the fourth payday all withholding was taken. He has one employee who owes him $4.70 each fourth payday. It only took one month to produce two hundred conservatives.

Are you willing to spend time studying the issues, making yourself aware, and then conveying that information to family and friends? Will you resist the temptation to get a government handout for your community? Realize that the doctor's fight against socialized medicine is your fight. We can't socialize the doctors without socializing the patients. Recognize that government invasion of public power is eventually an assault upon your own business. If some among you fear taking a stand because you are afraid of reprisals from customers, clients, or even government, recognize that you are just feeding the crocodile hoping he'll eat you last.

If all of this seems like a great deal of trouble think what's at stake. We are faced with the most evil enemy mankind has known in his long climb from the swamp to the stars. There can be no security anywhere in the free world if there is not fiscal and economic stability within the United States. Those who ask us to trade our freedom for the soup kitchen of the welfare state are architects of a policy of accommodation. They tell us that by avoiding a direct confrontation with the enemy he will learn to love us and give up his evil ways. All who oppose this idea are blanket indicted as war-mongers. Well let us set one thing straight, there is no argument with regard to peace and war. It is cheap demagoguery to suggest that anyone would want to send other peoples' sons to war. The only argument is with regard to the best way to avoid war. There is only one sure way—surrender.

Appeasement or Courage? The specter our well-meaning liberal friends refuse to face is that their policy of accommodation is appeasement, and appeasement does not give you a choice between peace and war, only between fight and surrender. We are told that the problem is too complex for a simple answer. They are wrong. There is no easy answer, but there is a simple answer. We must have the courage to do what we know is morally right, and this policy of accommodation asks us to accept the greatest possible immorality. We are being asked to buy our safety from the threat of "the bomb" by selling into permanent slavery our fellow human beings enslaved behind the Iron Curtain, to tell them to give up their hope of freedom because we are ready to make a deal with their slave masters.

Alexander Hamilton warned us that a nation which can prefer disgrace to danger is prepared for a master and deserves one. Admittedly there is a risk in any course we follow. Choosing the high road cannot eliminate that risk. Already some of the architects of accommodation have hinted what their decision will be if their plan fails and we are faced with the final ultimatum. The English commentator [Kenneth] Tynan has put it: he would rather live on his knees than die on his feet. Some of our own have said "Better Red than dead." If we are to believe that nothing is worth the dying, when did this begin? Should Moses have told the children of Israel to live in slavery rather than dare the wilderness? Should Christ have refused the Cross? Should the patriots at Concord Bridge have refused to fire the shot heard round the world? Are we to believe that all the martyrs of history died in vain?

You and I have rendezvous with destiny. We can preserve for our children this, the last best hope of man on earth, or we can sentence them to take the first step into a thousand years of darkness. If we fail, at least let our children and our children's children, say of us we justified our brief moment here. We did all that could be done.

NOTES

The following abbreviations are used throughout the notes in references to collections of papers and documents:

CPLB   The Collected Papers of Lemuel Boulware
GEC   The General Electric Collection
WPR   The Collections of the Archives of Labor and Urban Affairs

1. A New Dealer to the Core

1. Broder and Hess, *The Republican Establishment*, 253–54.
2. R. Reagan, *An American Life*, 132–34.
3. See draft letter of Lemuel Boulware dated June 18, 1958, CPLB.
4. Cannon, *Governor Reagan*, 70–71; Starpulse.com biography of Hal Roach, at http://www.starpulse.com/Actors/Roach,_Hal/Biography.
5. Brokaw, *The Greatest Generation*, xix–xx, xxx.
6. RR, *An American Life*, 106, 111–12.
7. Kirkpatrick, *The Reagan Phenomenon*, 10.
8. Reagan's terms as president of the Screen Actors Guild before his employment by GE are referred to in RR, *An American Life*, 130; Von Damm, *Sincerely, Ronald Reagan*, 111; and Edwards, *Early Reagan*, 494. SAG's opposition to right-to-work laws is described in an interview between RR and Hollywood columnist Charles Denton,

which was reprinted in GE's magazine, *Monogram* (June 1960): 22. Conservative and management support for right-to-work legislation is noted in Velie, *Labor USA*, 249–50.

9. RR, *An American Life*, 132–33, 105.

10. Gerald Ford, quoted in H. Thomas, *Thanks for the Memories, Mr. President*, 128.

11. References to RR's career at Eureka come from Edwards, *Early Reagan*, 79–97, unless otherwise noted. As to the economic downturn in the Midwest in 1928, also see RR, *An American Life*, 47.

12. Edwards, *Early Reagan*; also see RR with Richard G. Hubler, *Where's the Rest of Me?* 23–24.

13. Edwards, *Early Reagan*; also see RR, *An American Life*, 47–48.

14. Edwards, *Early Reagan*, 91; see 93–97 for references later in this section, and also RR, *An American Life*, 44–48.

15. See, e.g., Edwards, *Early Reagan*, 56–61; Fitzgerald, *Way Out There in the Blue*, 25, 43–44.

16. Edwards, *Early Reagan*, 37–40.

17. On RR's youthful interest in Edgar Rice Burroughs, see RR, *An American Life*, 53.

18. Edwards, *Early Reagan*, 37–38; N. Reagan, *My Turn*, 130; RR, *An American Life*, 31–32.

19. N. Reagan, *My Turn*, 130.

20. Dallek, *The Right Moment*, 197, quoting Kenneth Holden.

21. Gergen, *Eyewitness to Power*, 152.

22. Skinner, Anderson, and Anderson, eds., *Reagan: In His Own Hand*, 423–99, 423.

23. Ibid.

24. Edwards, *Early Reagan*, 105–6; for later references in this section, see Edwards, *Early Reagan*, 119, 126–29, and 136–37. See also RR, *An American Life*, 169.

25. RR, *Speaking My Mind*, 70.

26. For the references to Gergen in this section and to the academicians he quotes, see Gergen, *Eyewitness to Power*, 198–200, 223. Gergen also cites Lou Cannon's analysis of RR's intelligence, to which Gardner applies.

27. See Evans, "The New Mentors," *Teachers College Record* 102, no. 1 (February 2002): 244–63.

28. RR was with GE for eight years, from 1954 to 1962. Boulware was with the company for seventeen years but retired one year before RR left the company.

29. See Robinson, *How Ronald Reagan Changed My Life*.

30. Schweizer, *Reagan's War*, 51.

31. Skinner, Anderson, and Anderson, eds., *Reagan: In His Own Hand*, xiv.

32. RR with Richard G. Hubler, *Where's the Rest of Me?* 251.

33. RR, *An American Life*, 128–29.

34. Perlstein, *Before The Storm*, 123.

35. Jacobs, "Political Boulwarism," 350.

36. Larrabee, *Commander in Chief*, 414.

37. Larrabee, *Commander in Chief*, 414–15. Perret, *Eisenhower*, 84–89.

38. Humes, *Eisenhower and Churchill*, 104, 106.

39. Larrabee, *Commander in Chief*, 414–15.

40. Perret, *Eisenhower*, 89–95.

41. RR, *An American Life*, 118–19.

42. Editorial comments and excerpts from the "Remarks" themselves appear in RR, *Speaking My Mind*, 17–21.

43. Edwards, *Early Reagan*, 434.

44. The description of the ceremony is based on Kate Link, "When Reagan Came to Fulton," *Kingdom Dairy News*, March 22, 1981, 7; and from interviews with Pat O'Rourke and other students who attended the commencement.

45. See Candace Kacena, "Remembering Reagan," *Fulton Sun Gazette*, December 29, 1980.

46. Link, "When Reagan Came to Fulton."

47. Ibid. Also see Edwards, *Early Reagan*, 539–42.

48. The excerpts from the speech come from Edwards, *Early Reagan*, appendix, 539–42.

49. See Link, "When Reagan Came to Fulton."

50. See RR, *Where's the Rest Of Me*, 216–17. See also Edwards, *Early Reagan*, 518, 520.

51. Pat O'Rourke, interview, May 6, 2001, by phone, fax, and e-mail, included the letter of RR to Nancy Statton Korcheck, dated April 28, 1952.

52. Edwards, *Early Reagan*, 542 and 570.

53. *Fulton Daily Sun Gazette*, June 2, 1952, at p.1.

54. Johnson, *Sleepwalking Through History*, 59–60. In *Way Out There in the Blue*, Fitzgerald maintains that the incident occurred in the 1946 film, *A Wing and a Prayer* (58).

55. Von Damm, *Sincerely, Ronald Reagan*, 222–23.

56. Local background from O'Rourke, interview. RR's view of his work in *King's Row* from *Where's the Rest of Me?* 3–4.

57. RR's remarks and the attendant description come from the program for the *Breakthrough* dedication. Mikhail Gorbachev's remarks come from the program of his 1992 visit. Both programs were furnished to the author by Pat O'Rourke.

58. Margaret Thatcher's appraisal of Gorbachev is set out in, *The Downing Street Years*, 463. Specifically, she says, "This is a man with whom I could do business."

59. RR, *An American Life*, 112–15.

60. Bosch, *Reagan*, 62–66.

61. RR, *An American Life*, 106–15.

62. Ibid., 115.

63. Boulware, *What You Can Do*, 16.

64. RR, *An American Life*, 114.

65. Flynn, *The Road Ahead*, 9.

66. Edwards, *Early Reagan*, 209, 229–232, 294, 355.

67. Ambrose, *Nixon*, 541.

68. Boulware, letter to RR, June 5, 1985. Included in CPLB.

69. RR, *An American Life* at p. 138.

70. Fitzgerald, *Way Out There in the Blue*, 55, says that "GE had offered the package to several other actors ahead of [Reagan]." See also Edwards, *Early Reagan*,452–53. In *Where's the Rest of Me?* RR suggests that the package was designed with him in mind (251).

71. Edwards, *Early Reagan*, 522–23.

72. RR, *Where's the Rest of Me?* 247.

73. Ibid., 249–51; Bosch, *Reagan*, 77–78.

74. Edwards, *Early Reagan*, 447.

75. Ibid., 434–35.

76. In Dugger, *On Reagan*, 13, reporter Patrick Owen is given as the source of the information that RR was on Boulware's payroll. See also RR, *Where's the Rest of Me?* 251; Perlstein, *Before the Storm*, 123; and Jacobs, "Political Boulwarism," 349, 350.

2. Politics: War by Different Means

1. Von Clausewitz, *On War*, book 8, chapter 6. See also Beilenson, *Power Through Subversion*, 10, and online at clausewitz.com for this frequently rephrased quotation.

2. Boyle, *The UAW*, 30.

3. Boulware, *The Truth*, 160.

4. Walter Reuther, "Labor and the Community," speech delivered at Howard University, May 13, 1947, WRP.

5. Boulware, "Salvation Is Not Free," speech delivered at Harvard Business School, June 11, 1949, CPLB.

6. Northrup, *Boulwarism*, 20, 25–26.

7. The descriptions of both agencies come from Lichtenstein, *Labor's War at Home*, 4, 6.

8. Lichtenstein, *Labor's War at Home*, 41.

9. Lichtenstein, *Labor's War at Home*, 88–89.

10. As quoted in the frontispiece of Nelson Lichtenstein, *The Most Dangerous Man in Detroit*.

11. Unless otherwise noted, Reuther's biography comes from Boyle, *The UAW*. The book contains an extensive index of Reuther's life and politics.

12. Boyle, *The UAW*, 19.

13. Lichtenstein and various oral history interviews, cited in Boyle, *The UAW*, 21 n. 28.

14. Boyle, *The UAW*, 21.

15. Boyle, *The UAW*, 30.

16. Excerpts from an address by IUE president James B. Carey to the IUE Westinghouse Conference Board, February 9, 1965, 4, WPR.

17. Northrup, *Boulwarism*, 39.

18. Ibid., 40.

19. Ibid., 41.

20. The quotation comes from Galenson, *The CIO Challenge to the AFL*, 256, as quoted in Northrup, *Boulwarism*, 41.

21. *Business Week*, October 18, 1969, 73.

22. Northrup, *Boulwarism*, 40.

23. Ibid., 19.

24. Boyle, *The UAW*, 30.

25. Northrup, *Boulwarism*, 20.

26. Northrup, *Boulwarism*, 20.

27. Boyle, *The UAW*, 30.

28. Walter Reuther, "To Foster Fair Employment in Our Own Industries and to Act Vigorously in the Public Arena," article in booklet published by the National Conference of Christians and Jews, 1949, 21, WRP.

29. Boyle, *The UAW*, 28–31.

30. Boyle, *The UAW*, 31.

31. Reuther, "To Foster Fair Employment," 24–25, WRP.

32. Reuther, quoted in Boyle, *The UAW*, 32.

33. The foregoing union history comes primarily from Boyle, *The UAW*, 64.

34. Northrup, *Boulwarism*, 39–46.

35. Boulware, *What You Can Do*, 15–16, 25–28.

36. Historian Barton Bernstein, quoted in Boyle, *The UAW*, 206.

37. Boyle, *The UAW*, 207–8, for the description in this and the prior paragraph of the antiunion movement of the middle-sized companies.

38. Boyle, *The UAW*, 30.

39. Lichtenstein, *Labor's War At Home*, 230.

40. See, e.g., Velie, *Labor U.S.A.*, 249–50.

41. Northrup, *Boulwarism*, 21.

3. BOULWARISM

1. Boulware, *The Truth*, 1. See also, Northrup, *Boulwarism*, 25.

2. GE organization directory, 7, GEC.

3. Northrup, *Boulwarism*, 37–38.

4. Raymond Livingstone, interview by author, December 21, 2001, Boca Raton, Florida. Notes of the interview are in author's files.

5. Livingstone, interview.

6. Shames, *The Big Time*, 162–63.

7. Letter/press release of James B. Carey, dated February 2, 1965, WPR.

8. Boulware's educational background, his jobs, and his prior employment are taken from his obituary, *New York Times*, November 8, 1990; the archives of the Uni-

versity of Wisconsin; Livingstone, interview; and various texts that are set out in further notes below.

9. Livingstone, interview.

10. The program and the characterization of the panelists are taken from *The Har-
bus News*, May 12, 1949, 1, 8.

11. The physical description of Boulware is drawn from interviews with various
colleagues and fellow GE executives but especially from an extensive interview with
a GE executive secretary who worked for years in close proximity to Boulware and
requested to remain anonymous. She is hereafter referred to as "GE/EXSEC." Interview, February 12, 2000, at GE/EXSEC's home, audio recording. Tape, transcript,
and notes are in author's files.

12. Boulware's Alumni Day remarks are set out in full in Boulware, *The Truth*, 159–
67, under the title "Salvation Is Not Free," and in the appendix to this book. The address
and its public setting are also described in Shames, *The Big Time*, 162–65. Quotations
set out in this chapter come from both sources.

13. Boulware, *The Truth*, 162–64.

14. Brokaw, *The Greatest Generation*, xx.

15. Marvin Traub, Tom Murphy, and Bill Ruane, interviews with author, May
2001, New York City. Traub interview was at his office, the others by telephone. Author's
notes. All three are members of the class of 1949, and all are CEOs.

16. See Shames, *The Big Time*, especially the subtitle.

17. See Callahan, *Kindred Spirits*, subtitle.

18. *Fortune*, May 1974.

19. Shames, *The Big Time*, 6–7.

20. Traub, interview.

21. The *New York Times*, August 21, 2005. The full title of Roberts's senior paper
was "The Utopian Conservative: A Study of Continuity and Change in the Thought
of Daniel Webster."

22. Boulware, *The Truth*, 159.

23. Boulware, *What You Can Do*, 17.

24. Ibid., 16.

25. Boulware, *The Truth*, 90.

26. *The Truth About Boulwarism* was published by the prestigious Bureau of National Affairs in Washington, D.C., in 1969. Thousands of books were sold to individuals who worked in the labor field. Organizations that endorsed Boulware's policies
often distributed the books without charge.

27. Northrup, *Boulwarism*, 28.

28. Boulware, *The Truth*, 87.

29. Northrup, *Boulwarism*, 28.

30. *GE Schenectady News*, September 2, 1960, 2, GEC.

31. *NLRB v. GE*, 418 F. 2d 736 (2d Cir. 1969). Actually, Chief Judge Kaufman and
the NLRB before him spelled the word "Boulwareism," but they were alone in this

practice. The quotations from Kaufman in this paragraph all come from this reported decision.

32. Worthman and Randle, *Collective Bargaining*, 32.

33. Quoted in Bok and Dunlop, *Labor and the American Community*.

34. *Business Week*, October 18, 1969, 73.

35. Boulware, *The Truth*, 24; See also *NLRB v. GE*.

36. Boulware, *The Truth*, 21.

37. Ibid.

38. Gary Bridge, interview by author, by telephone and memoranda, December 24, 1990, New York, author's files. Bridge is an IBM executive and former Teachers College professor.

39. Boulware, *The Truth*, 22–23.

40. McQuaid, *Uneasy Partners*, 96–97.

41. This quotation and those which follow in this section, unless otherwise noted, come from Boulware, *The Truth*, 62, 21, 40, 29, and 7.

42. Boulware, *The Truth*, 19, quoting the Berkshire *Evening Eagle*, July 24, 1954.

43. Boulware, *The Truth*, 40–41.

44. Boulware, *The Truth*, 10, 50–51, and 121. The survey technique is described at 40–41.

45. These examples are reprints of *Works News* that were sent to directly to employees whose plants were too small to warrant separate publications; they are from Boulware, *The Truth*, 41–42. The direct communications to ERMs and other *Works News* mats set out in the next paragraph are from CPLB.

46. Boulware, *What You Can Do*, 119, 126.

47. Boulware, *The Truth*, 38, 39. The *News* and *Newsletter* are referred to throughout *The Truth*. See also GEC for all back issues of all publications.

48. Boulware, *The Truth*, 40–42.

49. *Employee Relations News Letter*, December 31, 1957, GEC.

50. Ibid., 14.

51. See back issues of *Monogram* and other GE publications at GEC.

52. *Forum*, January–March 1962 and October–December 1961.

53. Strausz-Hupe and Kintner, "Military Defense." The impact of the article on "The Speech" and Reagan administration policy is discussed below in chapters 8 and 13.

54. Boulware, *The Truth*, 35–38.

55. For Boulware's friendship with Hazlitt, see Livingstone, interview.

56. Boulware, *The Truth*, 37–38.

57. Ibid., 38.

58. Flynn, *The Road Ahead*, 7, 11.

59. After receiving his assignment from Charles Wilson to develop a new labor policy, Boulware established a "study group" to ascertain what employees really wanted from their company. The book clubs could be viewed as lineal descendants. See Northrup, *Boulwarism*, 26.

60. Northrup, *Boulwarism*, 25.

61. Boulware, *The Truth*, 2.

62. The source for the M, B, G diagram, and LB's explanatory words, is Boulware, *What You Can Do*, 19–21.

63. This point is the premise of almost all of Boulware's writings. A typical, more concentrated reference may be found in chapter 9 of *The Truth About Boulwarism*, entitled "Marketing the Improved Nine-Point Job."

64. RR, *An American Life*, 129.

4. The Plant Tour

1. Edwards, *Early Reagan*, 459–61; RR, *An American Life*, 128.

2. Ibid.

3. RR, *Where's the Rest of Me?* 255–56.

4. RR, *Where's the Rest of Me?* 257.

5. No one contests the vastness of GE's operations at this time, but the exact numbers vary almost every time they appear. The figures given at this point in the text are this author's best estimate. *National Labor Relations Board v. General Electric Company*, 204, mentions plants in twenty-nine states, and Chief Judge Kaufman's opinion (4), based on that record, states that GE manufactured its products in all fifty states. RR recalls "some forty states" (in *Where's The Rest of Me?* 257), while Francis Fitzgerald cites 139 plants in more than thirty-nine states (*Way Out*, 56) and Martin Anderson describes 135 plants (Skinner, Anderson, and Anderson, *In His Own Hand*, xiv). Ralph Cordiner, GE's CEO during this period, lists 138 plants in twenty-eight states (*New Frontiers*, 35). Some of the confusion comes from the definition of "plants," as compared to distribution centers and research facilities. In addition, the calculations that appear throughout this text may have been made at different times.

6. RR, *Where's the Rest of Me?* 257–58.

7. Ibid.

8. Edwards, *Early Reagan*, 454–55.

9. Earl B. Dunckel Jr., interview, April 27, 1982, Regional Oral History (ROH) Office, Bancroft Library, University of California at Berkeley. The quotations from Dunckel that appear in this chapter come from that interview, unless otherwise noted.

10. Langley's remarks, in this paragraph and set out below, come from an article he published in the *Knowxville Journal* over three days in July 1980, "Reagan Philosophy Changed," July 14, 15, 16. This quotation is from July 14.

11. Quoted in Catherine Drinker Bowen, *Adventures of a Biographer*, 94.

12. *The General Electric News* (Outdoor Lighting Department), March 8, 1957, 1, GEC. References to the day's schedule are also from this source.

13. Edwards, *Early Reagan*, 459–60.

14. RR, *An American Life*, 81–83.

15. Ibid., 89–90; Edwards, *Early Reagan*, 206, 321.

16. Langley, "Reagan Philosophy Changed," July 14.

17. Langley, "Reagan Philosophy Changed," July 15.

18. Ibid.

19. RR, *An American Life*, 128–29.

20. RR, *Where's the Rest of Me?* 253–55.

21. Langley, "Reagan Philosophy Changed," July 15.

22. RR, *Where's the Rest of Me?* 266.

23. Dunckel, interview, 17.

24. Ibid., 17–18.

25. RR, *Where's the Rest of Me?* 251.

26. Dunckel, interview, 17–18.

27. RR, *An American Life*, 127–28.

28. Reagan, *Where's the Rest of Me?* 266–67.

29. Langley, "Reagan Philosophy Changed," July 14.

30. Langley, "Reagan Philosophy Changed," July 15.

31. RR, *Where's the Rest of Me?* 267, 266.

32. RR, *Where's the Rest of Me?* 251, 263.

33. Ibid., 266–67.

34. Dunckel, interview, 29–30.

35. Reagan, *Where's the Rest of Me?* 266–68.

5. SCHOOLS, CLASSES, AND TRAINS

1. "The Powerhouse," *Time*, January 12, 1959, 76.

2. Krames, *Jack Welch Lexicon*, 68.

3. General Electric brochure, "GE Crotonville," which is distributed by the company to a few potential outside users of the campus. See also GE/EXSEC, interview.

4. See Cordiner, *New Frontiers*, 45; Boulware, *The Truth*, 3–6.

5. Cordiner, *New Frontiers*, 40–44, esp. 40.

6. Ibid., 27, 35. Boulware describes his assignment in 1947 to develop a "more rewarding approach" for GE at the outset of *The Truth* (1) and throughout that book.

7. Cordiner, *New Frontiers*, 8.

8. Ibid., 44–46, 8.

9. General Electric, "GE Crotonville."

10. "The Powerhouse," *Time*, January 12, 1959.

11. Physical descriptions and the information about the relationship between the two men was furnished by GE/EXSEC, who observed them closely for over a decade, and many other interviewees.

12. The honor was awarded to Cordiner in the annual economic and business review issue of the *Saturday Review of Literature* in 1960, as reported in *GE Schenectady News*, January 29, 1960, 5, GEC.

13. Boulware correspondence describing ethics taskforce, CPLB.

14. RR, *An American Life*, 127, 133.

15. Boulware to RR, December 17, 1974, CPLB.

16. Cordiner, *New Frontiers*, 106.

17. Welch, *Straight From The Gut*, 170.

18. Ibid.

19. Cordiner, *New Frontiers*, 48.

20. Collins and Porras, *Built to Last*, 298.

21. Cordiner, *New Frontiers*, 37.

22. Ibid., 23.

23. "The Powerhouse," *Time*, January 12, 1959, 86.

24. Boulware, *The Truth*, 34. Also see GE/EXSEC, interview, about HOBSO.

25. Boulware, *The Truth*, 32–35; also for the quotations in the next paragraphs.

26. RR, *An American Life*, 128–29.

27. Cannon, *The Role of a Lifetime*, 183.

28. Dunckel, interview.

29. RR, *Where's the Rest of Me?* 265.

30. RR, *An American Life*, 128. Also see *Where's the Rest of Me?* 252, where RR describes himself as a "train traveler."

31. Bowen, *Adventures of a Biographer*, 126.

32. Gergen, *Eyewitness to Power*, 152.

33. Edwards, *Early Reagan*, 171.

34. Fitzgerald, *Way Out There in the Blue*, 57.

35. Cited in Welch, *Straight from the Gut*, 170.

36. Skinner, Anderson, and Anderson, eds., *Reagan: In His Own Hand*, xviii, xix.

37. RR, *An American Life*, 130.

38. Boulware, *The Truth*, 35–38; Boulware to Hazlitt, December 22, 1960, CPLB.

39. Raymond Livingstone, interview by author, December 21, 2001, Boca Raton, Florida.

40. People for the American Way, "Voucher Veneer: The Deeper Agenda to Privatize Public Education," http://www.pfaw.org/pfaw/general/default.aspx?oid=11381.

41. Llewellyn H. Rockwell Jr., "Biography of Henry Hazlitt (1894–1993)," Ludwig von Mises Institute, http://www.mises.org/content/hazlittbio.asp.

42. Ibid.

43. In *The Truth*, 35, Boulware notes that "we distributed thousands of copies of [Haney's] book."

44. Quotations from Haney, unless otherwise noted, all come from *How You Really Earn Your Living*.

45. Joint Economic Committee (Jim Saxton, chairman), "Study: Budget Surpluses,

Deficits and Government Spending," December 1998, http://www.house.gov/jec/fiscal/budget/surplus2/surplus2.htm.

46. Quotations from Henry Hazlitt, unless otherwise noted, come from *Economics in One Lesson*.

47. GE, *Public and Employee Relations News*, December 31, 1957, 2, GEC.

48. Ibid.

6. The Campaign

1. Northrup, *Boulwarism*, xi.

2. Richards, *Early Reagan*, 463, 524.

3. Ibid., 528.

4. Cannon, *Governor Reagan*, 107; Richards, *Early Reagan*, 472.

5. Cannon, *Governor Reagan*, 109; Morris, *Dutch*, 305.

6. Perlstein, *Before the Storm*, 13; New York Times, *The New York Times Encyclopedic Almanac for 1970*, 154.

7. Velie, *Labor U.S.A.*, 250.

8. Perlstein, *Before the Storm*, 12.

9. Wuerthner, *The Businessman's Guide*, xiv. The author was a GE employee at the time of publication.

10. Ibid., xvi–xvii.

11. Ibid., xvii.

12. Boyle, *The UAW*, 101.

13. Ibid., 102.

14. Ibid., 102.

15. Ibid., 104, 105.

16. Perlstein, *Before the Storm*, 30–31.

17. See, e.g., press release of Hawaii's COPE director Terry W. T. Lau, September 2, 2005, http://www.hawaflcio.org/cope.html.

18. Wuerthner, *The Businessman's Guide*, 215.

19. Boulware, *The Truth*, 164.

20. Boulware, "Salvation Is Not Free," speech, in *The Truth*, 160.

21. Boulware, *What You Can Do*, 12.

22. Cordiner to Boulware, May 2, 1958, CPLB.

23. NLRB transcript in *GE and IUE* (Boulwarism Unfair Labor Practice Proceedings), 207n. 5, 212, 209, 246, referred to in appellate decision, *NLRB v. GE*, 418 F. 2d 736 (2d Cir. 1969).

24. Boulware, *What You Can Do*, 12.

25. Boulware memorandum to Parker, June 18, 1958, CPLB; quotations in this section are from the memo unless otherwise noted.

26. Boulware, *The Truth*, 106.

27. Boulware, *What You Can Do*, 100.

28. Memorandum, Boulware to Hoyt Steele, December 22, 1958, CPLB.
29. Ibid.
30. Memorandum, Boulware to Hoyt Steele, February 24, 1959, CPLB.
31. Wuerthner, *The Businessman's Guide*, 214–15, 163, 165, 166, 171, 178, 182, 191, 194. These are the citations to the quotations and references that follow.
32. See T. White, *The Making of the President, 1964*, 95.
33. Quotations set out below are from "The Powerhouse," *Time*, June 12, 1959, 76, 85.
34. A. C. Nielsen Jr. to Boulware, August 30, 1960, CPLB.
35. Boulware to Nielsen, September 1, 1960, CPLB.
36. Ibid.
37. *GE Schenectady News*, March 6, 1959, 6, GEC.
38. Wuerthner, *The Businessman's Guide*, 167.
39. Boulware, *The Truth*, 161.
40. Editorial, *GE Schenectady News*, June 3, 1955, 3, GEC. This portion of the plant newspaper was typically prepared centrally as part of Boulware's *Works News* project.
41. *The Monogram*, September 1958, cover photo, GEC.
42. *GE Schenectady News*, January 30, 1959, 3, citing YMCA speech, GEC.
43. RR, "Encroaching Government Controls," speech published in *Human Events* 18, no. 29 (July 21, 1961): 460.
44. *GE Schenectady News*, January 30, 1959, 3, GEC.
45. Boulware, *The Truth*, 31.
46. This math comes from the "Community Relations" chapter in Boulware, *The Truth*, esp. 58–60. There he uses the term "thought leaders" instead of "communicators" and "mass communicators," which he uses in his June 18 memo.

7. ALLIES

1. For the description of the meeting of the Wise Men and for the names of the attendees mentioned in this section, GE/EXSEC, interview, February 12, 2000, at GE/EXSEC's home, audio recording. Tape, transcript, and notes are in author's files.
2. Wuerthner, *The Businessman's Guide*, xvii.
3. Fuller, *The Gentlemen Conspirators*, 30–31, 36.
4. Ibid., 27.
5. Ibid., 29.
6. O'Mahoney and Cordiner are cited in Fuller, *The Gentlemen Conspirators*, 32–34.
7. William Ginn's GE press release and three subsequent *New York Times* articles are cited in Fuller, *The Gentlemen Conspirators*, 55–56.
8. GE/EXSEC, interview.
9. Fuller, *The Gentlemen Conspirators*, 38.
10. Boyle, *The UAW*, 137.

11. Boulware to Manion, June 10, 1960, CPLB.

12. Wuerthner, *The Businessman's Guide*, esp. 150–76.

13. See GE annual reports and other records, GEC; and Northrup, *Boulwarism*, 46.

14. McQuaid, *Uneasy Partners*, 19, 107–8.

15. Boulware, *The Truth*, 159, 169. The details of this setting come from Raymond Livingstone, interview by author, December 21, 2001, Boca Raton, Florida; Raymond Livingstone was a vice president of TRW and often spoke on panels with Boulware.

16. See Boulware to J. D. Tuller, February 24, 1960, CPLB; and Boulware to John G. Pew Jr., November 23, 1960, CPLB.

17. Boulware to Pew, November 23, 1960, CPLB.

18. Herb Berkowitz (of the Heritage Foundation), "Letter to the Editor," November 16, 1980, CPLB.

19. White and Gill, *Why Reagan Won*, quoting Senator Paul Laxalt, xi.

20. Boulware, *The Truth*, 39.

21. Ibid., 38–39.

22. Sam Tanenhaus, "The Buckley Effect," *New York Times Magazine*, October 2, 2005, 68.

23. Buckley to Boulware, September 21, 1960, CPLB.

24. White and Gill, *Suite 3505*, 43, 49.

25. Rusher, *The Rise of the Right*, 55.

26. Livingstone, interview.

27. Livingstone, interview. But see GE/EXSEC, interview. The secretary believed that Norma came from a "middle-class" background. She also found Norma "attractive."

28. Boulware to O. Glenn Saxon, August 16, 1960, CPLB.

29. Boyle, *The UAW*, 31.

30. Reuther, "To Foster Fair Employment," 28, WRP.

31. AFL-CIO Web site, "History: Walter Reuther (1907–1970)," http://www.aflcio.org/aboutus/history/history/reuther.cfm.

32. Perlstein, *Before the Storm*, 365.

33. Perlstein, *Before the Storm*, 307, 310.

34. Boulware to Saxon, August 16, 1960, CPLB.

35. Boulware to Lewis Jarvis, November 29, 1960, CPLB.

36. Boulware, "Statesmanship in Industrial Relations," speech to National Association of Manufacturers, Industrial Relations Division, 1964, quoted in Bok and Dunlap, *Labor and the American Community*.

37. Boulware, "Introduction of John Merril Olin," testimonial dinner, April 16, 1981, St. Louis Club, CPLB.

38. Livingstone, interview.

39. Livingstone, interview

40. CPLB. Another working title was *Responsible Citizenship*.

41. CPLB.

42. CPLB.

8. THE SPEECH

1. RR, *Where's the Rest of Me?* 267.

2. RR, *An American Life*, 130.

3. The incident is described in *Where's the Rest of Me?* at pp. 268–270.

4. M. Reagan, *First Father, First Daughter*, 110.

5. RR, *Where's the Rest of Me?* 267.

6. RR, *An American Life*, 129.

7. Ibid., 132–34. Actually, because he supported Richard Nixon in 1960 as a "Democrat for Nixon," at the candidate's request, he didn't change his party registration to Republican for another two years.

8. Ambrose, *Nixon*, 541.

9. RR, *Where's the Rest of Me?* 257–61.

10. The words spoken by RR in this section come from the then-current version of "The Speech," entitled "Encroaching Government Controls," given at the Business Institute of New Jersey and published in the July 21, 1961, issue of *Human Events*. The Reagan Library forwarded a slightly different version to the author, entitled "Encroaching Control" that was presented to the Phoenix Chamber of Commerce on March 30, 1961. The library's covering letter, dated January 3, 2000, noted that "we have no [Reagan] speeches given between 1958 and 1960."

11. RR, *An American Life*, 129.

12. Edwards, *Early Reagan*, 463.

13. *GE Schenectady News*, in sequence as the headlines appear in the text, July 18, 25, August 15, 1958; February 6, 27, May 8, 1959; April 8, September 16, 23, December 2, 1960, GEC.

14. Chief Judge Kaufman's opinion for the court in *NLRB v. GE*, 418 F. 2d 736, 758 (2d Cir. 1969).

15. *GE Schenectady News*, January 30, 1959, 3, GEC. This is also the source for later quotations from the interview.

16. See "A Time for Choosing," in RR, *Where's the Rest of Me?* 302–12, and in appendix of this volume.

17. Edwards, *Early Reagan*, 359, 436; see also Beilenson's biography on the jackets of his books, *The Treaty Trap* and *Survival and Peace in the Nuclear Age*; for Beilenson's role in the divorce proceedings and other points, see Schweitzer, *Reagan's War*, 85–86.

18. *The Treaty Trap* (1969), *Power Through Subversion* (1972), and *Survival and Peace in the Nuclear Age* (1980).

19. Skinner, Anderson, and Anderson, eds., *Reagan: In His Own Hand*, 8, 48, 51, 52, and 54.

20. RR, "Commencement Address at U.S. Military Academy," May 27, 1981, http://www.reagan.utexas.edu/archives/speeches/1981/52781c.htm. Former aide Martin Anderson, in *Revolution* (74), mentions RR recommending Beilenson.

21. RR, "Encroaching Control," 2.

22. Beilenson, *Power Through Subversion*, 201, 28, 158, 3, 9–10.

23. Beilenson, *The Treaty Trap*, 162, 212–213, 215, 221, 219; Beilenson, *Power Through Subversion*, 160.

24. Beilenson, *The Treaty Trap*, 221.

25. Beilenson, *The Treaty Trap*, 221.

26. See, e.g., George Shultz, *Turmoil and Triumph*, 1133; David Gergen, citing his own experience and an affirmation of it by Margaret Thatcher, *Eye Witness to Power*, 203.

27. Beilenson, *The Treaty Trap*, 221.

28. Beilenson, *Power Through Subversion*, 241.

29. Beilenson, *Survival and Peace*, 142.

30. Ibid., 154.

31. That precursor of "The Speech" was delivered in 1962 and is quoted in Edwards, *Early Reagan*, 559.

32. Cannon, *Reagan*, 19; Morris, *Dutch*, 169, 468–70.

33. Quoted in Beilenson, *Nuclear*, 56.

34. Ibid.

35. Ibid., 57.

36. Major A. Johnson (a GE Aerospace employee), *Progress in Defense and Space: A History of the Aerospace Group of the General Electric Company* (1993), 297–98, GEC; this self-published book may be obtained directly from Major Johnson or through Amazon.com.

37. Strausz-Hupé and Kintner, "Military Defense," 21–26.

38. Ibid., 23.

39. Ibid., 26.

40. Beilenson, *The Treaty Trap*, v–ix, 300, 310; Foreign Policy Research Institute, "In Memoriam: Robert Strausz-Hupé, Founder of FPRI," http://www.fpri.org/about/people/strausz-Hupe.html.

41. Beilenson, *Survival and Peace*, 56.

42. Ibid., 1, 4.

43. Ibid., 4–6, for this and the remaining Beilenson quotations in this section.

44. On use of word "evil" to describe communists, see RR, *An American Life*, 115.

45. Boulware, *What You Can Do*, 25.

46. Ibid., 15–16.

47. Ibid., 100.

9. TWO UNIONS

1. *Screen Actor*, March 1960, 14. This is the magazine of the Screen Actors Guild.

2. Wills, *Reagan's America*, 215.

3. Wills, *Reagan's America*, 222.

4. Prindle, *The Politics of Glamour*, 22–23.

5. *Screen Actor*, March 1995, Special Sixtieth Charter Anniversary Issue. The history of the guild and the staff and star statements below, unless otherwise noted, come from this special issue.

6. RR, *An American Life*, 107.

7. N. Reagan, *My Turn*, 95.

8. Ibid., 96–97.

9. See *Screen Actor*, special issue, 29. More detailed examination of the issues and references to specific sources are set out in the next chapter.

10. *Screen Actor*, January, 1998, "Fifty Years Ago: SAG Remembers the Blacklist"; RR, *An American Life*, 114–15; Wills, *Reagan's America*, 251–58.

11. Prindle, *The Politics of Glamour*, 78–82; Wills, *Reagan's America*, 263–66, 271–75; Cannon, *Governor Reagan*, 103–6; RR, *Where's the Rest of Me?* 286–87.

12. For this section on SAG, see *Screen Actor*, February 1960, 3; March 1960, 1–15; April–May 1960, 1–5 and editorial.

13. Boulware, *The Truth*, 107.

14. Northrup, *Boulwarism*, 67–68, 74–79; *NLRB v. GE*, 5.

15. Jack Welch to Boulware, July 11, 1988, enclosed the July 5, 1988, *Berkshire Eagle*, describing the 1955 necktie incident in an article by Thomas O. Morton, "On the picket line: strikes at GE." CPLB.

16. Northrup, *Boulwarism*, 66–69; GE and IUE, case nos. 2-CA-7581-1 et al, December 16, 1964, Intermediate Report, 210.

17. Northrup, *Boulwarism*, 41.

18. *Berkshire Eagle*, July 5, 1988, CPLB (see note 16, above).

19. Northrup, *Boulwarism*, 55.

20. Northrup, *Boulwarism*, 68n 6. The statement appeared in the July 27, 1959, issue of *Steel*. The subsequent quotation from the Schenectady local comes from the Northrup note.

10. THE ART OF NEGOTIATION

1. Shultz, *Turmoil and Triumph*, 164. This is the source for Shultz's further comment on RR's "self-confidence" in negotiating.

2. RR, quoted in Strock, *Reagan on Leadership*, 59.

3. The description of the March 13 meeting and the quotations set out in the next few pages come from *Screen Actor*, March 1960, 1–15, unless otherwise noted. The members of the SAG negotiating committee are named in *Screen Actor*, April–May 1960, 4.

4. McDougal, *Mogul*, 2, 243–44, 295–97.

5. Prindle, *The Politics of Glamour*, 86–87, also includes Mickey Rooney's statement, set out below.

6. The description of the later meeting (April 18) and the statements of Reagan and Dales come from *Screen Actor*, April–May 1960, 1–5.

7. *Monogram*, "So They Say" column, June 1, 1960, 22, GEC.

8. Northrup, *Boulwarism*, 84, for this and the following quotation.

9. *GE and IUE*, NLRB case nos. 2-CA-7581-1 et al., 207n. 5.

10. Letter from Boulware to manager of the Hillsboro Club, December 16, 1959, CPLB.

11. IUE Newsletter, September 1959.

12. Boulware, *The Truth*, 40–41, for his use of formal surveys and representative *Works News* issues.

13. *NLRB v. Herman Sausage Co, Inc.*, 122 NLRB 23, as affirmed in 275 Fed 2d 229 (1960) and cited in *GE and IUE*, case nos. 2-CA-7581-1 et al., 194–95.

14. *GE and IUE*, 210.

15. Ibid.

16. *GE and IUE*, 211.

17. Ibid., 211–12.

18. Northrup, *Boulwarism*, 27–30.

19. *GE and IUE*, 212.

20. The quoted descriptions of the visit in this section come from the *GE Schenectady News*, March 4, 1960, 1, GEC.

21. The article was distributed to plants throughout the country, to be placed in their local plant newspapers. Quoted portions come from the *GE Schenectady News*, September 2, 1960, 2, GEC.

22. *NLRB v GE*, 418 F. 2d 736, 4, 5, and 19; See also *GE and IUE*, 219–20.

23. *GE and IUE*, 219–20, 214–15.

24. Northrup, *Boulwarism*, 83.

25. Ibid., 96; *GE and IUE*, 208, 225, and 232.

26. *GE and IUE*, 233–34.

27. *NLRB v. GE*, 6.

28. *GE and IUE*, 244.

29. *NLRB v. GE*, 16.

30. The quotations and references to press coverage in this section come from reprints on a full-page spread appearing on in the *GE Schenectady News*, October 21, 1960, 4, GEC.

31. On October 22, the union signed the company's short-form settlement agreement. The union terminated its strike on October 24. Formal agreements were executed on November 10. *GE and IUE*, 253–55.

32. A.H. Raskin, *New York Times*, October 25, 1960, as cited in Northrup, *Boulwarism*, 90.

11. THE CAMPAIGN CONTINUES

1. RR's letter of November 5, 1994, http://americanpresidents.org/letters/39.asp.

2. RR, *An American Life*, 132–34.

3. See Koenig, *Bryan*, 10–11, 549–51.

4. RR, *An American Life*, 133–34.

5. Ambrose, *Nixon*, 570–75.

6. Boyle, *The UAW*, 146–47.

7. *GE and IUE*, 203–7.

8. Perlstein, *Before the Storm*, 123.

9. The case is found at 418 F. 2d 736 (2d Cir. 1969). All the quotations from the case set out hereafter in the text are taken from the opinion.

10. Stephen I. Schlossberg to UAW board, interoffice communication, November 6, 1969, WRP, box 136, folder 6.

11. Boulware, *The Truth*, x.

12. Fuller, *The Gentlemen Conspirators*, 175–76.

13. Ibid., 61, 70, 73–76.

14. Ibid., 78.

15. Ibid., 165–66 and (quoting the *Herald Tribune*), 183–85.

16. Ibid., 173.

17. Ibid., 165.

18. Ibid., 180.

19. Wiprud, "Antitrust Treble Damages," 29–32.

20. RR, *An American Life*, 137–38.

21. Edwards, *Early Reagan*, 478–79.

22. This and other references in this section come from Dallek, *The Right Moment*, 39–40, unless otherwise noted.

23. Wills, *Reagan's America*, 285.

24. Ibid., 287, 286.

25. RR, *An American Life*, 136.

26. T. Thomas, *The Films of Ronald Reagan*, 223–4; Edwards, *Early Reagan*, 483–84.

27. Dallek, *The Right Moment*, 39–41.

28. Von Damm, ed., *Sincerely Yours, Ronald Reagan*, 74.

29. The account of the Davis-Reagan contest is found in White and Gill, *Why Reagan Won*, 14–15. See also Dallek, *The Right Moment*, 66.

30. Perlstein, *Before The Storm*, 441.

31. New York Times, *The New York Times Encyclopedic Almanac 1970*, 155.

32. Rusher, *The Rise of the Right*, 158–59.

33. From White, *The Making of the President, 1964*, 405; Schlesinger, *The History of American Presidential Elections*, vol. 4, quoted in Perlstein, *Before The Storm*, 516.

34. See Perlstein, *Before The Storm*, 513–14.

35. See Northrup, *Boulwarism*, 46–47.]

36. LB to O. Glenn Saxon, August 16, 1960, CPLB.

37. See T. H. White, *The Making of the President, 1964*.

38. Broder and Hess, *The Republican Establishment*, 253–54.

39. See RR, *An American Life*, 139–41; also see Dallek, *The Right Moment*, 67; and Rusher, *The Rise of the Right*, 174.

40. Edwards, *Early Reagan*, 483, 485, 543–46. See also archives of the Ronald Reagan Library. "The Speech" was delivered in Phoenix on March 30, 1961.

41. See Dallek, *The Right Moment*, 26, 67.

42. John Wayne, letter to brothers of Sigma Chi, September 1964, CPLB; J.J. Wuerthner Jr. to Michael Deaver, May 4, 1984 and March 26, 1985, CPLB; and Wuerthner to Boulware, March 21, 1985, CPLB.

43. RR's October 27, 1964, speech in support of Barry Goldwater, "A Time for Choosing," is set out in its entirety in Edwards, *Early Reagan*, 561–70. A version of "The Speech" that RR gave before and after the Goldwater telecast is set out in full in the appendix to this volume.

44. See chapter 4.

45. RR, *An American Life*, 143.

46. Ibid. Also see Dallek, *The Right Moment*, 68.

47. Dallek, *The Right Moment*, 174.

48. Ibid., 120–24.

49. Ibid.

50. Ibid.

51. Ibid., 196–98, for this quote and subsequent ones in this section, except where noted otherwise.

52. Wills, *Reagan's America*, 296.

53. Dallek, *The Right Moment*, 196.

54. Cannon, *Governor Reagan*, 98.

55. The description of BASICO's work is found in Dallek, *The Right Moment*, 120, 196–97.

56. The background for the references to the social life of the group of friends who later became known as Reagan's "Kitchen Cabinet" is found in Bob Colacello, "Ronnie and Nancy, " parts 1 and 2, *Vanity Fair*, July (beginning on page 76) and August (beginning on p. 60), 1998, unless otherwise noted.

57. Lew Wasserman's longtime friendship with Reagan is documented throughout McDougal, *The Last Mogul*. Taft Schreiber's connection to the Kitchen Cabinet is mentioned at page 332 of that book.

58. Colacello, "Ronnie and Nancy, " part 1, 85.

59. See Dallek, *The Right Moment*, 74–76.

60. Ambrose, *Nixon*, 541.

61. Quotations from the official announcement of Reagan's candidacy come from Dallek, *The Right Moment*, 195–96.

62. The reactions to RR's candidacy set out on this date come from Dallek, *The Right Moment*, 174, 195. Some of them occurred before the official announcement.

63. Ibid., 174, 195, 235.

64. Ibid., 175.

65. Ibid.

66. Ibid.

67. See Edwards, *Early Reagan*, 253n.

68. Dallek, *The Right Moment*, 176.

69. Ibid., 210.

70. Ibid.

71. Ibid., 7–27.

72. Quoted in Ibid., 187.

73. Ibid., 186.

74. Smith et al., *Reagan*, 41.

75. Wills, *Reagan's America*, 303.

76. Cannon, *Governor Reagan*, 171.

77. As quoted in Bosch, *Reagan*, 108.]

78. Reeves, *President Nixon*, 246.

79. For this quotation and the section on welfare that follows it, see Bosch, *Reagan*, 108–11; also see footnotes in that text.

80. Boulware, *What You Can Do*, 47.

81. See LB to RR, December 17, 1974, CPLB.

82. Ibid.

83. RR to LB, January 2, 1975 (one of the governor's last days in office), CPLB.

84. LB to RR, December 17, 1974.

85. Robert Lindsey, in Smith et al., *Reagan*, 40.

86. D'Souza, *Ronald Reagan*, 68.

87. See Bosch, *Reagan*, 108–11.

88. Smith et al., *Reagan*, 45–46.

89. Michael Deaver, quoted in in Bosch, *Reagan*, 111.

90. Smith et al., *Reagan*, 40.

91. Ibid., 44.

92. Ibid, 43.

12. THE PRESIDENTIAL BUG

1. White and Gill, *Why Reagan Won*, 130.

2. AFL-CIO Web site, "History: Walter Reuther (1907–1970)," http://www.aflcio.org/aboutus/history/history/reuther.cfm.

3. The account of the convention comes from White and Gill, *Why Reagan Won*, 118–30.

4. Ibid., 118.

5. Ibid., 117.

6. Ibid., 119–25.

7. RR, *An American Life*, 203.

8. White and Gill, *Why Reagan Won*, 143.

9. Skinner, Anderson, and Anderson, eds., *Reagan: In His Own Hand*, xiv–xv.

10. Gergen, *Eyewitness to Power*, 117.

11. Skinner, Anderson, and Anderson, eds., *Reagan: In His Own Hand*, 380.

12. See Dallek, *The Right Moment*, 198.

13. See, e.g., Boulware, *What You Can Do*, 25–27.

14. The editors of *In His Own Hand*, reviewing the totality of Reagan radio scripts that they recently discovered, found only a tiny percentage devoted to the so-called social issues. See Skinner, Anderson, and Anderson, eds., *Reagan: In His Own Hand*, 330. They write: "A few were written on gun control laws; none on gay rights; only one on immigration; none on school prayer. Only one essay concerns abortion." In quoting from the radio addresses in this book, I have corrected or spelled out certain phrases where RR used a de facto shorthand. E.g., where he refers to "Democrats and Republicans" in the address on welfare reform, the original script simply says "D. & R."

15. See Von Damm, *Sincerely, Ronald Reagan*, 200.

16. See RR, *Abortion and the Conscience of the Nation*, esp. 8.

17. Skinner, Anderson, and Anderson, eds., *Reagan: In His Own Hand*, 389–90.

18. N. Reagan, *My Turn*, 149.

19. Cannon, *Governor Reagan*, 404; RR, *An American Life*, 200; White and Gill, *Why Reagan Won*, 172–73.

20. RR, *An American Life*, 199.

21. Boulware, *What You Can Do*, 16,17, 22, 117.

22. The ad, in both its handwritten and published versions is found in CPLB.

23. Cannon, *Governor Reagan*, 399.

24. White and Gill, *Why Reagan Won*, 179.

25. Langley, "Reagan Philosophy," July 14.

26. Unless otherwise noted, the description of the convention, including the quotation of the California observer, comes from White and Gill, *Why Reagan Won*, 182–91.

27. The speech, including the poem, are found in White and Gill, *Why Reagan Won*, 191.

28. Skinner, Anderson, and Anderson, eds., *Reagan: In His Own Hand*, 503.

29. Bosch, *Reagan*, 121.

30. Boulware, *What You Can Do*, 20–22.

31. Ibid.

32. James Reston of the *New York Times*, quoted in Meese, *With Reagan*, 40.

33. White, *America in Search of Itself*, 30–31; Cannon, *Governor Reagan*, 461–63.

34. White, *America in Search of Itself*, 303.

35. Cannon, *Governor Reagan*, 475.

36. RR, *An American Life*, 216.

37. White, *America in Search of Itself*, 412–13.

38. Bosch, *Reagan*, 139.

39. Quoted in Rusher, *The Rise of the Right*, 307.

40. Quoted in ibid., 308.

13. A President's Vision

1. *The Candidate*, a Wildwood-Ritchie Production, directed by Michael Ritchie, written by Jeremy Larner, from Warner Borthers, a Warner Communications Company, 1972.

2. Shultz, *Turmoil and Triumph*, 263; Meese, *With Reagan*, 10; Pemberton, *Exit with Honor*, 195, citing Ambassador Anatoly Dobrynin as the source for Gorbachev's description of Reagan as "a visionary making great 'decisions.'"

3. Clark Clifford, as cited in Johnson, *Sleepwalking Through History*, 447.

4. Gergen, *Eyewitness to Power*, 153.

5. Taranto and Leo, *Presidential Leadership*, 11, although the entire book is an exploration of the rating of U.S. presidents.

6. Schultz, *Turmoil and Triumph*, 263.

7. Boyle, *The UAW*, 1.

8. The description and the excerpts from the first Inaugural Address come from RR, *An American Life*, 226–27.

9. See, e.g., "Encroaching Control," presented at the annual meeting of the Phoenix Chamber of Commerce, March 30, 1961, excerpts from which are set out in Edwards, *Early Reagan*, 543–46.

10. Both the Sloan and Will quotations come from Sloan, "Meeting the Leadership Challenges," 796.

11. Hugh Sidey, Remarks at Florida International University, January 9, 2003.

12. The incident, the Reagan comments, and the appraisal of the public reaction all come from Gergen, *Eyewitness to Power*, 176–78.

13. RR, *An American Life*, 285.

14. Ibid., 263.

15. Ibid., 288.

16. RR, *An American Life*, 286; Wikipedia, s.v. "Phil Gramm," http://en.wikipedia.org/wiki/Phil_Gramm.

17. As quoted in D'Souza, *How an Ordinary Man*, 104.

18. Anderson, *Revolution*, 127, 130–32.

19. Richard Neustadt, foreword to *Saving the Reagan Presidency*, by David Abshire, vii.

20. D'Souza, *How an Ordinary Man*, 231.

21. Martin Anderson, interview, December 11–12, 2001, Palo Alto, California, Miller Center of Public Affairs, Presidential Oral History Program, Ronald Reagan Oral History Project, the Miller Center Foundation, University of Virginia.

22. Boyle, *The UAW*, 1.

23. Jacobs, "Political Boulwarism," 351.

24. Ibid., 350.

25. Ibid., 350.

26. Boulware, *The Truth*, 90; Northrup, *Boulwarism*, 85.

27. Dugger, *On Reagan*, 319.

28. *Who's Who in America*, 46th ed., 1990–91, 230.

29. Quoted by Maurice Berube, in *Encyclopedia of the American Presidency* (New York: Simon and Schuster, 1994), 2:404.

30. Ibid.

31. Comments from the press and press aides in this section come from Hertsgaard, *On Bended Knee*, 4–5, 47–48.

32. This quotation and the history of Reagan's transformation of the State of the Union speech come from a article by Stanford linguist Geoffrey Nunberg, "The Speech That Turns Mere Presidents Into Talk Show Hosts," *New York Times*, February 2, 2003.

33. Quoted in Shultz, *Turmoil and Triumph*, 266–67.

34. Mitchell, *Talking Back*, 97.

35. Boulware, *The Truth*, 164. RR had used the phrase elsewhere and employed a variation—"ant heap of totalitarianism"—in "A Time for Choosing." See Edwards, *Early Reagan*, 562.

36. Quoted by Harvey Mansfield, in Taranto and Leo, *Presidential Leadership*, 195.

37. Ibid., 196–97.

38. Quoted in Shultz, *Turmoil and Triumph*, 256.

39. Ibid., 261.

40. Ibid., 263.

41. Ibid., 259.

42. *Business Week*, June 20, 1983, as quoted in Dugger, *On Reagan*, 421.

43. The phrase "Let Reagan be Reagan" is generally attributed to his beleaguered secretary of the interior, James Watt. Originally intended as a "conservative mantra" to permit the president's conservative ideas to emerge, it took on another meaning, to permit the best utilization of Reagan's abilities, instead of micromanaging him. See Sloan, "Meeting the Leadership Challenges," esp. 798, 801.

44. Gergen, *Eyewitness to Power*, 152–53.

45. Quoted in ibid., 203.

46. Shultz, *Turmoil and Triumph*, 1135.

47. Schultz, quoted in Strober and Strober, *Reagan*, 97.

48. Kirkpatrick, *The Reagan Phenomenon*, 7.

49. Lou Cannon, quoted in J. W. Sloan, "Meeting the Leadership Challenges," 796.

50. Bosch, *Reagan*, 250.

51. Shultz, *Turmoil and Triumph*, 525.

52. Beilenson, *Power Through Subversion*, 241. See also chapter 8.

53. Quoted in Edwards, *Early Reagan*, 559.

54. Strausz-Hupé and Kintner, "Military Defense," 26.

55. See Shultz, *Turmoil and Triumph*, 607.

56. Ibid., 606, 607.

57. See author's comments and collection of others in Fitzgerald, *Way Out There in the Blue*, 351–56.

58. Shultz, *Turmoil and Triumph*, 264.

59. GE's *Public and Employee News*, "The Great Debate," December 31, 1957, 2, GEC.

60. Strausz-Hupé and Kintner, "Military Defense," 26.

61. Shultz, *Turmoil and Triumph*, 904.

62. Abshire, *Saving the Reagan Presidency*, 4.

63. Ibid., 5.

64. Shultz, *Turmoil and Triumph*, 263.

65. Cordiner, *New Frontiers*, 48; Mitchell, *Talking Back*, 112.

66. Collins and Porris, *Built to Last*, 170, 298.

67. Fuller, *The Gentlemen Conspirators*, 182–84 and generally.

68. Cannon, *Governor Reagan*, 238–55.

69. RR, *An American Life*, 316; RR, *Where's the Rest of Me?* 139.

70. Humes, *Speak Like Churchill*, 17. Humes also praises Churchill for his natural talent for acting.

71. Martin Anderson, quoted in Greenstein, *The Presidential Difference*, 151.

72. Meese, *With Reagan*, 60.

73. Greenstein, *The Presidential Difference*, 18.

74. Ibid.

75. Ibid.

76. For an analysis of those who were able to "Let Reagan be Reagan," see Sloan, "Meeting the Leadership Challenges," 798.

77. N. Reagan, *My Turn*, 313. Also see Bosch, *Reagan*, 302.

78. Greenstein, *The Presidential Difference*, 153.

79. Jackson, *That Man*, 154–55, 255n 33.

80. As cited by White House counsel Peter Wallison, who held a similar view, in *Ronald Reagan*, 104.

81. Morris, *Dutch*, 662.

82. Abshire, *Saving the Reagan Presidency*, 19 and throughout.

83. Bosch, *Reagan*, 308.

84. Shultz, *Turmoil and Triumph*, 702.

85. Reagan, *Speaking My Mind*, "Remarks at the Brandenburg Gate," 348, 352.

86. Shultz, *Turmoil and Triumph*, 1010.

87. Ibid.

88. Shultz, *Turmoil and Triumph*, 1081–85.

89. Pemberton, *Exit With Honor*, 196.

90. Thatcher, *The Downing Street Years*, 463.

91. Thatcher's 1991 Heritage Foundation speech, quoted in Fitzgerald, *Way Out There in the Blue*, 284.

92. Quoted in Edwards, *The Power of Ideas*, 128.

93. Fitzgerald, *Way Out There in the Blue*, 475–76.

94. Pemberton, *Exit with Honor*, 195.

95. Thatcher, *Statecraft*, 460.

96. As cited in Fitzgerald, *Way Out There in the Blue*, 466.

97. Frank Doyle, telephone interviews by author, December 2, 1999, and December 12, 1999.

98. RR to Boulware, May 30, 1985, CPLB.

99. Doyle, interviews.

100. Joan Cook, "Lemuel Ricketts Boulware, 95; Headed Labor Relations for G.E.," obituary, *New York Times*, November 8, 1990.

101. Reagan inaugural photo, CPLB.

REFERENCES

General Bibliography

Abshire, David. *Saving the Reagan Presidency*. College Station: Texas A & M University Press, 2005.

Aibel. H. J. "Corporate Counsel and Business Ethics: A Personal Review." *Missouri Law Review* 59, no. 427 (Spring 1994).

Ambrose, Stephen. *Eisenhower: Soldier and President,* New York: Simon and Schuster, 1990.

———. *Nixon: The Education of a Politician, 1913–1962*. New York: Simon and Schuster, 1987.

———. *To America*. New York: Simon and Schuster, 2002.

Anderson, Martin. *Revolution: The Reagan Legacy,* Stanford, Calif.: Hoover Institution Press, 1990.

Baum, Dan. *Citizen Coors: An American Dynasty,* New York: William Morrow, 2000.

Beilenson, Laurence W. *Power Through Subversion*. Washington, D.C.: Public Affairs Press, 1972.

———. *Survival and Peace in the Nuclear Age*. Chicago: Regnery/Gateway, 1980.

———. *The Treaty Trap*. Washington, D.C.: Public Affairs Press, 1969.

Bok, Derek, and John T. Dunlop. *Labor and the American Community*. New York: Simon and Schuster, 1970.

Bosch, Adriana. *Reagan: An American Story*. New York: TV Books, 1998.

Boulware, Lemuel. *The Truth About Boulwarism*. Washington, D.C.: BNA Books, 1969.

———. *What You Can Do About . . . Inflation, Unemployment, Productivity, Profit, and Collective Bargaining.* San Diego: Loefler, 1972.

Bowen, Catherine Drinker. *Adventures of a Biographer.* Boston: Little, Brown, 1959.

Boyle, Kevin. *The UAW and the Heyday of American Liberalism, 1945–1968.* Ithaca, N.Y.: Cornell Paperbacks, 1998.

Broder, David, and Stephen Hess. *The Republican Establishment: The Present and Future of the G.O.P.* New York: Harper & Row, 1967.

Brokaw, Tom. *The Greatest Generation.* New York: Delta, 1998.

Callahan, David. *Kindred Spirits: Harvard Business School's Extraordinary Class of 1949 and How They Transformed American Business.* New York: Wiley, 2002.

Cannon, Lou. *Governor Reagan: His Rise to Power.* New York: Public Affairs, 2003.

———. *The Role of a Lifetime.* New York: Public Affairs, 2000.

Colacello, Bob. "Ronnie and Nancy." *Vanity Fair.* Parts 1 and 2. July and August 1998.

Collins, James C., and Jerry I. Porras. *Built to Last.* New York: Harper-Collins, 1994.

Cordiner, Ralph. *New Frontiers for Professional Managers.* New York: McGraw-Hill, 1956.

Dallek, Matthew. *The Right Moment.* New York: The Free Press, 2000.

D'Souza, Dinesh. *Ronald Reagan: How An Ordinary Man Became an Extraordinary Leader.* New York: The Free Press, 1997.

Duberstein, Kenneth M. "Reagan's Second-Half Comeback." Op-ed article, *New York Times,* November 2, 2005.

Dugger, Ronnie. *On Reagan: The Man and His Presidency.* New York: McGraw-Hill, 1983.

Edwards, Anne. *Early Reagan: The Rise to Power.* New York: William Morrow, 1987.

Edwards, Lee. *The Power of Ideas.* Ottawa, Ill.: Jameson Books, 1997.

Evans, Thomas W. "The New Mentors." *Teachers College Record* 102, no. 1 (February 2000): 244–63.

Fitzgerald, Frances. *Way Out There in the Blue: Reagan, Star Wars, and the End of the Cold War.* New York: Simon and Schuster, 2000.

Flynn, John T. *The Road Ahead: America's Creeping Revolution.* New York: The Devin-Adair Company, 1950.

Fuller, John G. *The Gentlemen Conspirators.* New York: Grove Press, 1962.

Galenson, Walter. *The CIO Challenge to the AFL.* Cambridge, Mass.: Harvard University Press, 1960.

Gardner, Howard. *Frames of Mind.* New York: Basic Books, 1999.

Gergen, David. *Eyewitness to Power: The Essence of Leadership, Nixon to Clinton.* New York: Simon and Schuster, 2000.

Goleman, Daniel. *Emotional Intelligence.* New York: Bantam Books, 1995.

Greenstein, Fred I. *The Presidential Difference.* New York: The Free Press, 2000.

Haney, Lewis. *How You Really Earn Your Living.* Englewood Cliffs, N.J.: Prentice Hall, 1952.

Hannaford, Peter, ed. *Recollections of Reagan.* New York: William Morrow, 1997.

Hazlitt, Henry. *Economics in One Lesson.* New York: Pocket Books, 1948.

Hertsgaard, Mark. *On Bended Knee: The Press and the Reagan Presidency.* New York: Farrar Straus and Giroux, 1988.

Humes, James C. *Eisenhower and Churchill: The Partnership That Saved The World.* New York: Forum, 2001.

——. *Speak Like Churchill, Stand Like Lincoln.* New York. Three Rivers Press, 2002.

Jackson, Robert H. *That Man: An Insider's Portrait of Franklin D. Roosevelt.* Ed. John Q. Barrett. New York: Oxford University Press, 2003.

Jacobs, David C. "Political Boulwarism: Bargaining During the Reagan Years." *Negotiation Journal* 5, no. 349 (October 1989).

JFKLibrary.org/rfk-reag.htm. Town Meeting of the World: "The Image of America and the Youth of the World." As broadcast over the CBS Television Network, on Monday, May 15, 1967.

Johnson, Haynes. *Sleepwalking Through History.* New York: W. W. Norton, 1991.

Kacena, Candace. "Remembering Reagan." *Fulton Sun Gazette,* December 29, 1980.

Kirkpatrick, Jeane J. *The Reagan Phenomenon.* Washington, D.C.: American Enterprise Institute, 1983.

Kissinger, Henry. *Does America Need A Foreign Policy?* New York: Simon and Schuster, 2001.

Koenig, Louis W. *Bryan: A Political Biography of William Jennings Bryan.* New York: G. P. Putnam's Sons, 1971.

Korda, Michael. *Another Life: A Memoir of Other People.* New York: Random House, 1999.

Krames, Jeffrey A. *The Jack Welch Lexicon of Leadership.* New York: McGraw-Hill, 2002.

Langley, Ed. "Reagan Philosophy Changed by GE Years." *Knoxville Journal,* July 14, 15, 16, 1980.

Larrabee, Eric. *Commander in Chief: Franklin Delano, His Lieutenants, and Their War.* New York: Simon and Schuster, 1988.

Lichtenstein, Nelson. *Labor's War at Home: The CIO in World War II.* New York: Cambridge University Press, 1991.

——. *The Most Dangerous Man in Detroit: Walter Reuther and the Fate of American Labor.* New York: Basic Books, 1995.

Link, Kate. "When Reagan Came to Fulton." *Kingdom Dairy News,* March 22, 1981, 7.

Lowry, Rich. Introduction to *Tear Down This Wall: The Reagan Revolution—A National Review History,* compiled by the editors of *National Review.* New York: Continuum, 2004.

McDougal, Dennis. *The Last Mogul.* New York: Crown Publishers, 1998.

McQuaid, Kim. *Uneasy Partners: Big Business in American Politics, 1945–1990.* Baltimore, Md.: Johns Hopkins University Press, 1994.

Meese, Edwin III. *With Reagan: The Inside Story.* Washington, D.C.: Regnery Gateway, 1992.

Mitchell, Andrea. *Talking Back . . . to Presidents, Dictators, and Assorted Scoundrels*. New York: Viking, 2005.

Morris, Edmund. *Dutch: A Memoir of Ronald Reagan*. New York: Random House, 1999.

New York Times. *The New York Times Encyclopedic Almanac 1970*. New York: The New York Times Book and Educational Division, 1969.

Nixon, Richard. *Leaders*. New York: Warner Books, 1982.

Northrup, Herbert. *Boulwarism*. Ann Arbor: Bureau of Industrial Relations, University of Michigan, 1964.

Nunberg, Geoffrey. "The Speech That Turns Mere Presidents Into Talk Show Hosts." *New York Times*, February 2, 2003.

Ogden, Christopher. *Legacy: The Biography of Moses and Walter Annenberg*. Boston: Little, Brown and Company, 1999.

Pemberton, William E. *Exit With Honor: The Life and Presidency of Ronald Reagan*. Armonk, N.Y.: M. E. Sharpe, 1997.

Perlstein, Rick. *Before the Storm*. New York: Hill & Wang, 2001.

Perret, Geoffrey. *Eisenhower*. New York: Random House, 1999.

Prindle, David F. *The Politics of Glamour*. Madison: University of Wisconsin Press, 1988.

Reagan, Maureen. *First Father, First Daughter*. Boston: Little, Brown, 1989.

Reagan, Nancy. *I Love You, Ronnie*. New York: Random House, 2000.

Reagan, Nancy, with William Novak. *My Turn: The Memoirs of Nancy Reagan*. Paperback ed. New York: Dell, 1989.

Reagan, Ronald. *Abortion and the Conscience of the Nation*. Afterwords by C. Everett Koop and Malcolm Muggeridge. Nashville, Tenn.: Thomas Nelson, 1984.

——. *An American Life*. New York: Simon and Schuster, 1990.

——. *Speaking My Mind—Selected Speeches*. New York: Simon and Schuster, 1989.

Reagan, Ronald, with Richard G. Hubler. *Where's the Rest of Me?* New York: Duell, Sloan and Pearce, 1965.

Reagan, Ronald, and others. *Ronald Reagan: An American Hero*. Presented by the Ronald Reagan Presidential Foundation. London: Dorling, Kindersley, 2001.

Reeves, Richard. *President Nixon: Alone in the White House*. New York: Simon and Schuster, 2001.

Robinson, Peter. *How Ronald Reagan Changed My Life*. New York: Harper Collins, 2003.

Rusher, William A. *The Rise of the Right*. New York: William Morrow, 1984.

Shames, Laurence. *The Big Time: The Harvard Business School's Most Successful Class—and How It Shaped America*. New York: Harper and Row, 1986.

Schweizer, Robert. *Reagan's War*. New York: Doubleday, 2002.

Shultz, George P. *Turmoil and Triumph: My Years As Secretary of State*. New York: Scribner's, 1993.

Skinner, Kiron, and Annelise Anderson, and Martin Anderson, eds. *Reagan: In His Own Hand*. New York: The Free Press, 2001.

Sloan, Irving J., ed. *Ronald W. Reagan, 1911– : The Presidential Chronology Series.* Dobbs Ferry, N.Y.: Oceana Publications, 1990.

Sloan, John W. "Meeting the Leadership Challenges of the Modern Presidency: The Political Skills and Leadership of Ronald Reagan." *Presidential Studies Quarterly* 26, no. 3 (Summer 1996): 795–804.

Smith, Hedrick, et al. *Reagan: The Man, The President.* New York: Macmillan, 1980.

Spada, James. *Ronald Reagan—His Life in Pictures.* New York: St. Martin's Press, 2000.

Strausz-Hupé, Robert, and William R. Kintner. "Military Defense: Free World Strategy in the 60's." *General Electric Forum* 5, no. 1 (January–March 1963): 21–26.

Strober, Deborah Hart, and Gerald S. Strober. *Reagan: The Man and His Legacy.* Boston: Houghton Mifflin, 1998.

Strock, James M. *Reagan on Leadership.* Rocklin, Calif.: Forum (Prima), 1998.

Taranto, James, and Leonard Leo, eds. *Presidential Leadership—Rating the Best and Worst in the White House.* New York: A Wall Street Journal Book published by Free Press, 2004.

Thatcher, Margaret. *The Downing Street Years.* New York: Harper Collins, 1993.

———. *Statecraft—Strategies for a Changing World.* New York: Harper Collins, 2002.

Thomas, Helen, *Thanks for the Memories, Mr. President: Wit and Wisdom from the Front Row at the White House.* New York: Simon and Schuster, 2002.

Thomas, Tony. *The Films of Ronald Reagan.* Secaucus, N.J.: Citadel Press, 1980.

Von Clausewitz, Carl. *On War.* Paperback ed. New York: Penguin Classics, 1982.

Von Damm, Helene, ed. *Sincerely, Ronald Reagan.* New York: Berkley Books, 1980.

Velie, Lester. *Labor U.S.A.* New York: Harper, 1958.

Wallison, Peter. *Ronald Reagan.* New York: Westview Press, 2002.

Welch, Jack, with John Byrne. *Jack Welch—Straight from the Gut.* New York: Warner Books, 2001.

White, F. Clifton, and William J. Gill. *Politics As A Noble Calling.* Ottawa, Ill.: Jameson Books, 1994.

———. *Suite 3505: The Story of the Draft Goldwater Movement.* Ashland, Ohio: Ashbrook Press, 1992.

———. *Why Reagan Won.* Chicago: Regnery Gateway, 1981.

White, Theodore H. *America in Search of Itself: The Making of the President, 1956–1980.* New York: Harper & Row, 1982.

———. *The Making of the President, 1964.* New York: Atheneum, 1965.

Wills, Garry. *Reagan's America.* New York: Doubleday, 1987.

Wiprud, Grant W. "Antitrust Treble Damages Against Electrical Manufactures: The Statute of Limitations and Other Hurdles." *Northwestern University Law Review* 57, no. 29 (1962): 29–52.

Worthman, Max, and C. Wilson Randle. *Collective Bargaining: Principles and Practices.* 2nd ed. Boston: Houghton Mifflin, 1966.

Wuerthner, J.J., Jr. *The Businessman's Guide to Practical Politics*. Chicago: Henry Regnery, 1959.

COLLECTIONS

The Collected Papers of Lemuel Boulware. Van Pelt Library, University of Pennsylvania.

The General Electric Collection. Museum of Electricity, Schenectady, New York.

The Collections of the Archives of Labor and Urban Affairs. Walter P. Reuther Library, Wayne State University Library, Detroit, Michigan.

CASES

U.S. v. General Electric Company (1961). The criminal cases against GE and Westinghouse and other antitrust conspirators have numerous citations. The most comprehensive discussion of the merits of the charges, particularly by Chief Judge Gainey, is found in the transcript of the Rearraignment Hearings of November 1960 at *U.S. V. Westinghouse Elec. Corp.*, Criminal No. 20399 (E.D. Pa.1960). The final judgment in the criminal cases is reported in *U.S. V. General Electric Company et al.*, 1962 Trade Cas. Par 70,488, at 76,984–76,994.

U.S. V. MCA, 1962 Trade Cas. (CCH) Par. 70,414. Ronald Reagan appeared before a grand jury in this litigation and was questioned about the blanket waiver and other matters. The case was filed in a federal district court in California on July 13, 1962, and terminated in an order agreed to by the government and the defendant corporation ten days later.

The City of Burbank v. General Electric Company, 329 F. 2d 825 (1964). Four thousand utilities, some of them municipally owned, commenced civil actions against General Electric and the other companies that had been defendants in the criminal cases. These lawsuits, brought under the Clayton Act, permitted plaintiffs to recover three times the amount of the damages actually proved. *The City of Burbank* decision of the U.S. Court of Appeals for the Ninth Judicial Circuit covers some 124 companion cases on the issue of the precedental value of guilty and nolo pleas in the earlier criminal cases. Writing for the court is Judge Stanley Barnes, who, in his earlier role as head of the Antitrust Division in the Eisenhower administration, spoke highly of GE's policy of internal antitrust enforcement.

National Labor Relations Board v. General Electric Company, 418 F. 2d 736 (2d Cir. 1969). This is the "Boulwareism" decision of the U.S. Court of Appeals for the Second Judicial Circuit, setting out Chief Judge Irving Kaufman's opinion, along with Judge Waterman's concurrence and Judge Friendly's dissent. Also of interest are the proceedings appealed from, GE and IUE cases, nos. 2-CA-7581-1, 2-CA-7581-2, 2-CA-7581-4, and 2-CA-7864 (post 10-CA-4682), December 16, 1964.

U.S. v. General Electric Company, 1977-2 CCH Trade Cas. Par. 61,660. The Department of Justice alleged that GE and Westinghouse had entered into a course of conduct starting in 1963 that constituted a "tacit cartel" to fix prices. The defendants denied any wrongdoing. This decision embodies the consent decree that ended the government's pursuit of the alleged conspiracy.

INTERVIEWS

CONDUCTED BY AUTHOR UNLESS OTHERWISE NOTED.

John Anderson

Martin Anderson

———. Miller Center of Public Affairs, Presidential Oral History Program, Ronald Reagan Oral History Project, the Miller Center Foundation, University of Virginia.

David Burke

Frank Doyle

Earl B. Dunckel, Jr. Regional Oral History Office, Bancroft Library, University of California at Berkeley

Edwin Feulner

Anon. GE executive secretary ("GE/EXSEC")

Nancy Cordiner Judge

Ned Landon

Frederic Lione

Raymond Livingston

J. William Middendorf

Victor Millione

Thomas Murphy

Patricia O'Rourke

William Ruane

Marvin Traub

ACKNOWLEDGMENTS

Among those who sustained me in this book when it was just an idea and very little material seemed to be available were two prolific authors, bibliophile-historian William Alexander Johnson and novelist Warren Adler. Carol Saltz of Teachers College Press was also an early and persistent advisor. My greatest debt is to a woman who will not let me use her name, and who is identified in my endnotes as "GE/EXSEC." A former executive secretary at General Electric, she gave me an extensive interview and led me to the collected papers of Lemuel Boulware, which she had organized and sent to the University of Pennsylvania.

Archivists, historians, and librarians helped me with sources that had never been used before or hadn't been published since GE first sent them out to their workers or to "thought leaders" half a century ago. Nancy Shaw-cross and John Pollack at the Annenberg Collection at the University of Pennsylvania; Chris Hunter at the Schenectady Museum (where GE has housed hundreds of thousands of pages of documents); Ray Wilson at the Ronald Reagan Library; Mark Renovitch at the Franklin D. Roosevelt Library; William Lefevre of the Walter Reuther Collection in the Wayne State University Archives; and Valerie Yaros of the Screen Actors Guild all fall into this category.

Great libraries at Harvard, Yale, and the Gottesman at Columbia's Teachers College, were also locales for research. Greg Gallagher, the librarian at The Century Association was most helpful with obscure current sources. Local libraries, for which I have great enthusiasm generally, played a significant role, especially Southbury, Connecticut, where Judith Stark is in charge of research, and Surf-Bal-Bay of Surfside, Florida, where Suzanne McGlynn and Leslie Liebesman hold forth. In addition to their considerable skills, these librarians and others gave new dimensions to the scope of inter-library loans.

David Fromkin read my manuscript in roughly its present form, and, as a result, the book is shorter and, I believe, more readable. Others who also deserve great thanks are John Moore, Chela Scott, Pat O'Rourke, Arthur Levine, Gary Bridge, Bill Summerscales, Suzanne Spear, Becky Black, John Ottaviani, and Richard Baumfield. The editorial team with whom I worked at Columbia University Press has been outstanding. Peter Dimock, Michael Haskell, and Kabir Dandona have improved my manuscript. My wife, Lois, and my children, Heather, Logan, and Paige have been extremely supportive over the years.

T. W. E.

INDEX

COLUMBIA STUDIES IN CONTEMPORARY AMERICAN HISTORY

Alan Brinkley, General Editor